A YEAR WITH PETER DRUCKER

ALSO BY JOSEPH A. MACIARIELLO
Lasting Value: Lessons from a Century of Agility at Lincoln Electric

WITH PETER DRUCKER
The Daily Drucker
Management: Revised Edition
The Effective Executive in Action

WITH KAREN LINKLETTER
Drucker's Lost Art of Management

A Year *with*

PETER DRUCKER

---

52 WEEKS OF
COACHING *for* LEADERSHIP
EFFECTIVENESS

BASED ON THE WORK OF PETER F. DRUCKER

JOSEPH A. MACIARIELLO

HARPER
BUSINESS
An Imprint of HarperCollins*Publishers*

HarperCollins books may be purchased for educational, business, or sales promotional use. For information, please e-mail the Special Markets Department at SPsales@harpercollins.com.

FIRST EDITION

Grateful acknowledgment is made for permissions to reprint material from the following books, articles, and Internet passages:

The Drucker Literary Trust has granted permission to use quotations from the books cited by Peter F. Drucker.

Permission to use excerpts from WBUR's On Point with Tom Ashbrook, a radio interview of Peter Drucker by Tom Ashbrook on December 8, 2004.

Permission of *Leadership Journal* to include excerpts of the interview "MANAGING TO MINISTER: An interview with Peter Drucker," by the editors of *Leadership Journal*, April 1, 1989.

Permission granted by Pastor Rick Warren to include his material in this book.

Consent to reprint excerpts from "The Future of Evangelicals: A Conversation with Pastor Rick Warren," November 13, 2009, Pew Research Center.

Permission granted to use excerpts from a Drucker interview by Joseph A. Maciariello in *Shine a Light*, a special issue of the Leader to Leader Institute's journal published in 2005.

Permission to use Peter Drucker's consultation with Chuck Smith and Chuck Fromm on Succession Planning at Calvary Chapel, December 3, 2003.

Permission to include an interview by Derek Bell and Joseph Maciariello with Jim Mellado on Diffusion of Innovations in Society and Mega-Churches.

Reprint permission permitted by Capital Research Center for an excerpt from *Compassion and Culture* by Gwen Purtill, pp. 1, 2.

Permission to reprint responses by Peter F. Drucker to Lord Brian Griffiths of Fforestfach, "The Business of Values," in C. William Pollard (ed.), *The Heart of a Business Ethic*, University Press of America, September 8, 2005.

Limited license agreement from PARS INTERNATIONAL CORP. to reproduce excerpts from the interview by Rich Karlgaard, "Drucker on Leadership: An Interview with Peter F. Drucker," *Forbes Magazine*, November 19, 2004.

Library of Congress Cataloging-in-Publication Data has been applied for.

ISBN: 978-0-06-231567-0

14 15 16 17 18 OV/RRD 10 9 8 7 6 5 4 3 2 1

This book is dedicated to my sons, Pat and Joe, with love.

Acknowledgments

I first want to thank Bob Buford. Bob is the founder of Leadership Network and the Halftime Institute, and an author of numerous books including the best-selling book *Halftime* and the recently released book *Drucker & Me*.

Bob gave me access to recordings and transcripts of what is referred to in the book as "The Drucker-Buford Dialogue Project." The dialogue is a series of mentoring consultations between Bob and Peter Drucker, and includes consultations with a number of other leaders in private and social sector organizations. These consultations took place from 1984 to September 2005, the last one just two months before Drucker's death on November 11, 2005. Bob and his assistant Derek Bell provided me with available source materials, CDs, and transcripts in 2008, and Bob encouraged me to engage in the research necessary to write this book. Derek and I consulted with Bob and many other leaders in the social sector between 2009 and 2013. Without Bob's support and encouragement, and Derek's help, this book would not have been possible. Bob's personal assistant, BJ Engle, was a source of information and encouragement to me. Thank you, BJ.

Steve Hanselman, my friend and agent, worked with me over a two-year period to help design the structure of the book so that it would provide a yearlong mentoring experience for executives and those aspiring to become executives. Thank you, Steve.

I would like to thank Hollis Heimbouch, Vice President/ Publisher of HarperBusiness. Hollis helped to refine the structure of the book at a critical point in the writing process. Eric Myers served as my editor throughout and helped me immensely with the detailed editorial issues that we confronted in creating a book that would mentor executives in both business and public service. Thank you, Eric. The copyeditor, Ms. Susan Gamer, did the most thorough job of copyediting I have ever experienced. I am grateful to Hollis, Eric, Penny Makras, Joanna Pinsker, Anna Brower, Oliver Munday, and all those involved at HarperBusiness.

Mr. Ming Lo Shao, founder and chairman of the Bright China Group, has provided me with research support during this and several previous research and publication projects. Thank you, Mr. Shao.

Kathy Holden, my assistant at the Peter F. Drucker and Masatoshi Ito Graduate School of Management of Claremont Graduate University, was available to provide assistance I needed during the entire time I worked on this book. Thanks, Kathy.

The Drucker Literary Trust cooperated with me in writing this book by granting permission to use relevant passages from Peter Drucker's books. In addition, Doris Drucker has been a constant source of friendship and inspiration to me as I have tried to advance the legacy of Peter Drucker. At 103 years old she continues to provide encouragement and she is waiting to read this book!

In addition to the transcripts, Derek and I interviewed Jim Mellado. Jim, now president of Compassion International, Colorado Springs, Colorado, gave of his time to discuss with Derek Bell and me the work of the Willow Creek Association and its premier event, the Global Leadership Summit, whose purpose is to diffuse innovations throughout society. Thank you, Jim.

I had numerous conversations with Dr. Chuck Fromm, president of Maranatha Music for twenty-five years and founder and president of *Worship Leader* magazine. Chuck participated in a number of Drucker-Buford meetings and was very helpful to me in contextualizing issues of succession, especially those issues involved in succeeding charismatic founders of large organizations.

Three friends, with expertise in the subject matter of this book, listened and encouraged me throughout the entire research and writing process. Thanks to Professors Steve Davis and Donald Griesinger, and to John Pusztai.

Finally and most important, my wife, Judy, listened and commented on the numerous drafts this book went through. To say that she helped and encouraged me is an understatement because no one knows what went into this book and no one gave more support to me than Judy. Thank you once again, Judy.

Contents

MAINTAINING YOUR ORGANIZATION THROUGH CHANGE

STRUCTURING YOUR ORGANIZATION

MANAGING YOUR MEMBERS

CHARACTER AND LEGACY

Introduction

Peter Drucker mentored executives and other knowledge workers for over a half century through his consulting, teaching, and publications. As a longtime student and colleague of his, I have had the opportunity to observe his mentoring directly and I have benefited from his counsel. It began in 1981, when I attended a PhD seminar he taught in Claremont. I also had the opportunity to learn from him during the twenty-six years I spent as his colleague at what is now the Peter F. Drucker and Masatoshi Ito Graduate School of Management of Claremont Graduate University.

When Drucker reduced his teaching, I had the opportunity to teach the course "Drucker on Management" to executives and MBA students in Claremont and around the world for approximately ten years. I then coordinated a team-taught course, "The Drucker Difference," involving the entire Drucker faculty. Finally, I had the extraordinary opportunity to work directly with him during the last six years of his life. Then in 2008, Bob Buford asked me to assemble, analyze, edit, and study the transcripts and listen to the recordings of Drucker's mentoring of him and a number of other leaders associated with his Leadership Network and the Halftime Institute. In addition, I later conducted and transcribed interviews related to what I have called the Drucker-Buford Dialogue Project, which took place from 1984 to 2005. I have devoted much of my time during the past six years to developing the ideas contained in this mentoring book, an opportunity given to me by Bob Buford.

The purpose of this book is to share Drucker's management techniques with fans the world over. Through a year of readings, lessons, and questions, you will get a chance to experience Drucker's mentorship. The objective is to share Drucker's mentorship program with you just as he shared it with Buford and with a number of others.

Drucker's work has had a tremendous impact on the management of large-scale organizations, a product of the twentieth century. Drucker codified the practice of management in 1946 and 1954, largely on the basis of his consulting experience and his knowledge of the social sciences and humanities, including history, political science, psychology, and economics.

Drucker had a number of very unusual qualities. First, he believed that the discipline of management should be organized by looking at good practice. He believed that practice organizes reality and therefore good practice should organize the discipline of management. Second, he was an astute observer of reality, always learning from the people and organizations with whom he associated. Third, he was able to integrate his vast knowledge and bring it to bear on specific problems faced by executives in their organizations. Fourth, as a person trained in international law and political science, he looked at organizations from the outside in. This viewpoint led him to become interested in all of society's organizations—not just for-profit institutions, but also social sector and public sector organizations. He felt that to tolerate substandard performance in any one sector dissipates wealth and is detrimental to society's overall welfare. His driving force was to provide for the needs of citizens of free societies so they would never be tempted to turn to authoritarian substitutes, which history, and his own early life experiences, had shown to be disastrous. His domain included private, nonprofit, and governmental organizations and his writings and mentoring were filled with examples from all walks of life. He did see differences among organizations in these three sectors but he saw many more similarities. As you read this book and work through the exercises, you will see the value that Drucker saw in taking such a broad perspective.

There are fifty-two entries in the book, one for each week of the year. They are subdivided into thirteen major topics. Each topic has important contributions to make in helping you become an effective leader. Some entries use unexpected examples and applications from organizations that may surprise you, but they are all important to Drucker's worldview, and to his principles of management.

Each entry begins with an introduction and examples introducing the week's lessons and context. The introduction is then followed by a three-part sequence: readings, reflections, and exercises. There is a new reading from Drucker on the topic in each entry, generally in part I. In part II there are several readings from Drucker along with my reflections, which set the context for the readings. Finally, part III consists of "practicum-prompts" that help you to apply what you have learned to your own life and work. Some of the questions are too broad to be handled in the space that follows them; some others are simply reflections entailing no need to write.

My advice is to concentrate first on those entries that have immediate application to your life and duties. Work these through and try to implement them. Think through what you expect to happen as a result of your actions and then compare actual results with your expectations. This process is called *feedback analysis*. It should help you to determine what you did right and what still needs improvement.

Some of the entries may also apply to other people in, and other units of, your organization. You might suggest that relevant people take a look at and work out these entries. In this way you will make a contribution to the organization as a whole and to other organizations whose mission and welfare you care about.

Throughout the book, you will be introduced to Drucker's principles of management. These principles are also summarized in "Lessons Learned" and itemized in the Appendix. Effective leadership is a practice, and like every other practice it is mastered through an iterative process of learning and doing and learning more. "Lessons Learned" and the Appendix will help you in this iterative process.

My hope is that this book will become an indispensable guide. That it will lead you deeply into Drucker's knowledge and wisdom, and allow you, as a leader and a person, to convert this wisdom into effective action. Good luck!

Effective Leaders

Developing Leaders, Not Functionaries

Effective Leaders *Get the Right Things Done* and *You Can Trust Them*

Introduction

Peter Drucker had great hopes for business executives in the United States. These hopes gradually faded, as he saw one scandal after another and as he found leaders to be self-serving. Drucker hoped that the large industrial organization would provide a place where employees could find community, citizenship, meaning, and purpose for their lives.

Drucker wished the business organization would create a functional relationship between individuals and the ideals we hold as a nation, such as equality of opportunity, personal freedom, and personal responsibility. This would help establish a working philosophy of life for individuals and serve as a remedy for the failures of totalitarianism. The lack of such a workable philosophy under totalitarianism was the subject of his first book, *The End of Economic Man* (1939).

In his second book, *The Future of Industrial Man* (1942), he brought these concepts together under the framework of the *self-governing plant community* for the rapidly emerging industrial organization, without applying it to any specific organization. A self-governing plant community consists of empowered and responsible employees who, by assuming managerial responsibility as individuals, could meet their personal and social needs while contributing to the wealth-creating activities of their organization. The concept of the self-governing plant community became an integral element for a stable society of organizations.

In his first book devoted to management, *Concept of the Corporation* (1946), Drucker proposed this idea for General Motors, but the company rejected it. He then reluctantly abandoned the idea of the plant community although a number of organizations, mostly in Japan and more recently in South Korea, have used a very similar system, creating conditions under which associates, by assuming certain managerial responsibilities, do find *citizenship*, *meaning*, and *purpose* for their lives.

On completion of his *Management: Tasks, Responsibilities, Practices* (1974), and because of his growing disappointment with business management in the United States, he intensified his efforts, which he had begun in the 1950s, to help executives of social sector institutions manage themselves in a professional way. These organizations help change for the better the lives of people they serve and in the process provide high levels of *community, citizenship,* and *meaning* for their employees and volunteers. Executives in the best-run of these social sector organizations provide examples for all executives to follow.

In Week 1, we begin with a consultation Drucker had in early 2002 with senior executives of World Vision International. His subject was "What Do Effective Leaders Do to Create High-Performing Organizations?" His objective was to help develop effective leaders, rather than what he referred to as "functionaries."[1]

I. Read

The only definition of a leader is someone with followers. When you do it, do it your way, what works for you. Do not try to be anybody else. Leadership is an achievement of trust. You know what to expect, and you see performance and achievement. What matters is "Leadership for what purpose?" *Leadership means getting the right things done.* No two leaders are alike. Some are very gregarious, some are very aloof, some are charmers, and others are like a dead mackerel. Some are communicators, and some praise, and others may never praise. They all have two things in common: they get things done, and you can trust them.

Let me give you an example of effective leadership. I was in Vermont during World War II, at a small women's college, but I was also available to the War Department, and I worked for the assistant secretary of war on specific assignments. I had one qualification: I was not in uniform. So a general could scream at me, but he could not give me orders. That was very important.

One of the assignments I received was a relationship with the nonexistent Dutch army. The guests and very close friends of President Roosevelt—Princess Beatrix, who became queen of the Netherlands; her husband, who was a German prince; and three of his brothers, who ran the German army—wanted supplies that fitted Dutch specifications. However, the Dutch army was nonexistent, and I was not going to recommend interrupting war production.

I said, "No." They apparently complained to President Roosevelt or General Marshall, the chief of staff, [hoping] to get rid of me. Now, I did not work for General Marshall. However, General Marshall called me and said, "What's going on?" I told him. He responded, "You are doing what you are supposed to be doing; forget about it. I'll take care of it." I never heard of it again. That is leadership. I could trust Marshall absolutely. If he said, "It is my job now; forget about it," I could trust him.

> Peter F. Drucker, *Executive Summary: A Conversation with Peter Drucker on Leadership and Organizational Development.* February 5, 2002, p. 5, as edited by author.

II. Reflect

- A focus on mission and purpose and the creation of trust are among the key differences between effective leaders and functionaries.

- Organizations are built on trust, and trust is built on communication and mutual understanding. To achieve mutual understanding you must understand what information your colleagues need from you to perform their function, and they must understand what you need from them.

1. EARNING TRUST IS A MUST

To trust a leader, it is not necessary to like her. Nor is it necessary to agree with her. Trust is the conviction that a leader means what she says. It is a belief in integrity. A leader's actions and a leader's professed beliefs must be congruent, or at least compatible. Effective leadership—and again this is very old wisdom—is not based on being clever; it is based primarily on being consistent.

> Peter F. Drucker as revised and updated by Joseph A. Maciariello, *Management: Revised Edition*, 2008, pp. 290–91.

2. TRUST AND INTEGRITY

In order to be a leader a man must have followers. And to have followers, a man must have their confidence. Hence, the supreme quality for a leader is unquestionably integrity. Without it, no real success is possible, no matter whether it is on a section gang, a football field, in an army, or in an office. If a man's associates find him guilty of being phony, if they find that he lacks forthright integrity, he will fail. His teachings and actions must square with each other. The first great need, therefore, is integrity and high purpose.

> Dwight David Eisenhower, Supreme Allied Commander during World War II and thirty-fourth president of the United States, n.d.

- Manual, service, and knowledge workers are all capable of assuming managerial responsibilities. In the knowledge economy it is no longer "job enrichment" to delegate responsibility to knowledge workers. Empowerment, based on competence and trust, is essential to the productivity of the knowledge worker and to the welfare of the organization.

3. DELEGATE RESPONSIBILITY TO ALL EMPLOYEES ONCE THEY HAVE BEEN TRAINED TO ASSUME RESPONSIBILITY

Of all my work on management, I consider my ideas for the self-governing plant community and for the responsible worker to be the most important and most original. A self-governing plant community is the assumption of managerial responsibility by the individual employee, the work team, and the employee group alike for the structure of the individual job, for the performance of major tasks, and for the management of such community affairs as shift schedules, vacation schedules, overtime assignments, industrial safety, and above all employee benefits. But managements have tended to reject these ideas as "encroachment" on their prerogatives. And labor unions have been outright hostile: they are convinced that they need a visible and identifiable "boss," who can be fought as "the enemy."

Peter F. Drucker, June 23, "Self-Governing Communities," *The Daily Drucker*, 2004.

- If leaders in business are to regain their status as a leading group in society, they must seek a society in which the public good is reflected in their actions. They must make their institutions perform for the society and economy, for the community, and for the individual. This requires a focus on the interests of all stakeholders of the organization, which in turn requires a shift from maximizing shareholder value and short-term profitability to *maximizing the long-term wealth-producing capacity of the enterprise.* This focus involves consideration of the welfare of employees and society as well as customers, suppliers, and stockholders.

4. EVERYONE IS AN ORGAN OF SOCIETY

None of our institutions exist[s] by itself and as an end in itself. Everyone is an organ of society and exists for society. Business is no exception. "Free enterprise" cannot be justified as being good for business. It can be justified only as being good for society.

> Peter F. Drucker, *Management: Tasks, Responsibilities, Practices*, 1973, 1974, p. 41.

III. Practicum-Prompts

Are you developing leaders in your organization, or are you developing bureaucratic, rule-following functionaries? What can you do to enhance leadership development? What practices can you institute or recommend for increasing trust in your organization?

Are you a part of a functioning community in your organization where your citizenship, sense of community, and personal responsibility are being developed? If you are not, what is missing? How can you use whatever influence you have in your organization to bring into being a highly functioning community?

Is the authority of the leadership group in your organization grounded in responsibility, integrity, and service? Does it bring out whatever strength is present in each person? Does it foster a sense of community and citizenship? What can you do to enhance the legitimacy of the leadership group in your area?

Questions to Ask Before Committing a Portion of Your Life to the Service of an Organization

Introduction

Peter Drucker had a very high opinion of what human beings could become if properly led. He also experienced firsthand the destruction bad leaders could inflict on human beings and society. Yet he chose to focus on the positive in his management books. He observed in his first book devoted exclusively to management: "It is typical of the most successful and durable organizations that they induce in their members an intellectual and moral growth beyond a . . . [person's] original capacities" (*Concept of the Corporation*, 1946, p. 28). This kind of development requires the right kind of leadership. It is therefore very important for young people to know that organizations differ and that their choices will affect their growth and development. Week 2 provides Drucker's wisdom regarding how young people should proceed in developing their careers. They should take their time, and come to understand the mission and leadership of the organization they are joining and just how they might make a contribution while developing themselves in the process.

I. Read

Peter Drucker was asked by the president of a leading educational institution: "What kinds of questions should MBA students ask prospective employers about leadership and mission as they make a decision to commit at least a portion of their life to the service of an organization?"

I would probably tell that student of mine that he should hold that question a couple of years until he knows a little more both about himself and the organization, but then I would ask him, "Are you learning enough?" That is always my question. "Are you challenged enough?" "Does the organization make use of your strengths or what you can do? All together as a group of human beings, "does the organization constantly challenge and make you more ambitious in terms of contribution?" "Are you acutely suffering from creative discontent?" I hope at age thirty that you are not content. That's for six-year-olds. Being content is being a child, but there is a difference between negative and positive discontent. If you say, "They aren't any good; nothing ever gets done; and all they want is for me to come in from nine to five." And if you say, "You know, the nice thing about this organization is that it gives me so much time to play tennis," basically you are too young to retire. If you say, "You know, I wish I had more time for my family, and my tennis game has gone to hell because we have that big project starting that new trauma unit, and it's really not my job but I am on the team," or, "We have that enormous job here in the new school we are building and [we are] recruiting faculty and so I spend all my weekends with the prospective faculty people"—OK, then you are growing but also the organization meets the first test, which is that it *mobilizes human resources, challenges them, grows them.* My next question is: Look at the mission. Is it one in which you can make a difference? Sure, none of us make a great difference. No institution is that important, but is it one that makes—I wouldn't say [makes] the world richer; that's such an ambitious statement—but it makes a difference. That emphasizes the more responsibility we as human beings have. Or is it one that just won't really be missed? All right, none of us are going to achieve a great deal. But everyone has a chance to achieve.

Peter Drucker–David Hubbard dialogue, February 2, 1988.

II. Reflect

- You cannot fully answer the question about leadership and mission in the organization in which you belong, and the answer is likely to change from time to time. At first you can only do your homework on the organization you have an opportunity to join, take inventory of your own strengths and deficiencies, and focus on the strengths. You will make much more progress in your career by working to improve your strengths than by trying to turn your weaknesses into strengths.

1. MANAGING ONESELF

"Knowledge workers must take responsibility for managing themselves."

Knowledge workers are likely to outlive their employing organization. Their average working life is likely to be fifty years. But the average life expectancy of a successful business is only thirty years. Increasingly, therefore, knowledge workers will outlive any one employer, and will have to be prepared for more than one job. And this means most knowledge workers will have to *manage themselves*. They have to place themselves where they can make the greatest contribution; they will have to learn to develop themselves.

They will have to learn how and when to change what they do, how they do it and when they do it.

The key to managing oneself is to know: Who am I? What are my strengths? How do I work to achieve results? What are my values? Where do I belong? Where do I not belong? Finally, a crucial step in successfully managing oneself is *feedback analysis*. Record what you expect the results to be of every key action or key decision you take, and then compare *actual results* nine months or a year later [with] your expectations.

> Peter F. Drucker, June 1, "Managing Oneself," *The Daily Drucker*, 2004.

2. HOW TO DO FEEDBACK ANALYSIS

There is only one way to find out [one's strengths] and that is through *Feedback Analysis*. Whenever one makes a key *decision* and whenever one takes a key *action*, one writes down what one expects to happen. And nine months or twelve months later, one then feeds back from results to expectations. . . . Within a fairly short period of time, maybe two or three years, this simple procedure will tell people, first, where their strengths are—and this is probably the most important thing to know about oneself. It will also show them what they do or fail to do that deprives them of the full yield from their strengths. It will show them where they are particularly competent. And, finally, it will show them where they have no strengths and cannot perform. . . . Concentration should be on areas of high skill and competence. It takes far more energy and far more work to improve from mediocrity to first-rate performance than it takes to improve from first-rate performance to excellence.

> Peter F. Drucker, and Joseph A. Maciariello, *Management: Revised Edition*, 2008, pp. 481, 482, 483.

3. AIM FOR RESULTS THAT MAKE A DIFFERENCE

"To start with the question 'What should I contribute?' gives freedom because it gives responsibility."

One question has to be asked to decide "What should I contribute?" *"Where and how can I have results that make a difference?"* The answer to this question has to balance a number of things. Results should be hard to achieve. They should require "stretching," to use the present buzzword. But they should be within reach. To aim at results that cannot be achieved—or can be achieved only under the most unlikely circumstances—is not being "ambitious." It is being foolish. At the same time, results should be meaningful. They should make a difference. And they should be visible and, if at all possible, measurable.

The decision "What should my contribution be?" balances three elements. First comes the question: "What does the situation require?" Then comes the question: "How could I make the greatest contribution with my strengths, my way of performing, my values, to what needs to be done?" Finally, there is the question: "What results have to be achieved to make a difference?" This then leads to the *action conclusions*: what to do, where to start, how to start, what goals and deadlines to set.

Peter F. Drucker, *Management Challenges for the 21st Century*, 1999, pp. 182–83.

• It may take some time to know the organization in which you belong. You must know as much as possible about yourself. If you are in the wrong position you must be prepared to move when the opportunity presents itself, and not wait for better timing in your personal life. Opportunities do not come according to your schedule. Your job is to be prepared to recognize and seize opportunities as they come.

III. Practicum-Prompts

Do you know your strengths? Do you periodically perform feedback analysis? Are your strengths changing as you gain more experience? Parents, teachers, and coaches may identify outstanding strengths early in your life, but then you must do it.

Do you know where to place yourself to make contributions that are significant to your organization and also bring you great satisfaction? Where can you do this?

Does your organization have a systematic program to help associates identify strengths and make sure these strengths are fully utilized? Drucker knew about various instruments for assessing strengths but preferred feedback analysis, and used it himself because people have used it for centuries to produce outstanding results.

How many diet books have had positive long-term results? Not many. Do not jump onto every fad. Make sure the instruments you use are grounded in a history of proven success in accurately identifying strengths.

Management Is a
Human Activity

Three Fundamental Questions for a Functioning Society of Organizations

Introduction

During a celebration of Peter Drucker's eightieth birthday, in 1989, Bob Buford, the host, distributed a gift to each of those in attendance.[2] Many distinguished associates of Peter Drucker attended the event. Guests included executives from all three sectors of American society.[3]

Buford commissioned a calligrapher, Timothy Botts, to create a print. He made a tapestry, or mosaic, of interwoven, interacting hands of various colors. There is diversity in those hands. There is warmth in the interactions among them. The interwoven hands represent human transactions to meet human needs. And that idea is central to Drucker's life and work, and to his often-repeated saying, "Management is a human activity." When a friend of Peter's and Bob's, Chuck Fromm, presented the print to Drucker for his approval and signature, Drucker said to Fromm, in his deep Austrian accent, *"This is my life."*

Drucker believed that management in all three sectors should focus on satisfying the needs of human beings in society. Across the bottom of the print are Peter Drucker's three fundamental questions. The first question—"What is our business?"—starts with a human being and depends on interactions of human beings, whether in a business furnishing women's cosmetics or a shipyard building an aircraft carrier to further the mission of the U.S. Navy. The second question—"Who is our customer?"—is the most human of the three questions. The third—"What does the customer consider value?"—is simultaneously the most knowable but also the most unstable trait of the customer.

I. Read

Tom Ashbrook of National Public Radio interviewed Peter Drucker on December 8, 2004. Drucker had lost his hearing by then, and he responded to written questions prepared in advance by an aide of his own, and by Ashbrook. It was a remarkable interview covering a broad range of topics, a few of which are included as entries in this book.

Drucker never stated the three questions in exactly the same way and sometimes expanded them to four or five depending on the context. Yet the questions were always focused on satisfying needs of human beings. In this interview Drucker used a variation of the three questions to explain the similarities and differences between business and social sector organizations.

I always ask the same three questions whether I am meeting with a church or a business or a university, and whether it is American or Japanese makes no difference. The first question is: *What is your business?* What are you trying to accomplish? What makes you distinct? The second question is: *What are results?* This is much tougher for a nonbusiness than for a business. And the third question is: *What are your core competencies?* What do you have to do with excellence or great competence to have results? And that is really all. There are few differences between this century [the twenty-first] and the last century [the twentieth]—only there are so many more organizations. We have become a society of organizations in the last hundred years. We now need an enormous number of managers so we have to organize their development.

> "Management Guru Peter Drucker," WBUR for National Public Radio, December 8, 2004.

II. Reflect

- The editors of *Leadership Journal* asked Peter Drucker why he had turned away from for-profit toward nonprofit, volunteer, and public service organizations, including churches. Here is Drucker's answer.

1. "I TEACH THEM MANAGEMENT"

"After a lifetime of studying management, why are you now turning your attention to the church?" Drucker replied: "As far as I'm concerned, it's the other way around: I became interested in management because of my interest in religion and institutions. I started out teaching religion, and all of my personal experience in management has been with nonprofits—working in academia and serving on boards of everything from Blue Cross to museums. . . . Your question shows that you, like most everyone else, think of the word 'management' as business management. Many people are surprised to find out that for thirty-five years I have been working with nonprofit institutions—hospitals, schools, and charitable organizations. They'll ask, 'What do you do for them? Advise them on fund-raising?' I reply, 'No, I don't know a thing about fund-raising. I teach them management.'" [4]

- Drucker devoted his life to the practice of management after studying the emergence of fascist and communist governments in Europe during the twentieth century. A functioning society of organizations that satisfies the needs of its citizens is a safeguard against the temptation to resort to dictators as a solution for a dysfunctional society. Effective leadership and management of society's organizations is therefore the alternative to tyranny and the remedy for preserving responsible freedom and equality of opportunity.

2. "MANAGEMENT AS THE ALTERNATIVE TO TYRANNY"

If the institutions of our pluralist society . . . do not perform in responsible autonomy, we will not have individualism and a society in which there is a chance for people to fulfill themselves. We will instead impose on ourselves complete regimentation in which no one will be allowed autonomy. We will have Stalinism rather than participatory democracy, let alone the joyful spontaneity of doing one's own thing. Tyranny is the only alternative to strong, performing autonomous institutions.

Tyranny substitutes one absolute boss for the pluralism of competing institutions. It substitutes terror for responsibility. It does indeed do away with the institutions, but only by submerging all of them in the one all-embracing bureaucracy of the *apparat* [or cabal]. It does produce goods and services, though only fitfully, wastefully, at a low level, and at an enormous cost in suffering, humiliation, and frustration. To make our institutions perform responsibly, autonomously, and on a high level of achievement is thus the only safeguard of freedom and dignity in the pluralist society of institutions. Performing, responsible management is the alternative to tyranny and our only protection against it.

Peter F. Drucker, *Management: Tasks, Responsibilities, Practices*, 1973 (Hardcover Edition), pp. ix–x.

- This is why Drucker argues that *the purpose of a business* is to create a customer and to satisfy human needs. Marketing thus becomes the primary function of a business and the lens through which the entire business should be viewed. We now look at the three questions in more detail.

3. DEFINING PURPOSE AND MISSION

"What is our business?"

Nothing may seem simpler or more obvious than to know what a company's business [or mission] is. A steel mill makes steel; a railroad runs trains to carry freight and passengers; an insurance company underwrites fire risks; a bank lends money. Actually, "What is our business?" is almost always a difficult question and the right answer is usually anything but obvious.

A business is not defined by the company's name, statutes, or articles of incorporation. It is defined by the want the customer satisfies when she buys a product or a service. To satisfy the customer is the mission and purpose of every business. The question "What is our business?" can, therefore, be answered only by looking at the business from the outside, from the point of view of customer and market. What the customer sees, thinks, believes, and wants, at any given time, must be accepted by management as an objective fact and must be taken as seriously as the reports of the salesperson, the tests of the engineer, or the figures of the accountant. And management must make a conscious effort to get answers from the customer herself rather than attempt to read her mind.

Peter F. Drucker, February 27, "Defining Business Purpose and Mission," *The Daily Drucker*, 2004.

- Drucker was asked to assist the board of directors of ServiceMaster in answering this question. So at a meeting of the board he simply asked, "What is your business?" After listening to the board members try to answer, Drucker responded in a way that startled everyone, as reported by C. William Pollard in his book *The Soul of the Firm* (1996, p. 113). Here is his response: "Your business is simply the training and development of people. You package it in all different ways to meet the needs and demands of the customer, but your basic business is people training and motivation. You are delivering services. You can't deliver services without people. You can't deliver quality services to the customer without motivated and trained people."

- Drucker's question "What is your business?" is not an easy one to answer and has many variations depending on the specific business in a multi-product, service, or social sector organization.

4. DEFINING BUSINESS PURPOSE AND MISSION

"Who is the customer?"

"Who is the customer?" is the first and the crucial question in defining business purpose and business mission. It is not an easy, let alone an obvious, question. How it is being answered determines, in large measure, how the business defines itself. The consumer—that is, the ultimate user of a product or a service—is always a customer.

Most businesses have at least two customers. Both have to buy if there is to be a sale. The manufacturers of branded consumer goods always have two customers at the very least: the housewife and the grocer. It does not do much good to have the housewife eager to buy if the grocer does not stock the brand. Conversely, it does not do much good to have the grocer display merchandise advantageously and give it shelf space if the housewife does not buy. To satisfy only one of these customers without satisfying the other means that there is no performance.

Peter F. Drucker, February 28, "Defining Business Purpose and Mission: The Customer," *The Daily Drucker*, 2004.

5. DEFINING PURPOSE AND MISSION

"What does the customer value?"

The final question needed to come to grips with business purpose and business mission is: "What is value to the customer?" It may be the most important question. Yet it is the one least often asked. One reason is that managers are quite sure that they know the answer. Value is what they, in their business, define as quality. But this is almost always the wrong definition. The customer never buys a product. By definition the customer buys the satisfaction of a want. He buys value.

For the teenage girl, for instance, value in a shoe is high fashion. It has to be "in." Price is a secondary consideration and durability is not [of] value at all. For the same girl as a young mother, a few years later, high fashion becomes a restraint. She will not buy something that is quite unfashionable. But what she looks for is durability, price, comfort and fit, and so on. The same shoe that represents the best buy for the teenager is a very poor value for her slightly older sister. What a company's different customers consider value is so complicated that it can be answered only by the customers themselves. Management should not even try to guess at the answers—it should always go to the customers in a systematic quest for them.

Peter F. Drucker, February 29, "Understanding What the Customer Buys," *The Daily Drucker*, 2004.

III. Practicum-Prompts

Your organization is an organ of society. Do you and your colleagues understand the importance of integrating the interests of your organization with the public interest? What results should your organization be delivering? Is it doing so?

How would you answer the question: "What is our business?" (Note: The nonprofit should substitute "What is our mission?") The question may generate a fair amount of conflict among the leadership group in order to arrive at an accurate answer, but an accurate definition can be used to guide many decisions and is worth the conflict the question may create.

While a customer always includes the ultimate user of a product or service, there are often many customers, such as doctors for hospitals and retailers for consumer goods. Consider a specific business, or nonprofit, that you are involved in and identify all its customers, perhaps ranking them as primary, secondary, and tertiary.

Ask your customers what they consider value for one of your products or services. What customer needs are satisfied by your product? How did your customers respond to the question? Do not assume that your customers' responses are irrational.

The question What are results? is much tougher to answer for social sector institutions than for business organizations. What is the most important social sector institution you are associated with? How does it define and measure results? Are these accurate indicators of progress toward achieving the mission of the organization and changing the lives of those in need in society?

Education and Management

Keys to Economic Development

Introduction

In 2008–2010 I had the privilege of working with Father Ben Beltran, founder of the E-Veritas Trading Network in Manila, Philippines, as he organized an electronic trading network with and for the people in the Basic Ecclesiastical Communities (BECs) of the Tondo District of Manila. Beltran founded the network to engage the people of Manila in bulk ordering, purchasing, receiving, and distribution of fresh food and produce, daily and at much lower prices than they could obtain these goods in local markets. In the process, E-Veritas trained and educated "knowledge workers" to handle the electronic trading activity involved in taking orders, accumulating orders, placing orders with reputable suppliers, distributing food to customers, and managing the financial transactions. In addition the people were also trained how to manage the infrastructure of the organization. Father Beltran and his staff trained electronic traders and organized a network of suppliers while learning and teaching the basic principles of leadership and management to employees. No amount of corruption by government can take away the knowledge absorbed by these workers, because this knowledge now resides within human beings and travels with them. E-Veritas is creating human capital within people at the bottom of the economic and social pyramid so they can develop rapidly and escape poverty.

E-Veritas (or "economic truth") is organized as a "business enterprise with a moral purpose," the economic and social well-being of the people of the Tondo District. It reports to a board of directors, just like a normal corporation. But in addition to the excess revenue over cost earned by its activities, E-Veritas receives contributions from sources around the world that are committed to microfinance investments, the elimination of poverty, and the promotion of economic development.

The moral purpose of the business enterprise is clear. Smoky Mountain, in the Tondo District of Manila, is a garbage dump[5] that emits poisonous gases. Scavengers search the smoldering mountain all day long for food and other necessities of life. Father Beltran was chaplain to 25,000 of these scavengers. Many of the employees of E-Veritas were recruited from among the scavengers and were subsequently trained in information technology and management to operate the electronic trading network.

As a result of Father Beltran's association with the Peter F. Drucker and Masatoshi Ito Graduate School of Management[6] and with sympathetic philanthropists, he was able to raise funds necessary to design and construct a water-filtration plant to help provide clean water for the people of the district.

Evidence is accumulating that through *education and management*, E-Veritas has been turned into an organization of knowledge workers, lifting up those at the bottom of the economic and social pyramid. It provides a workable model for developing segments of the underdeveloped world. But before an economic entity like E-Veritas can be organized, the long and difficult task of community organizing must be done, because something comparable to BECs or community action councils must be established before a community is ready for education and management.[7] The advantage of the BECs is that they are somewhat sheltered from corruption by the people in power because of support from the cardinal of the Philippines, Province of Manila.

Corporations doing business globally can help shelter local people from corruption to allow these locals to engage in at least small-scale economic activity. We explore this further below.

I. Read

Our traditional development theories to date have been total failures. Fifty years ago, I was an advisor to the first two presidents of the World Bank, Eugene Meyer, 1946, and John J. McCloy, 1947. We believed that capital investment should create development. However, this analogy proved erroneous. Otherwise, Egypt would be the Japan of today. There is a similar inverse relationship between capital investment and development.

The Exception: Korea and Capital
Investment in Education

Post–Korean War development is possibly the most amazing case where capital investment has created development. After seeing the devastation in Japan, Russia, and Germany, [I found that] postwar Korea was infinitely worse. During the Korean War, each of the six times the North advanced on the South, upon their retreat they shot every male, leaving only women and children.

President Dwight D. Eisenhower introduced a development strategy, placing a high priority on education. Approximately 200,000 young Korean students per year came to the United States at our expense. The overwhelming majority went back to Korea with exceptional high school educations.

Korea now has high schools. Even though the Japanese harassed the missionaries, and, at one time shot 5,000, they realized they could not impede progress. Therefore, missionaries, missions, and higher education became acceptable. For that reason, educating the Koreans laid the foundation for [South] Korea, twenty years later, to be on the brink of becoming a world economic power. Missions and education played key roles in [South] Korea's development. Every town in [South] Korea has a Catholic and Protestant high school.

Islam has been an economic development failure. In the entire Islamic world, Indonesia is where you see entrepreneurship. The only countries where there has been any development are those with minority Chinese influence, such as Indonesia and Malaysia. Again, education is the key. The Chinese place high priority on education.

> Peter F. Drucker, *Executive Summary: A Conversation with Peter Drucker on Leadership and Organizational Development*, February 5, 2002, p. 1.

II. Reflect

- Management is becoming the dominant resource in developed and developing countries. It is more effective to allocate resources to educate leaders and would-be leaders in developing countries than it is to provide financial aid.

1. EDUCATION AS A DRIVER OF KOREAN ECONOMIC DEVELOPMENT

Within twenty years—from the 1950s, when the American occupation of Japan ended, to the 1970s—Japan became the world's second economic power, and a leader in technology. When the Korean War ended in the early 1950s, South Korea was left more devastated than Japan had been seven years earlier. And it had never been anything but a backward country, especially as the Japanese systematically suppressed Korean enterprise and higher education during the thirty-five years of occupation. But, by using the colleges and universities of the United States to educate their able young people, *and by importing and applying the concepts of management* [italics mine], Korea became a highly developed country within twenty-five years.

Peter F. Drucker, *Post-Capitalist Society*, 1993, p. 44.

2. THE CENTER OF THE KNOWLEDGE SOCIETY

"Education will become the center of the knowledge society, and schooling its key institution."

Throughout history, the craftsman who had learned a trade after five or seven years of apprenticeship had learned, by age eighteen or nineteen, everything he would ever need to use during his lifetime. The new jobs require a good deal of formal education and the ability to acquire and apply theoretical and analytical knowledge. They require a different approach to work and a different mind-set. Above all they require a habit of continuous learning to prevent obsolescence.

What mix of knowledges is required for everybody? What is "quality" in learning and teaching? All these will, of necessity, become central concerns of the knowledge society, and central political issues. In fact, it may not be too fanciful to anticipate that the acquisition and distribution of formal knowledge will come to occupy the place in politics of the knowledge society that the acquisition of property and income have occupied in the two or three centuries that we have come to call the Age of Capitalism.

Peter F. Drucker, May 9, "The Center of the Knowledge Society," *The Daily Drucker*, 2004.

- A management that commits itself and its organization to developing human beings will foster a durable organization because as its people grow they will increase their managerial and entrepreneurial capacity, yielding higher levels of productivity and innovation to the organization, both directly through their work and indirectly through their suggestions.

- The Yuhan-Kimberly case below illustrates two points: first, manufacturing workers can become knowledge workers if given the opportunity; and second, manufacturing workers can take on certain levels of managerial responsibility. In other words, they can learn how to practice "responsibility-based management" and undertake functions associated with Drucker's "plant community."

3. LIFELONG LEARNING PARADIGM

Kook-Hyun Moon, the former CEO and president of Yuhan-Kimberly [Y-K], is emphatic in his belief that organizational restructurings and large layoffs are *old* and unproductive *practices*. He argues that most leaders in the current business environment do not understand that the *practice* of investing in employee development is the most beneficial one an organization can adopt. . . . Instead of large layoffs [during the Asian financial crisis of the late 1990s] Mr. Moon suggested a job-sharing system, a system that came to be known as the "four crew/two shift system." The system could have led to even greater financial difficulties because its immediate implementation actually increased labor costs. However, Mr. Moon believed that application of Y-K's human principle and the decision not to lay off Y-K's employees would overcome increased costs. . . . Under the system, a team works the day shift for four days, from 7 a.m. to 7 p.m., and then another team works the night shift for four days, from 7 p.m. to 7 a.m. After four days,

another set of two teams takes over the two shifts and the
previous two teams have four days off (three days of rest
and one day of paid training). . . . Y-K offered employees
corporate-sponsored in-house educational opportunities
in areas such as beginning and advanced computer
skills, foreign languages, and job-related skills. Y-K also
encouraged employees to further their education outside
the workplace and the company agreed to support 70% of
the costs. The implementation of the new system brought
about a "lifelong learning paradigm" among employees
and produced impressive financial results within two years
of implementation. Mr. Moon strongly believes in the
importance of continuous learning to transform manual
workers into knowledge workers. These workers in turn
generate more ideas [innovate] and are able to make more
decisions on their own.

> Peter F. Drucker and Joseph A. Maciariello, *Management
> Cases: Revised Edition*, HarperCollins, 2009, pp. 4, 5, 7.

• The current McDonald's Corporation is a product of applying
knowledge to the process of making hamburgers. Ray Kroc, a
salesman for milk shake machines, noticed that one of his fast-
food customers in California was making forty milk shakes at
once. Curious, he visited the restaurant. He learned that it had
applied something like an assembly line for turning out fast-food.
He was impressed and formed a partnership with the owners, the
McDonald family. They began turning out hamburger meals of
uniform quality. Starting with the hamburger and knowledge of
what the customer valued as the end product, Kroc redesigned
and then automated the entire management process. Tools were
designed to produce every ingredient required in a hamburger
meal at uniform quality. Kroc then trained each member of a
store to carry out operations in a standard way and made sure that
all facilities were clean and customers were treated courteously.

Ray Kroc thus increased the productivity of knowledge and produced enormous value for both customers and the business. (This
short example of applying knowledge to management—which
is itself knowledge—at McDonald's is adapted from Drucker's
1985 book *Innovation and Entrepreneurship*, pp. 17 and 18.)

4. THE PRODUCTIVITY OF KNOWLEDGE

The productivity of knowledge is going to be the
determining factor in the competitive position of a company,
an industry, or an entire country. No country, industry,
or company has any "natural" advantage or disadvantage.
The only advantage it can possess is the ability to exploit
universally available knowledge. The only thing that
increasingly will matter in national as in international
economics is management's performance in making
knowledge productive.

Peter F. Drucker, *Post-Capitalist Society*, 1993, p. 193.

- When I first learned about McDonald's I advised the investment
  committee of the organization I was with that all McDonald's
  was doing was making "hamburgers," which was not a sustainable competitive advantage. How wrong I was. Ray Kroc applied
  knowledge to the operations, marketing, and service of the organization he took over. He vastly raised the productivity of the
  organization by applying knowledge to the existing management
  process.

III. Practicum-Prompts

Identify the employees in your organization who have the potential
to become knowledge workers and to grow in managerial responsibility. Discuss with your superiors the possibility of training these

people to assume more responsibility. How can this be accomplished in the most effective manner and in the shortest period of time?

If you and your organization operate in developing countries, what actions can you take to raise the educational and managerial competencies of people there—not only to enhance their education and development but to further encourage them to do business with you and your organization in the future?

Does your organization make the best interests of the societies in which you operate your best interests? If not, what initial steps can you propose to your management so that this can be done?

Have you made learning a lifelong habit? If not, chart a plan this week. Begin by making sure you know the answer to the question "How do I learn?" Do not limit yourself to new technical and organizational knowledge but seek to broaden yourself.

Management Rooted in the Nature of Reality

Introduction

As you will see in this entry, Peter Drucker believed that Cyrus the
Great, in the fourth century B.C., was one of the outstanding leaders of
all time, no doubt because of his integrity (Hedrick, *Xenophon's Cyrus
the Great*, p. xiv), and that his biography, *Cyropaedia* by Xenophon,
is one of the best books on leadership. Drucker also believed Harry
S. Truman was one of the most effective presidents of the United
States.[8] What did these two leaders have in common? First, Cyrus
the Great was one of Truman's heroes (McCullough, *Truman*, p. 58).
Second, Truman thought that his recognition of Israel immediately
after the United Nations had granted it statehood earned him the
title of a present-day Cyrus because, like Cyrus, he acted benevolently
on behalf of the Jews. Truman, although educated only through high
school, was very well read in history and knew that Cyrus the Great,
as king of Persia, captured the Babylonian empire and in 538 B.C.
returned the Jews to Jerusalem after their seventy years of Babylonian
captivity. Cyrus also believed the Babylonians who had captured the
Jews had been punished because of their irreverence.

What leadership traits did Cyrus the Great and Harry S. Truman
share? Cyrus and Truman were both men of integrity who had sym-

pathy for the human condition. Both Cyrus and Truman did the right thing by making possible the return of the Jews to the land of Israel. Integrity, and doing the right thing, is the essence of leadership. Truman was not engaging in self-glorification; the political risks were way too high for that. Perhaps his biggest risk was that General George Marshall, then secretary of state, was intensely against recognition because of the almost certain impact on the flow of badly needed Arab oil for Europe. Interruption in the supply of oil would interfere with the objectives of the Marshall Plan in Europe. Truman decided to do the right thing first and then worry about the oil.

Clark Clifford, Truman's adviser, sums up Truman's motives as follows:

> The ethical and moral humanitarian and sentimental
> reactions that the president felt toward Israel were very
> important to him. I know why he fought for Israel. I know
> that for instance he believed that in the Old Testament there
> were references to the fact that ultimately there would be
> a Jewish homeland. . . . He felt a desire to see that these
> people who had been so mistreated all through their lives
> and all through their history would be given a chance.[9]

Therefore, leadership at the highest level is shown here to be rooted in history, religion, sympathy, and human reality.

I. Read

David Hubbard once said to Peter Drucker: "So much of your vision is rooted in the very nature of reality. One of the blessed things about you is that most of those burdens in the graduate schools of management are all common steps from mathematics, or economics, or whatever and students don't know beans about philosophy, or theology or history. They don't get back to the way life is."

Peter Drucker

Will you stop; will you accept a theological precept?
The best thing about being dead is that you don't hear
your obituary, and I am not modest, I'm honest, but will
you also accept the fact that this isn't the way things
work? One of the troubles you have in the management
schools, as in the seminaries too, is [that] they are heavily
vocational, and have to get the students their first job, and
for that they have to have a salable skill. One hundred
and fifty years ago in the commercial sector, basically
they focused on penmanship, which is the mathematics of
today, because that is how the cleric got the job in 1830.
The ones who stayed clerks are the ones who became the
chief clerks, but the people who taught penmanship, I
can assure you, believed that that was really what made
the wheels of commerce turn. So that is something. Now
I would say what you are doing, what you are beginning
to do, is the right way to go, and it isn't intended to cast
any one human being [i.e., Drucker] into bronze, but it
establishes . . . the true mechanism, an organism that sets
an example, and responds to a need and an opportunity. I
think it's the right time, and I think it is the right people
[leaders of social sector institutions at first, then leaders of
all institutions].

David Hubbard and Peter Drucker, February 24, 1987.

II. Reflect

- Shaker A. Zahar interviewed Peter Drucker on the fiftieth anniversary of the publication of his book *The Practice of Management*
  (1954). The reading below is adapted from the published interview.[10]

1. MANAGEMENT EDUCATION

Shaker Zahar

How do you feel about the practice of management as a profession today? About the study of management as a field of scholarly inquiry?

Peter Drucker

That would require a book of its own. What I like to see—and what I have practiced now for many years in my own teaching—is:

(1) Management education *only* for already successful people. I believe management courses for people without a few years of management experience are a waste of time.

(2) Management education for people from the private, the public, and the not-for-profit sectors *together*.

(3) Planned, systematic work by the students while at school in *real* work assignments in real organizations—the equivalent [of] the MD residency.

(4) *Far more emphasis* on government, society, history, and the political process.

(5) Teachers with real management experience and enough of a consulting practice to know real challenges. . . .

(6) Major emphasis on the *nonquantifiable* areas which are the real challenges—and especially on the nonquantifiable areas *outside* the business; i.e., in understanding both the limitations of the available numbers and how to use numbers.

From Shaker A. Zahar, "An Interview with Peter Drucker," *Academy of Management Executive*, August 2003, pp. 11–12.

- The ability to quantify is very important in management, yet the unique event that can be observed only through human perception is often more important. Shifts in attitudes, for example, can have a major impact on economic activity. We in the United States have changed our attitudes toward health care. The glass is "half empty" rather than "half full." Not only has this affected our political debate, and the passage of the Affordable Care Act, which became law on March 23, 2010, but the Internet, television programs devoted to health care, commercials, and wellness publications are providing an avalanche of information on health care because it has become more a matter of personal responsibility. Opportunities are opening up for new outpatient centers, as provision of health services is being unbundled and as more attention is being given to physical fitness and to reducing stress. "Mindfulness" is being used by a number of organizations to reduce stress and enhance creativity. And the list of new opportunities for provision of wellness products and services is growing. This increase in health and wellness products and services is a result of the shift in perception from health care as "half full" to health care as "half empty." It is an example of a unique event that could have been spotted only through perception. Its effects are still hard to quantify. But perception can be trained so we can spot the unique event as it begins to unfold. We can spot it through the use of our human faculties in addition to examining relevant statistics. What we can perceive is shaped by what we know and that can be aided by broadly educating ourselves.

2. MANAGEMENT AND THE LIBERAL ARTS

"Management Is a liberal art"

Forty-five years ago, the English scientist and novelist C. P. Snow talked of the "two cultures" of contemporary society. Management, however, fits neither Snow's "humanist" nor his "scientist." It deals with action and application;

and its tests are results. This makes it a technology. But management also deals with people, their values, their growth and development—and this makes it a humanity. So does its concern with, and impact on, social structure and the community. Indeed, as everyone has learned who, like this author, has been working with managers of all kinds of institutions for long years, management is deeply involved in spiritual concerns—the nature of man, good and evil.

Management is thus what tradition used to call a liberal art—"liberal" because it deals with the fundamentals of knowledge, self-knowledge, wisdom, and leadership; "art" because it deals with practice and application. Managers draw upon all of the knowledges and insights of the humanities and social sciences—on psychology and philosophy, on economics and history, on the physical sciences and ethics. But they have to focus this knowledge on effectiveness and results—on healing a sick patient, teaching a student, building a bridge, designing and selling a "user-friendly" software program.

Peter F. Drucker, *The New Realities*, 1989, p. 231.

• The following question was preceded by Zahar's comment on Drucker's repeated emphasis in *The Practice of Management* on the need for integrity in management which Drucker answers indirectly below by providing an example of a leader with integrity, and then discussing recurring patterns of corruption among leaders throughout history.

3. THE ONES WITH INTEGRITY SURVIVE

Shaker Zahar
With recent scandals revealing corporate greed and corruption, how can integrity be restored?

Peter Drucker

"Adversity is the test of leadership," said Xenophon 2,500 years ago in the *Cyropaedia*—still the best book on leadership (next to the Epistles of St. Paul). It's easy to look good in a boom. But also every boom—and I have lived and worked through four or five—puts crooks in at the top. I came into the world of business and work when, not quite 19 and a trainee, I was put in charge of liquidating the first great "scandal" of the early Depression: the Belgian Baron Lowenstein's systematic looting of the synthetic-fiber companies of Europe, which he himself had largely created. A year later, January 1930, my first assignment as a young journalist was to cover the trial of the top management of what had been Europe's biggest and proudest insurance company (the Frankfurter Allgemeine), who had systematically plundered their company—and so it goes after every boom. But then, the ones with a little integrity survive and, in the Depression, they prosper—nothing new. The only thing new is that the last boom considerably increased the temptation to fake the books—the exclusive emphasis on quarterly figures, the overemphasis on the stock price, the well-meant but idiotic belief that executives should have major stakes in the company, the stock options (which I have always considered an open invitation to mismanagement), and so on. Otherwise, no difference.

Shaker Zahar, "An Interview with Peter Drucker," *Academy of Management Executive*, August 2003, p. 11.

- The widespread use of stock options, the subsequent overemphasis by executives on stock price, and the temptation to "cook" the books are significant differences between more recent economic crises and those of the past.

III. Practicum-Prompts

Develop a plan to broaden yourself in the humanities, social sciences, and technology as it applies to the problems faced in your position, organization, and industry.

Consider reading *Cyropaedia* by Xenophon, to learn lessons of leadership from Cyrus the Great.

A study of the Pauline epistles shows just how Drucker was influenced by Paul's writings in *developing, secularizing, and applying* key concepts of management. These concepts include the simultaneous need for freedom and responsibility in executive practice, the importance of focusing on the strengths of people in selection and placement, and methods for achieving unity in diversity among people within an organization. The concepts of freedom and responsibility are especially central to Drucker's ideas. They are at the heart of his philosophy of management by objectives. Does this surprise you? Might it explain why Drucker read so widely outside the field of management and perhaps why you should continue to develop yourself in the same direction?

Reducing temptations to cheat by imposing severe penalties on perpetrators is helpful, but it will not eliminate such temptations, especially during boom periods. Integrity in leadership and strong controls are also helpful. Nevertheless, history teaches us to be vigilant against fraud and abuse. What preventive steps are you and your organization taking? What has been your record in the recent past? If it is poor, how can you improve it?

Setting Your Sights on the Important, Not the Urgent

Make the *Important* Rather Than the *Urgent* Your Priority in Life

Introduction

The reading from Drucker this week has to do with Peter's personal choices in focusing his time on the important, not the urgent. There is a lot to be learned from his example that can be applied to our own lives.

Many of the readings in this volume come out of his work during the last third of a very long and productive life. This is work he considered *important*. Each of us can learn how to distinguish between the important and the urgent from the example of the way Peter Drucker did it himself. Drucker lived to be almost ninety-six, but many of us will not. Acting on the lessons in this reading should be a priority for us right now!

I had the opportunity to watch Peter Drucker allocate his time during the twenty-six years I served with him. Since then I have been digesting his mentoring and interactions with a larger group. These were acquaintances who became good friends over the many years of mentoring. He helped them sort out the important from the urgent.

I saw as he aged that he turned down a number of requests to write forewords for the books of others. He gave up serving on committees at the university; supervising doctoral students (with one or two exceptions); traveling, which took a great deal of energy; and his vacations at his cabin in Estes Park, Colorado, because he was unable to tolerate the altitude. The one exception regarding travel was a cross-country trip he made to Washington, D.C., in July 2002 to receive the Presidential Medal of Freedom from George W. Bush.

Peter Drucker led a focused life doing what he felt he was called to do. He made peace about how he used his time. He *managed it* by maintaining a detailed calendar of activities and projects that he and his wife, Doris, worked together to prioritize and carry out.

He knew there came a time in a person's life when a choice had to be made to work with energy restrictions. He had enough experience observing the handicapped to know that especially at such a time, working on the truly important issues and abandoning all the rest was more important than ever. He chose to work with his mind, which was brilliant—not with his legs, which were weak. He also knew that he wanted to be remembered for developing human potential, so he focused his limited energy on mentoring a number of people, some of whom are mentioned in this book. Finally, he was a writer, so he made sure that he made provision for his writings to be available after his death.

One had the sense that Peter Drucker finished all that he was called to do two weeks before he died on November 11, 2005, when he saw an advance copy of his last book, *The Effective Executive in Action* (2006). Although Drucker's life is instructive, each one of us is, as he would say, a "special Peter." We have our own purpose in life that should include balance between work and pleasure. But there will always be a decision to make between the important and the urgent. While Drucker's personal life is instructive on that topic, this entry is devoted to the priorities you establish in your life.

I. Read

By 1989 Drucker regretted not having spent more time earlier in his career on the management of social sector organizations—a regret he then resolutely addressed until his death in 2005. Drucker expressed this regret in an interview with a good friend of his:

> If I look back, my greatest frustrations are probably, in retrospect, this is hindsight, that I have, far too often, made the urgent rather than the important my priority and that as a result, some of the books I should have written I haven't written. And I have written the books that were urgent, or I have taught the things that they needed at the moment rather than the things that were needed five years since. I have been willing to run shorter rather than long-term. But that's hindsight.
>
> Peter F. Drucker, Interview with Reverend James Flamming, 1989.

Peter Drucker went on to spend a large part of his last twenty-plus years of life advising leaders of social sector organizations including, but by no means limited to, pastors of large church and para-church organizations. His focus was always on how to improve their *processes of leadership, organization* and *management*, including the *development of people, building community*, and *planning for succession* of leaders at the top of their organizations. As we will see, he and his mentees combined to produce astounding results.

II. Reflect

• You are responsible for allocating your life.

1. LEARN FROM THE HANDICAPPED HOW TO SEPARATE THE IMPORTANT FROM THE URGENT

[T]he best proof that the danger of overpruning
[eliminating urgent activities] is a bugaboo is the
extraordinary effectiveness so often attained by severely
ill or severely handicapped people. A good example was
Harry Hopkins, President Roosevelt's adviser in World
War II. A dying man for whom every step was a torment,
he could only work a few hours every other day or so. This
forced him to cut out everything but truly important
vital matters. He did not lose effectiveness thereby; on the
contrary he became as Churchill called him once "Lord
Heart of the Matter" and accomplished more than anyone
else in wartime Washington. This is an extreme example
of course. But it illustrates both how much control one
can exercise over one's time if one really tries and how
much of the time-wasters one can cut out without loss of
effectiveness.

Peter F. Drucker, *The Effective Executive*, 1967, p. 40.

- Drucker was very successful as a writer, teacher, and consultant
  for business executives, yet he was able to make a change from
  the urgent to what he considered important at the peak of his
  success, when he had other opportunities in abundance that he
  refused. This is a powerful example for each one of us to focus
  on what is important.

2. ASK WHAT NEEDS TO BE DONE, NOT WHAT DO I WANT TO DO

Regardless of their almost limitless diversity with respect to
personality, style, abilities, and interests, the effective leaders
I have met, worked with, and observed also *behaved* much the
same way: They did not start off with the question, "What

do I want?" They started out with the question, *"What needs to be done?"*

Peter F. Drucker, "Not Enough Generals Were Killed,"
1996, pp. xii–xiii.

- "If there is any one 'secret' of effectiveness, it is concentration." All the more so for executives, since demands on their time from others tend to be continuous. It follows that the need to engage in multitasking tends to be a reality for the executive. But he or she must learn, in the midst of multiple demands, to give priority, and the necessary amount of time and focus, to the *important* rather than to the *urgent*.

3. EVERYTHING MAY JUST NOT BE AS IMPORTANT AS SOME THINGS ARE

Being an executive means having no time. It means that everybody moves in on your time. Everybody wants time from you. There is always more work to be done than [there are] hours in a day. And everything always takes so much longer than it should. And then twice as long as the boss thinks it should. And there is a difference in the way effective executives use their time and in the way that most of us do. The important thing is that you know how many hours you really have and where they are going. Everything may just not be really as important as some things are. Do you really know how much solid time you give to activities that really deserve it? Now isn't it possible that a lot of time is simply slipping through your fingers?

Peter F. Drucker, transcript of videotape series, 1968.

- Feedback analysis is a very old technique employed by Saint Ignatius of Loyola for developing himself and the priests of the Jesuit order. His meditations, and their modern variations and secular adaptations, provide a tool for analyzing our performance from time to time by comparing results with our expectations. It is a tool that can be used to determine our strengths, and the areas in which we are likely to make our greatest contribution. These are the areas to which we should consider allocating our time.

III. Practicum-Prompts

"People decisions"—hiring, promoting, and firing—are almost always among the most *important* decisions you will have to make. Take your time making these decisions because if you make a mistake you will spend a long time regretting and undoing it!

I use a little pamphlet, *The Tyranny of the Urgent*[11] by Charles Hummel, as a reminder of the difference between urgent and important tasks. While I have had success with this specific approach for time management, consider placing your own prompts in key places where requests on your time come in, and form a habit of pausing to distinguish between the important and the urgent demands on your time.

Drucker used feedback analysis to help him make decisions about how to allocate his life, including decisions about what he wanted to be remembered for. What do you want to be remembered for?

The answer to the question "What do I want to be remembered for?" will change as you age, so it is important to ask and answer it a number of times during your life. The answer will give your life focus and purpose. The tendency to avoid the question is great, especially as we become absorbed in day-to-day activity. Crises play a major role in helping us stop and come to grips with the question but you do not need a crisis to do so. I have found the first few days of a new year are a good time to ask the question. But if you have not already answered it, why not try to answer the question now?

Manage in Two Time Dimensions

Introduction

CEOs are acutely aware of the need to balance short-term results with long-term results. They recognize and take into account the trade-offs. For example, it is easy to reduce research and development and employee development allowances in times when meeting short-term profit goals is in jeopardy. But if you do this, make sure you restore the resources and activities as soon as possible to maintain the innovation, knowledge, and skill levels you will need to successfully compete in the future. Restoring the funds will help to keep your strategic plan intact.

And this is the essence of strategic planning—making resource allocation decisions today that will affect the future. It requires deliberately allocating people and funds to projects that are directed toward securing the future of your organization. Yet short-term results are necessary, and this necessity may require you to make trade-offs between short-term and long-term results.

Because executives usually do not have a "bag of gold" to simultaneously spread around to both existing and future products and services, they must calculate what new investments in existing products and services, including people development, will take away from investments in the future prospects of the organization. If the trade-off is acceptable, then the decision is right. If not, resource allocation between the present and the future must be rethought until the trade-off is appropriate.

Let's now consider the statement by the CEO in this week's reading. She is trying to recover past losses *before* focusing on future products and services: *"The basic value, she says, is that first, we have to regain what we have lost in the past, and then build for the future."* Drucker issues a warning about consistency between this short-term action and the longer-term welfare of the organization.

I. Read

There are both short-term and long-term missions [and they] have to be compatible. But when you look at some modern organizations—for example, here is a very able woman who just took over for Hewlett–Packard. She wrote a short-term and a long-term mission for Hewlett–Packard when she took over, but the two missions are not compatible. She knows it by the way. She is very bright. *The basic value, she says, is that first, we have to regain what we have lost in the past, and then build for the future* [italics mine]. By the way, this old consultant said then and often before that it never works. But that doesn't matter. But that's everybody's problem [managing in two time dimensions], that's what you need. You have to have results in the short term and you have to have results in the long term. The old medical proverb says it doesn't help you much if the old woman, the sick woman, knows the surgery tomorrow would save her life, if she dies during the night. But it doesn't help you very much either if she survives at night if you don't do the surgery tomorrow and save her life. So you have to have short-term and long-term missions and the two have to be compatible. And yet they are often different.

Peter F. Drucker, at http://www.youtube.com/
watch?v=V1xppECWZPw, February 2, 2009.

II. Reflect

- There are always trade-offs between actions that serve the present and those that further long-term performance. When making these trade-offs, executives should know the costs imposed on the long term by short-term actions.
- The missions in these two time dimensions may be different but they should be compatible.

1. THE MANAGER'S TASKS

"A manager must, so to speak, keep his nose to the grindstone while lifting his eyes to the hills—quite an acrobatic feat."

A manager has two specific tasks. The first is creation of a true whole that is larger than the sum of its parts, a productive entity that turns out more than the sum of the resources put into it. The second specific task of the manager is to harmonize in every decision and action the requirements of [the] immediate and long-range future. A manager cannot sacrifice either without endangering the enterprise.

If a manager does not take care of the next hundred days, there will be no next hundred years. Whatever the manager does should be sound in expediency as well as in basic long-range objective and principle. And where he cannot harmonize the two time dimensions, he must at least

balance them. He must calculate the sacrifice he imposes
on the long-range future of the enterprise to protect its
immediate interests, or the sacrifice he makes today for the
sake of tomorrow. He must limit either sacrifice as much as
possible. And he must repair as soon as possible the damage
it inflicts. He lives and acts in two time dimensions, and is
responsible for the performance of the whole enterprise and
of his own component in it.

> Peter F. Drucker, *Management: Tasks, Responsibilities,*
> *Practices,* 1973, 1974, chap. 31, pp. 398–99.

• Executives must fix the problems of the past but the real job of
the executive is to commit the organization's resources to opportunities in the future.

2. COMMIT TODAY'S RESOURCES TO THE FUTURE

Executives, whether they like it or not, are forever bailing
out the past. This is inevitable. Today is always the result
of actions and decisions taken yesterday. Man, however,
whatever his title or rank, cannot foresee the future.
Yesterday's actions and decisions, no matter how courageous
or wise they may have been, inevitably become today's
problems, crises, and stupidities. Yet it is the executive's
specific job—whether he works in government, in a business,
or in any other institution—to commit today's resources to
the future.

> Peter F. Drucker, *The Effective Executive,* 1967, pp. 103–4.

• A mission statement must reflect results in the short term as well
as results in the long term.

3. A MISSION IS ALWAYS LONG RANGE

[T]he mission is always long range. It needs short-range efforts and very often short-range results. And it starts out with a long-range objective. There is a wonderful sentence in one of the sermons of the great poet and religious philosopher of the seventeenth century, John Donne. "Never start with tomorrow to reach eternity. Eternity is not being reached by small steps." So we start always with the long range, and then we feed back and say, What do we *do today?* Do is the critical word. . . . We have had some amazingly successful long-term companies . . . They all started out with a very clear long-range concept.

Peter F. Drucker, *Managing the Non-Profit Organization*: *Principles and Practices*, 1990, p. 46.

• An executive cannot sacrifice either dimension without threatening the survival of the organization.

III. Practicum-Prompts

Are both short-range and longer-range objectives spelled out in your organization's mission statement? What are they?

Are the short-term and long-term objectives in your mission statement compatible?

Does your organization focus most of its time and effort on problems related to past decisions?

How can you free up some of your time and resources to focus on opportunities that serve the future of your unit?

The Road Map
to Personal
Effectiveness

Week 8

Concentration

Introduction

Peter Drucker wrote a detailed letter to Bob Buford dated September 22, 1986, following a Drucker Summit Conference sponsored by Buford at Estes Park, Colorado. The letter contains principles of effectiveness and a personal work plan for Bob himself. In the letter Drucker reviews many aspects of executives' personal effectiveness and applies them directly to Bob's work. This letter was pivotal in Bob's work plan for the rest of his life and contains many lessons we can use in our own lives and work.

The letter provides a study of the principles of effectiveness contained in Peter Drucker's classic book *The Effective Executive* (1967) and his article "Managing Oneself" in the *Harvard Business Review* (1999). The article is itself an excerpt from Drucker's book *Management Challenges for the 21st Century* (1999, pp. 161–96).

The first topic is the cornerstone of personal effectiveness, *concentration of effort*—a key practice in getting the right things done and therefore a key practice for personal effectiveness.

I. Read

How should you define the specific pieces of work to be tackled? And how should you define what not to do? Should you be willing to admit everyone who wants your services and who needs them? Or should you focus on targets of opportunity only? And should you say "no" ever—and to whom and on what? I think you know that I consider these to be important questions. They are really the questions "What is our business?" "What should it be?" "What should it not be?" "Who is our customer?" "What is value to the customer?"

I would submit that you should target yourself on the areas where a little success on your part will have the greatest impact, both because it will be highly visible [and] also because it will make a genuine difference. This would indicate I think that you do not worry about the ones who are not yet ready for you. You, I submit, are likely to have more customers than you can possibly satisfy and very soon. . . .

I would . . . exclude [programs] where even great success is unlikely to make a real difference. In other words, you will have such a tough time satisfying the demands on you, that there is no point in splintering your very scarce resources. But also the need is in the large congregation [the pastoral church][12] and that is where you can make a real contribution. The small congregation basically does not need what you have to offer and will not be able to use it until it has become quite large. I foresee, and in the not too distant future, the possibility of your converting a lot of your experience into manuals, courses, books, and so on, which the small church then can use effectively. And then, needless to say, I foresee that one does some piloting—though not necessarily as part of the work of your Foundation. But your work, I would argue, should, for the foreseeable future, be focused on the large church and should therefore exclude, or at least discourage, others.

You pointed out that very much the same problems exist throughout the public service sector. Actually, I would say that quite a few public service institutions would need what you are offering just as badly as the large [pastoral] churches, and perhaps more so.

Peter F. Drucker, selected passages from correspondence with Robert Buford, September 22, 1986.

II. Reflect

- The most capable human resources of an organization, including managerial talent, should be allocated to the most promising opportunities of that organization.

1. CONCENTRATE ON THE SMALLEST NUMBER OF ACTIVITIES THAT WILL FOCUS ON THE GREATEST PRODUCTIVITY

Concentration is the key to economic results. Economic results require that managers concentrate their efforts on the smallest number of products, product lines, services, customers, markets, distributive channels, end uses, and so on that will produce the largest amount of revenue. Managers must minimize the amount of attention devoted to products that produce primarily costs because, for instance, their volume is too small or splintered.

Economic results require that staff efforts be concentrated upon the few activities that are capable of producing significant business results. . . .

Finally, human resources must be concentrated on a few major opportunities. This is particularly true for high-grade human resources through which knowledge becomes effective in work. And above all it is true of the scarcest, most expensive, but also potentially most effective of all human resources in a business: managerial talent.

Peter F. Drucker, *Managing for Results*, 1964, pp. 11–12.

- Knowing your mission or purpose is essential in choosing from among all available opportunities those that have the highest probability of producing *the right results.*

2. "KNOWING YOUR PURPOSE ALLOWS CONCENTRATION"

The fact is that you don't have time to do everything in life, and the good news is that not everything in life is worth doing anyway. So knowing your purpose allows concentration. Here's a quote from Peter: "Concentrate on the smallest number of activities that will focus on the greatest productivity." Focus on your core competencies; focus on your strengths; don't major in the minors. You know when you take a light that is unfocused it has no power at all, but if you take a magnifying glass and focus that light on a piece of grass you can burn it. If you want your life to count, if you want your organization to count, the secret is focus, focus with your life. Do a few things well.

> Rick Warren, "The Influence of Peter Drucker on My Life,"
> November 13, 2004.

- One just cannot keep adding initiatives without removing some. You should ask yourself, "What am I (or what are we) going to give up?" One should abandon programs where even great success is unlikely to make a real difference.

3. ABANDONMENT

"There is nothing as difficult and as expensive, but also nothing is as futile, as trying to keep a corpse from stinking."

Effective executives know that they have to get many things done effectively. Therefore, they concentrate. And the first rule for the concentration of executive efforts is to slough off the past that has ceased to be productive. The first-class resources, especially those scarce resources of human strength, are immediately pulled out and put to work on the opportunities of tomorrow. If leaders are unable to slough off yesterday, to abandon yesterday, they simply will not be able to create tomorrow.

Without systematic and purposeful abandonment, an organization will be overtaken by events. It will squander its best resources on things it should never have been doing or should no longer do. As a result, it will lack the resources, especially capable people, needed to exploit the opportunities that arise. Far too few businesses are willing to slough off yesterday, and as a result, far too few have resources available for tomorrow.

Peter F. Drucker, January 5, "Abandonment," *The Daily Drucker*, 2004.

III. Practicum-Prompts

What are some examples of "right results" for you and your organization? Pursue them.

What are those areas in your work and life in which you have high competence and skill? Seek to apply these competencies to activities and programs that if done well will produce extraordinary, "right" results.

You and your organization are likely to be overtaken by future events, unless you practice systematic abandonment of old products, programs, and processes, and redirect your activities and resources to programs and activities that have high potential impact.

How do we "create tomorrow"? Changes in trends are much more important than existing trends in spotting opportunities for creating a new and better future for your organization. Think about *creating tomorrow* by focusing on *changes in trends* rather than on just the current trends affecting your organization.

Once your primary opportunities have been converted to right results, think through how these efforts can be adapted to other opportunities or markets.

Week 9

Organize Work for Effectiveness

Introduction

Drucker, in *The Effective Executive* (pp. 25–26), argues, "Effective executives know that time is the limiting factor" of effectiveness. For a given day, week, month, year, etc., it is a fixed quantity and we all have the same amount. Therefore, we should attempt to plan our time, making sure that our most important tasks are done first, and—as much as possible—resist pressures to engage in multitasking. Both empirical evidence and common practice confirm that multitasking reduces our overall effectiveness.

In other words, we should plan our time, since it is our most limiting factor, and we should fit our tasks into our available time. Put another way, we should "cut the pattern to fit the cloth." But how to do this? Should we bypass unexpected opportunities because we have no time for them? Or, should we evaluate promising new opportunities as they occur and decide on the basis of their merits to take or reject them? If we want to accept an unexpected new opportunity, we must decide what to abandon or delegate, for if we keep adding new opportunities we will surely jeopardize our effectiveness and perhaps jeopardize our well-being.

The readings, reflections, and prompts in this entry teach us how to manage our time to achieve overall effectiveness in our work.

I. Read

"How did you go about developing yourself?"

This is a question Peter Drucker asked Andy Grove, one of the three founding members of Intel.

Andy Grove

I get my nose into a new activity; I spend some amount of time on it. I find that I put pressure on my time. At some point I find that something has to go. I begin to scan what I do. I look for opportunities. I look for activities that I participate in that I could stop participating in. [For] most of the things that have to go I can find some substitute arrangement. For example, I changed our management meeting from one each week to one each two weeks. In every case the pressure is around time. I ask, "What am I doing that I shouldn't be doing?" I force myself to get overloaded and then I look at the whole stack for something to throw out. I look at what I do. Should I still be doing it? Am I doing it well? Am I adding enough value to what I am doing? Is it more worthwhile or less worthwhile than something else? I negotiate with myself. Perhaps what happens is that I won't immediately stop something but I start the machinery to stop within a certain period of time, such as six months.

> Peter F. Drucker and Joseph A. Maciariello, "Andy Grove
> of Intel: Entrepreneur Turned Executive," in *Management
> Cases: Revised Edition*, 2009, pp. 186–87.

II. Reflect

- As demands on executives grow, they must create time for important ones by delegating certain activities, abandoning other activities, or relaxing the frequency of the performance of repetitive duties. They should embrace opportunities as these arise and use one or more of the above practices to make time for the new opportunities.

- The specific executive tasks are setting objectives, organizing, motivating, communicating, measuring performance, and developing people. Each task involves decision making and tools of executive effectiveness. But most executives spend a fair amount of their time on tasks that usually are not considered to be among these. The additional, operational tasks may include taking care of the organization's most important customers; negotiating major financing; recognizing longtime serving people, including those who are retiring; etc. These are important tasks, and although some of them are purely ceremonial, they have to be done well and usually cannot be delegated.

1. ORGANIZE WORK FOR EFFECTIVENESS

One area that is quite clear from the little I have seen of your associates, the pastors, is that they all need to organize their own work and effectiveness. They are people of tremendous energy. And they all get an enormous amount done in a very short time. Still the demands on them are growing faster than their time and energy allow. What have they found that enables [each] to remain effective and active as a Pastor, as a professional, as a leader—in addition to preaching? We know that in any professional work the leaders must not allow themselves to become merely "executives," but must remain active as "professionals," otherwise they lose their skill fast. This is surely just as true of the pastor as it is of the surgeon or the lawyer. Which of these men have successfully handled this and how? Is it simply a matter of setting aside time? Is it a matter of thinking through what the individual's own strength is and of making sure that the key activities that utilize this strength remain his [or her] "activities" rather than being delegated to others?

Peter F. Drucker, correspondence with Robert Buford, September 22, 1986.

• Successful executives are not afraid of strong subordinates. Strong subordinates help executives fulfill their own responsibilities. And giving subordinates expanded responsibility helps to develop them. Abraham Lincoln selected as cabinet members four of his opponents for the Republican nomination for president in 1860. At least two of them, William H. Seward and Salmon P. Chase, on the basis of formal qualifications, including education and experience, were more qualified for the presidency than Lincoln. His second secretary of war, Edwin Stanton, a Democrat and former attorney general in the Buchanan administration, previously thought dimly of Lincoln's ability as a lawyer. Yet Lincoln knew he was dealing with very serious problems and needed to assemble the most talented team available to help him carry out his responsibilities.

2. PICKING STRONG SUBORDINATES

"Making a leader effective."

Precisely because an effective leader knows that he, and no one else, is ultimately responsible, he is not afraid of strength in associates and subordinates. Misleaders are, they always go in for purges. But an effective leader wants strong associates, he encourages them, pushes them, indeed glories in them. Because he holds himself as ultimately responsible for the mistakes of his associates and subordinates, he also sees the triumphs of his associates as his triumphs, rather than as threats. A leader may be personally vain—as General MacArthur was to an almost pathological degree. Or he may be personally humble—both Lincoln and Truman were so almost to the point of having inferiority complexes. But all three wanted able, independent, self-assured people around them, they encouraged their subordinates, praising and promoting them. So did a very different person: Dwight "Ike" Eisenhower, when supreme commander in Europe.

Peter F. Drucker, *The Essential Drucker*, 2008, pp. 270–71.

- To establish standards, top executives must engage in activities that include developing, reiterating, and setting examples of the vision and values of the organization. People quickly forget the vision, values, and standards of an organization and treat these as "trophies" unless they are reinforced by management. Reinforcement of mission and values has to be done a number of times each year by the people in charge of an organization. Such reinforcements are sometimes referred to as "conscience activities." They establish what the organization stands for and aspires to, and its reason for being.

3. LEADERSHIP IS RESPONSIBILITY

"Not enough generals were killed."

All the effective leaders I have encountered—both those I worked with and those I watched—knew four simple things: a leader is someone who has *followers*; popularity is not leadership, *results are*; leaders are highly visible, they set *examples*; leadership is not rank, privilege, titles, or money, it is *responsibility*.

When I was in my final high school years, our excellent history teacher—himself a badly wounded war veteran— told each of us to pick several of a whole spate of history books on World War I, and write a major essay on our selections. When we then discussed these essays in class, one of my fellow students said, "Every one of these books says that the Great War was a war of total military incompetence. *Why was it?*" Our teacher did not hesitate a second but shot right back, "Because not enough generals were killed; they stayed way behind the lines and let others do the fighting and dying." Effective leaders delegate but they do not delegate the one thing that will set the standards. *They do it.*

> Peter F. Drucker, April 8, "Leadership Is Responsibility," *The Daily Drucker*, 2004.

III. Practicum-Prompts

Are demands on you growing faster than your time allows? What concrete steps can you take to "cut the pattern of your work to fit the cloth of time available"? Can you delegate some activities? Can you abandon some? Can you change the frequency of performing others? Can you get relief from your superior?

Andy Grove, who was a very effective CEO of a large public company, explained that he set his priorities by putting pressure on his time. As new opportunities arose that required his time, he identified other activities that he should either abandon or delegate to others. Would "putting pressure on your time" work for you?

Do not delegate standard-setting activities. And lead by example on these most important activities.

Select subordinates on the basis of their strengths. Do not be afraid of selecting strong subordinates. They will help you fulfill your responsibilities.

We tend to learn by teaching others. When we develop others we simultaneously develop ourselves because we have to figure out how to raise the capacity of the people we are trying to develop—which is a stretching exercise. Who should you reach out and help develop?

Humility is not a problematic personality trait in achieving executive effectiveness. Are you a humble person? Is your humility creating an inferiority complex? What steps can you take to retain your humility while shedding any sense of inferiority?

Information Literacy for Executive Effectiveness

Introduction

The "knowledge organization" is structured around information, not hierarchy. For example, Drucker states, "The typical business will be knowledge-based, an organization composed largely of specialists who direct and discipline their own performance through organized feedback from colleagues, customers, and headquarters. For this reason it will be what I call an information-based organization." [13] He often cited two examples of information-based organizations; the modern hospital, which is organized around a patient and a multitude of medical specialties and subspecialties, employed in diagnosing and caring for patients; and the symphony orchestra, which is organized around the musical composition, and around four families of musical instruments each consisting of several different instruments. The lead physician coordinates information flow among specialists and manages patient care with the assistance of nurses. The conductor communicates to different musicians who are all directed to perform according to the musical score.

Both the modern hospital and the modern symphony orchestra are examples of typical information-based or knowledge organizations. They are flat and rely for their effectiveness on a multitude of specialists who must communicate with one another. Moreover, information-based organizations call on executives—the lead physician and the conductor in these examples—to be technologically literate about the role of each member of the team so that all members' efforts can be coordinated. This is the role of the executive in the knowledge society.

Executives must make sure that they can analyze data effectively, and that these data are communicated to members of the organization who need the information if they are to be effective. An example from a very successful college basketball coach, Brad Stevens, clearly illustrates each of these requirements. Stevens, a former head coach of men's basketball at Butler University, led his teams to the NCAA Division I Championship Finals in 2010 and 2011 and is now head coach of the Boston Celtics of the National Basketball Association.

When asked how he uses the data he and his staff collect, he describes the process as follows:

> I first break down all of the statistics that I can on opponents
> to try to get my mind wrapped around what their trends
> are. I'll look for how many three-point attempts per field
> goal attempt—that tells you what kind of team they are
> right away. You can look at offensive-rebound percentages.
> Defensive—and offensive—turnover percentages. How
> teams shoot against them. What they defend well. What
> they try to defend well.[14]

He goes on to explain that opponents change their behavior during the season. He is observant of the most recent trends. In addition, the most important part of the job is getting his players to understand the information and to act on it. If his players do not understand and act on the information, it is worthless. So too in the management of all knowledge-based organizations, and that is why Drucker stresses the need for effective communications between those needing information to perform and those who possess the information others need. Brad Stevens provides us with the simplest complete example of how the knowledge organization is based on information, information literacy, and information responsibility.

I. Read

INFORMATION LITERACY FOR EXECUTIVE EFFECTIVENESS

There is a famous old joke about leadership. A man in the hot air balloon gets lost over Kansas, or Iowa, has no idea where he is or where he is going, he does not see anybody, nothing but grass. Finally, he sees a woman down in a field. He goes down and hollers to her, "Where am I? I'm already an hour late for an appointment!" She hollers back, "You're at 42 degrees 8 minutes and 4 seconds North latitude and 94 degrees longitude." He replies, "You must be an accountant." She says, "How did you know?" He says, "Your information is absolutely accurate, and totally useless." Then she says, "You must be an executive." He says, "Yes, but how did you know?" She says, "You're higher up, you do not know where you are, you do not know where you're going, you're over scheduled, and you blame your subordinates, someone below you."

From Peter F. Drucker, *Executive Summary: A Conversation with Peter Drucker on Leadership and Organizational Development*, 2002, p. 6.

II. Reflect

• In order to move from data literacy to information literacy executives must answer two specific questions: "What information does my organization need?" and "What information do I need?" This requires placing more emphasis on how to convert raw data to useful information than on how to acquire information technology—more emphasis on the "I" than on the "T." In this new era of "big data" it is even more important to convert raw data to true information.

1. ASKING WHAT INFORMATION I OWE TO OTHERS ESTABLISHES COMMUNICATIONS

To produce the information managers need for their work,
they have to begin with two questions:

[First:] "What information do I owe to the people with
whom I work and on whom I depend? And in what form?
And in what time frame?"

[Second:] "What information do I need myself? And from
whom? And in what form? And in what time frame?"

These two questions are closely connected. But they
are different. *What I owe* comes first because it establishes
communications. And unless that has been established there
can be no information flow.

> Peter F. Drucker and Joseph A. Maciariello, *Management: Revised Edition*, 2008, p. 349.

• Information literacy requires us to separate from an enormous amount of data, which is now available through our almost unlimited storage technology, the part that is true information. How do we tell the difference? True information is those data that are important to the solution of specific problems faced by the organization. The question then is not "Are the data interesting?" but rather "Are the data important and useful for making decisions to solve problems and seize new opportunities?"

2. NO SURPRISES: THE TEST OF INTELLIGENCE INFORMATION

The ultimate test of an information system is that there are
no surprises. Before events become significant, executives
have already adjusted to them, analyzed them, understood
them and taken appropriate action.

One example [is] the very few American financial
institutions that, in the late 1990s, were not surprised
by the [financial] collapse of mainland Asia. They had
thought through what "information" means in respect to
Asian economies and Asian currencies. They had gradually
eliminated all the information they got from within their
own subsidiaries and affiliates in these countries—these,
they had begun to realize, were just "data." Instead, they
had begun to organize their information about such things
as the ratio between portfolio investment (i.e., short-term
borrowing) and the country's balance of payments and with
it the amount available to service foreign short-term debt.
Long before these ratios turned so unfavorable as to make
a panic in mainland Asia inevitable, these executives had
realized that it was coming. They realized that they had
to decide whether to pull out of these countries for short-
term growth, or to stay for the very long term. They had,
in other words, realized what economic data are meaningful
in respect to emerging countries, had organized them, had
analyzed them and had interpreted them. They had turned
the data into information—and had decided what action to
take long before that action became necessary.

Peter F. Drucker, *Management Challenges for the 21st Century*,
1999, pp. 128–30.

• Most changes that have transformed organizations originate *outside* the specific industry of the organization. For example, the
discipline of *Sabermetrics*, developed in 1980 by historian and stat-
istician Bill James, involves the application of data analysis to the
evaluation of professional talent in baseball and basketball, and
to a lesser extent football. The Oakland Athletics in 2002 under
General Manager Billy Beane hired Paul DePodesta, a 1995 economics graduate of Harvard University, to apply data analytics to
evaluate and select talent in order to exploit market inefficiencies

and compete more successfully with the larger-market baseball teams. Sabermetrics is now widely used in professional baseball and basketball.

- Daniel Hertzberg reports in his June 7, 2014, entry in the *Wall Street Journal* online edition on Billy Beane's new efforts using a 3-D tracking system called *Statcast* that is designed both as a more enjoyable viewing system for fans and a tool to "enable management to assemble players in new ways, emphasizing their ability to complement one another" and "measure a player's value in the context of the rest of the team." This is precisely the challenge faced by executives of all organizations. Therefore, we can predict that data systems similar to Statcast will be used in industries outside of professional sports.

> Daniel Hertzberg, JOURNAL REPORTS: LEADERSHIP,
> "Billy Beane on the Future of Sports: A Tech-Driven
> Revolution," *Wall Street Journal* online edition, June 7, 2014.

3. NEED FOR OUTSIDE INFORMATION

Major changes always start outside an organization.

For *strategy*, we need organized information about the environment. Strategy has to be based upon information about markets, customers and noncustomers; about technology in one's own industry and others; about worldwide finance; and about the changing world economy. For that is where results are. Inside an organization there are only cost centers. The only profit center is a customer whose check has not bounced. . . . It is always with noncustomers that basic changes begin and become significant.

> Peter F. Drucker, *Management Challenges for the 21st Century*,
> 1999, p. 121.

III. Practicum-Prompts

The first step in moving from data to information literacy is for you to ask and answer two specific questions: What external, internal, and cross-organizational information does my organization need? What information do I need to be effective in my position?

Identify the key variables for your organization in the environment in which you operate. Develop a system for keeping track of them.

Focus data on the information needed for decision making. Eliminate data that do not pertain to the information you need. Organize, analyze, and interpret the data you do need so that they become true information.

Test the database and information derived from it for effectiveness by asking: "Have we experienced any events we have not anticipated?"

Explore data systems that have originated outside your industry for adaptation and use in your organization.

Principles of Professional Leadership and Management

Introduction

This entry describes the principles of professional leadership and management that Drucker hammered out with leaders in the Drucker-Buford Dialogue Project. Drucker's recommendations for a functioning board are also presented. I then elaborate on these recommendations. My commentary is based on the internal operations of one of the excellent social sector boards Drucker referred to, but did not describe, in his 1989 article in the *Harvard Business Review*. In Note 15 I cite five of the ten recommendations from the recent literature on corporate boards contained in my book *Drucker's Lost Art of Management* (2011, pp. 174–77).[15]

I. Read

As you will see in a number of places in this book, Peter Drucker had tremendous difficulty with what he considered a "craze" for leadership, especially in course offerings at graduate and undergraduate schools of management. The emphasis on charisma drew his ire. He was fearful of it because of his early experiences with charismatic leaders who were toxic or misleaders. Yet in his work with social sector executives, he encountered a number of very effective executives who were often charismatic leaders. So it was not charisma per se that he so vehemently opposed, but the kind of charisma that leads subordinates to yield their judgment and will in all matters to the leader. This to him was immoral.

There also is little question that Drucker realized that there is a distinction between leadership and management:

> Leadership is lifting a person's vision to higher sights, the raising of a person's performance to a higher standard, the building of a personality beyond its normal limitations.
>
> Peter F. Drucker and Joseph A. Maciariello, *Management: Revised Edition*, 2008, p. 288.

Drucker was quite sure we could teach people how to be effective executives but less sure that we could teach people to be leaders. But by creating organizations with a high spirit of performance, we could create the climate in which leaders could develop and emerge.

> Nothing better prepares the ground for such leadership than a spirit of management that confirms in the day-to-day practices of the organization strict principles of conduct and responsibility, high standards of performance, and respect for individuals and their work.
>
> Peter F. Drucker and Joseph A. Maciariello, *Management: Revised Edition*, 2008, p. 288.

Drucker also had great difficulty, which he never overcame, with what he believed were nonperforming boards of directors in business. In a powerful early article published in the *Wharton Magazine* (Fall 1976), and included in chapter 7 of his *Towards the Next Eco-*

nomics and Other Essays (reissued in 2010 by Harvard Business School Publishing), there is a tongue-in-cheek advertisement that he wrote, recruiting a board member for a private corporation (p. 109):

> Major Multibillion dollar corporation seeks professional member on board of directors. We have a job enrichment plan to convert position from rubber stamping to active policy-making. Requires 40–50 days per year intensive work. Salary high. Rare opportunity. Corporation Presidents and attorneys need not apply.

Drucker goes on to say that the advertisement reflects what he would like to see candidates consider before they apply for a position on a board of directors. Needless to say, he thought corporate boards were critical to the performance of any institution but were as a group underperforming in both for-profit and nonprofit organizations. Testimony to his assessment is the frequency of scandals that have beset American corporations leading up to the AIG economic meltdown of 2008 and its disruptive effects on economies and societies worldwide. He thought corporations could learn a lot from functioning boards of certain social sector organizations and said so in his *Harvard Business Review* article "What Business Can Learn from Nonprofits" (July–August 1989).[16] Drucker devotes approximately 20 percent of the space in this article to the problems of for-profit boards. He also believed it was the role of CEOs to make their boards effective and that if they did so, the CEO as well as the entire organization would also become more effective.

A leading authority in corporate governance, Robert A. G. Monks, in a letter of June 2, 2003, to Jonathan G. Katz, secretary of the Securities and Exchange Commission, recommended that the Securities Exchange Act of 1934 "be amended to include shareholder nominated candidates in the company proxy statement and proxy card."[17] This, he believed, would strengthen the effectiveness of the board. To support his recommendation he cited Drucker's argument in the *Wharton Magazine* article:

Whenever an institution malfunctions as consistently as boards of directors have in nearly every major fiasco of the last forty or fifty years it is futile to blame men. It is the institution that malfunctions.[18]

The letter from Monks seemed eventually to have an effect on the regulators. Following enactment of the Dodd-Frank Wall Street Reform and Consumer Protection Act in July 2010, making explicit provision for shareholders' access to proxy material, shareholders were given the right to nominate directors if they own "at least 3 percent of the company's shares continuously for at least the three prior years."[19] Nevertheless, this change alone did not solve the problems associated with corporate governance.

II. Reflect

- Professional leadership and management involve numerous activities: establishing the vision, defining the mission, making sure that resources are applied to the right tasks, making effective decisions, implementing and following up on these decisions, taking criticism, and working very diligently to establish and maintain a functioning board of directors to assist top management in performing its duties.

1. LEADERSHIP PRINCIPLES

(1) A leader sees the vision and sees what can be done, the opportunities for the organization.

(2) Defining mission is one of the most difficult things organizations have to do. The obvious answer is usually wrong. A common tendency is to develop a statement that looks good, but is not operational. It becomes a motto mission.

(3) A leader makes the fit between resources and needs, bringing those together, like a tailor . . . making a suit.

(4) A leader is a catalyst for making the right things happen. The "right things" are determined by matching inside resources to outside opportunities. If opportunities do not exist, an organization is wasting its resources. And if strength and competencies don't exist, futility will be the result.

(5) A leader takes responsibility, willingly absorbs criticism, and accepts the loneliness of command.

(6) Decision-making is central to the role of the leader. Decision-making takes courage as well as intelligence. Not everyone is constituted to make tough decisions. But everyone can learn effectiveness for her position.

(7) Popularity is not a criterion for leadership. Nor is a charismatic personality.

(8) A leader must sometimes create controversy to prevent satisfaction and a bureaucratic mindset from setting into an organization.

(9) The [CEOs are] responsible for making their boards effective.[20]

2. "BEWARE CHARISMA"

Charisma is "hot" today. There is an enormous amount of talk about it, and an enormous number of books [are] written on the charismatic leader. But the desire for charisma is a political death wish. No century has seen more leaders with more charisma than the twentieth century, and never have political leaders done greater damage than the four giant leaders of the twentieth century—Stalin, Mussolini, Hitler, and Mao. What matters is not charisma. What matters is [that] the leader leads in the right direction or misleads. The constructive achievements of the twentieth century were the work of completely uncharismatic people. The two military men who guided the Allies to victory in World War II were Dwight Eisenhower and George

Marshall. Both were highly disciplined, highly competent, and deadly dull.

Perhaps the greatest cause for hope [and] for optimism is that to the new majority, the knowledge workers, the old politics make no sense at all. But proven competence does [make sense].

> Peter F. Drucker, February 14, "Demands on Political
> Leadership: Beware Charisma," *The Daily Drucker*, 2004.

- The most important function of the executive is decision making. Effective leaders and executives make effective decisions. They follow a disciplined process, first defining the problem they face. If the problem is not defined properly, there is no way to tell if a decision moves one closer to a solution to the real problem. The situation is similar to that of a physician who is trained in diagnosis. If he or she diagnoses a problem incorrectly, the prescribed remedy will fail to cure the patient, and the physician will not learn anything from the process. The feedback from diagnosis to results does not provide any help in getting closer to the cure. If the problem is diagnosed correctly, and the treatment comes up short, then the physician knows what won't work and goes on to another alternative that moves closer to a cure. Learning takes place. For this reason, Drucker insisted that executives first *correctly define the problem* they are facing.

- Once the problem is defined correctly, the next step is to establish the boundary conditions the decision has to meet. For a decision to be an effective decision, what purposes must it fulfill, and what is the range within which acceptable solutions must fall?

3. THE STRUCTURE OF A BUSINESS DECISION

In *Management Cases: Revised Edition* (2009, Case 35, pp. 167–69), Drucker wrote about a decision facing Nakamura

Lacquer Company in Kyoto, Japan. Nakamura produced lacquerware such as tableware, including dishes. Its "Chrysanthemum" was Japan's best-known and best-selling brand, and became very popular in the United States after World War II.

As a result of lacquerware's popularity in the United States, Nakamura received two unsolicited expansion offers from reputable companies there. The two offers, however, were very different and difficult to compare. The first came from National China Company, which believed it could successfully promote lacquerware in the United States under its own Rose & Crown brand.

Here is an outline of National China's proposal, followed by an outline of the second proposal:

National China

(1) Three-year contract for 400,000 sets per year.

(2) Five percent premium above current price—the title shifts when Nakamura Lacquer delivers the sets to National China in Japan.

(3) The sets would be made for Rose & Crown and would carry the "Rose & Crown" trademark.

(4) Nakamura Lacquer would be prohibited from selling competing products in the United States during the life of the contract.

The second offer came almost immediately and was from SSW, a U.S. provider of hotel and restaurant supplies.

SSW

SSW believed the market in the United States was at least 600,000 sets a year, with an even larger potential—of a couple of million sets per year after five years—but it offered no firm orders.

SSW would budget $1.5 million for two years for

introduction and promotion and it would receive the exclusive right to represent Nakamura's "Chrysanthemum" brand for five years—but under Nakamura's label.

The first 20 percent on all sales would be used to pay for introduction and promotion expenses and the Nakamura brand would be established in the United States.

Analysis: Problem and Boundary Conditions

- A decision must satisfy the *boundary conditions* if it is to be effective. It must be adequate to its purpose.
- What must this decision accomplish? What objectives must the decision achieve?
- Nakamura must establish boundary conditions in order to accurately compare these two alternatives.

In other words, under what circumstances does each alternative make sense? The first proposal involves immediate profit, no risk, and no capital outlays for Nakamura, assuming it has excess capacity and no plans to expand into the United States. The disadvantage is that its products in the United States would be sold under National China's brand.

The second proposal would establish Nakamura's brand in the United States at no additional cost, again assuming it did not want to expand capacity in Kyoto, at least not right away.

Mr. Nakamura must answer the following questions to decide whether to accept the first or second offer or to reject both offers:

- Does he want Nakamura to expand and become a big company?
- Does he want it to remain only in the domestic market?
- Can he raise capital on his own to expand his plant when and if expansion is necessary?

The first offer gives Nakamura immediate profits but does not establish its brand name in the United States. There is a risk of losing the U.S market again if National China switches suppliers after three years.

National China is the right decision if Nakamura wants to eventually expand in Japan and needs capital to do so.

The second offer, from SSW, means no profit for some time but also no capital investment (assuming excess capacity currently exists) and no risk.

The second establishes Nakamura's brand name in the United States if the venture succeeds.

This decision is right if Nakamura wants to become a global company by expanding in the United States.

Mr. Nakamura currently has no basis for making a decision between these two alternatives because he has not thought through his objectives. If he wants to expand abroad, a choice between the two would be easy. And if he merely wants to remain domestic, a decision between the two would be easy. It all depends on his definition of the problem he is facing and thus the appropriate conditions that have to be met for this decision to be effective. These are always the two critical issues in decision making.

- Board members and boards of directors should provide leadership to an organization. They do have legal, fiduciary responsibility for the public corporation, and for the nonprofit organization they serve. Without a functioning board an organization will almost certainly underperform. Typically, the board appoints the CEO and is actively engaged in reviewing and approving major strategic initiatives. The board also monitors performance of the CEO and other top executives and is the legal agent of owners of the organization. Reading 4 provides a summary of the functions of the board.

4. THREE FUNCTIONS OF THE BOARD

There are actually three different tasks for which a company, and especially a large one, needs a functioning board.

(1) The Enterprise, First, Does Need a Review Body

It needs a group of experienced people, people of integrity and stature, people of proven performance capacity and proven willingness to work, who counsel and advise and deliberate with top management. It needs people who are not part of top management but who are available to it, and who can act with knowledge and decision in a crisis.

The big company is too important to society not to have a "control" in its own structure. Somebody has to make sure that top management thinks through what the company's business is and what it should be. Somebody has to make sure that objectives are being set and strategies are being developed. Somebody has to look critically at the planning of the company, its capital-investment policy, and its managed-expenditures budget. Somebody has to monitor people decisions and organization problems. Somebody has to watch the organization's spirit, has to make sure that it succeeds in utilizing the strengths of people and in neutralizing their weaknesses, that it develops tomorrow's managers and that its rewards to managers, its management tools and management methods strengthen the organization and direct it towards objectives.

The board also meets an important top management need. It is an informed, intelligent outsider to talk and confer with. Having someone to talk to is especially important in a small company where top management otherwise tends to be isolated. Small-company managements, without easy, continuous access to outside advisors, such as experienced lawyers and consultants, need to have available a few people who are experienced, and who are still part of the company.

Small-company top managements need, therefore, a true board of directors—yet small companies, as a rule, have even less of a functioning board than the large ones.

(2) An Effective and Functioning Board Is Needed to Remove a Top Management That Fails to Perform

A board capable of removing incompetent or nonperforming top managements has real power. But only a weak top management is afraid of it. No society can tolerate top-management incompetence in its large businesses. If top managements do not build boards that will remove weak and incompetent chief executives, government will take over the job.

There is another alternative: the "takeover" by the "financial raider" [or increasingly, the private equity firm]. Top managements—most of them seemingly all-powerful, seemingly deeply entrenched, seemingly in complete control—have been toppled by stockholder revolts organized by the financial raiders and their "takeover bids." The raiders [do] not aim at companies in trouble. They aim at companies that are not living up to their potential, companies the top managements of which did not perform adequately.

(3) The Enterprise Needs a "Public and Community Relations" Organ

It needs easy and direct access to its various "publics" and "constituents." It needs to hear from them and to be able to talk to them. The need is readily apparent for the big company, of course. But it may be even greater for the small or fair-sized company which is a major employer in a small or medium-sized community. The modern enterprise has many constituencies. The shareholders are one. But they are no longer *the* one, as traditional legal theory has it. Instead of being "owners" they have become "investors." The employees are clearly also such a constituency, but they are not *the* constituency. There are also the communities where a major company has its plants. There are consumers, suppliers, and distributors. All of them need to know what goes on in a major business, what its problems, its policies, and its plans are. The business needs to be understood by them. Top management needs to be known by them, respected by them, accepted by them. Top management needs even more, perhaps, to understand what these constituencies want, understand, misunderstand, see, question. A board involving these different constituencies could serve this two-way public relations need.

The governing board of directors must be a board that represents no one except the basic long-term interests of the enterprise. It must be capable of discharging its function as the review organ and as the supervisor of top-management performance.

But the enterprise also needs a board that is, in effect, an organ of information, advice, consultation, and communication—that is, the public and community relations board. If the enterprise and its top management do not create this board, it will be imposed on them in wrong and harmful form, that is, as an organ of antagonism, control, and restraint. That is what worker representation on the German board, government representation on the Swedish board, and minority-group representation on the American board are. This will not only further undermine the board, but it also undermines the authority of [companies] and reduces their capacity to perform.

> Peter F. Drucker, *Management: Tasks, Responsibilities, Practices*, abridged, 1999, pp. 538–41.

• In addition to these three broad functions, it is possible to identify a series of internal behaviors that facilitate the effective functioning of the board from one of Drucker's examples of exemplary nonprofit boards ("What Business Can Learn from Nonprofits," 1989, p. 4 of the reprint). The following example, Fuller Seminary under President David Hubbard, 1963–1993, is not described in Drucker's article.

A. Board members are *governors*—they help steer the institution toward its mission by assisting the CEO and top executives with strategic and policy-making decisions. They are expected to act as ambassadors and *explain* the mission of the organization to outsiders. And they are *consultants* to the organization's executives in their area of professional expertise.

B. Trustees, under Hubbard, were expected to give eight to ten days of service per year including attendance at three board meetings. In addition, they were expected to serve on committees of the board and to undertake specific projects between board meetings.

C. There was one person in the president's office dedicated specifically to board work involving continuous communications with board members.

D. It was Hubbard's policy to share bad news first at each board meeting and to overemphasize it relative to good news. In this way he avoided the common tendency of CEOs to want to look good before the board. He thought that avoiding difficult problems at the board level was irresponsible behavior. Confronting difficult problems helped to focus the energies of the board on problem solving activities and innovation, thus discouraging the tendency of some board members to meddle in the internal affairs of the institution. An open period was set aside at each meeting during which board members could bring up items not on the agenda.

E. The president dealt with upcoming board problems and issues with the chairs of the subcommittees of the board. He would educate each chair in various aspects of the problem so that the chair came to meetings very well informed. He then asked the chairs to lead discussion on specific problems at board meetings, thus encouraging the board to take ownership. He desired to be passive at board meetings and very active in cultivation and education of board members in between board meetings. If contention developed over an issue, he saw his role as trying to provide direction for resolution of the issue. Once the meeting was over, he sought to comfort those who were on the losing side of a particular issue.

F. It is difficult or perhaps impossible for an organization to reach its potential without an effective board of trustees or directors. This reflection provides us with an example of just how to develop an outstanding, functioning board, which Drucker believed to be the exception rather than the rule in organizations.

• This Drucker reading, the reflections on additional internal board processes, and the recommendations in Note 15 meet the requirements stipulated in Drucker's tongue-in-cheek advertisement and form the support necessary for professional leadership of an organization from the board down.

III. Practicum-Prompts

Is the mission of your organization both clear and operational?

What resources and competencies does your organization possess? Do these resources and competencies match the opportunities available to your organization? If not, what resources and competencies must you acquire or develop to capitalize on these opportunities?

Do you overvalue charisma rather than the right results in your leaders?

Do you avoid hard decisions in order to be popular? Do you follow the procedures for effective decision making defined and illustrated in Reading 3? If not, why not?

Do you readily assume responsibility for your people as well as for results in your organization? If not, why not?

Do you have a well-functioning board that serves the mission and stakeholders of your institution? If not, what can you learn from Readings 3 and 4 to help you develop a functioning board of directors in your organization?

Management in a Pluralistic Society of Organizations

Management: "The Governing Organ of All Institutions of Modern Society"

Introduction

Drucker believed *The Federalist Papers* to be one of the two great contributions of America to Western thought (*Practice of Management*, 1954, p. 282), primarily because of the pluralism contained within these documents, which support the checks and balances in the U.S. Constitution. The three branches of government provide checks and balances on each other. In addition, there is the concept of federalism: all powers not specifically delegated to the federal government are left to the states. The concepts of federalism and pluralism were expressed in the Tenth Amendment to the Constitution: "The powers not delegated to the United States by the Constitution, nor prohibited by it to the States, are reserved to the States respectively, or to the people."[21]

Drucker applied these principles to the modern society of organizations. The three sectors of society should take care of the needs of all the people and provide checks and balances on one another. In practice, each sector has its own mission and there are significant needs that "fall through the cracks." Drucker therefore recommended that while each institution should fulfill its primary mission, it also should seek to "lead beyond borders."

Here is the way Frances Hesselbein, former president and CEO of the Peter F. Drucker Foundation, and founder, current president, and CEO of the Frances Hesselbein Leadership Institute, summarizes Drucker's views on corporate responsibility in her *HBR* Blog Network post of June 9, 2010, "How Did Peter Drucker See Corporate Responsibility?" [22]

> Leaders in every single institution and in every single sector . . . have two responsibilities. They are responsible and accountable for the performance of their institutions, and that requires them and their institutions to be concentrated, focused, limited. They are responsible also, however, for the community as a whole.

Drucker supported executive sabbaticals for a number of reasons. First, he believed that by serving in the public or social sector corporate executives could broaden their understanding of the values held by people in different walks of life and that this could help them become more effective executives within their organizations. In addition the corporation has most of society's executive expertise and it is badly needed to solve social problems. Executive talent, for example, was used to advise the government of the city of Cleveland. My research at Lincoln Electric uncovered a most inspiring story. It is summarized beautifully by Professor Rosabeth Moss Kanter of the Harvard Business School in her *New York Times* article of September 27, 1995. Kanter, commenting on the renewal of downtown Cleveland, reports, "The turnaround of Cleveland in the last 15 years was orchestrated by a few dozen chief executive officers of big companies with headquarters there." [23]

We find another great example in a television interview of Ronald Reagan conducted by William F. Buckley Jr. on July 6, 1967, during the first year of Reagan's tenure as governor of California. [24] California then had the highest per capita state taxes in the United States, yet it was running an unconstitutional budget deficit. One major effort Reagan introduced to reduce cost and improve efficiency was to enlist the support of two hundred of the most successful executives in the state, who were able to take a sabbatical of four to six months from their organizations to study the effectiveness of state agencies and come back to the governor's office with recommendations for improved operations. Reagan found the enthusiasm for volunteer and sabbatical work overwhelming. Regarding volunteers, he said, "For every problem there are 10 people waiting to volunteer if someone could give them the lead and show them where they can be useful."

Regarding work done by the two hundred executives, Reagan provided the following summation:

> They are going to every department and agency of state government and coming back to the governor's office with their recommendations as to what they would do in that department as businessmen to make government more efficient. The other day I was able to simply cancel a $4 million, 10-story building that was going to be built in Sacramento because they found that the two agencies that were going to occupy that building already have more space than they can possibly need beyond 1980. That building was to be started next month and won't be built. There are going to be other buildings that will disappear that way.

Professional management in all three sectors of society in the United States is badly needed. Peter Drucker believed management is among the major social innovations of the twentieth century; this is if anything an *understatement*, given the executive talent we possess in the United States, the enormous progress we have made, and the serious problems we face.

I. Read

Tom Ashbrook

You have been writing, teaching, and consulting about management for over 60 years, both as a thinker and communicator. You have ranked management as among the major social innovations of the 20th century. Why? What in your view does society owe to management?

Peter Drucker

The word "management" was coined in 1911. It was unknown before then. Before that, everybody assumed that the owner ran a business. Nonowners, professionals, came in shortly before World War I. Simultaneously, J. P. Morgan invented professional management in America, [Eiichi Shibusawa in] Japan, and [Georg] Siemens in Germany. Management was a new social function, which made possible a new society, a society of organizations. And let me say that while business management was the first to emerge, it was not the most important. The most important ones are the management of nonbusinesses, such as hospitals, universities, and churches. They are the most interesting organizations because they have to define what they mean by results. How do you define the results of the large church I'm working with, which has grown from five hundred to six thousand members? . . . There is no great difference between this century and the last century, except there are so many more organizations today. We became a society of organizations in the last century. When managers were very rare you could depend on the naturals. Now you need enormous numbers of them.

"Management Guru Peter Drucker," WBUR for National Public Radio, December 8, 2004.

II. Reflect

1. DRUCKER'S MOST IMPORTANT CONTRIBUTIONS

Peter Drucker was asked by Jack Shaw, dean of the Drucker School of Management, in early 1999, "What do you consider to be your most important contribution?"

Drucker

- That I early on—almost sixty years ago—realized that *management* has become the constitutive [or essential] organ and function of the *Society of Organizations*.
- That *management* is not "Business Management"—though it first attained attention in business—but the governing organ of *all* institutions of modern society.
- That I established the study of *management* as a discipline in its own right, and;
- That I focused this discipline on people and power; on values, structure, and constitution [or rules of conduct]; *and above all on responsibilities*—that is, focused the discipline of management on management as a truly *liberal art*.

> Peter F. Drucker and Joseph A. Maciariello, *Management: Revised Edition*, 2008, p. vi.

- If each institution in our pluralistic society of organizations looks out merely for its narrow interests, and for doing no harm, who will take care of the issues that "fall into the cracks"? In other words, who will take care of the common good?

2. WE ARE BECOMING A SOCIETY OF PLURALISTIC INSTITUTIONS

Society in all developed countries has become pluralist and is becoming more pluralist day by day. It is splintering into a myriad of institutions each more or less autonomous, each requiring its own leadership and management, each having its own specific task.

This is not the first pluralist society in history. But all earlier pluralist societies destroyed themselves because no one took care of the *common good*. They abounded in *communities* but could not sustain *community*, let alone create it. If our modern pluralist society is to escape the same fate, the leaders of *all* institutions will have to learn to be *leaders beyond the walls*. They will have to learn that it is not enough for them to lead their own institutions—*though that is the first requirement*. They will also have to learn to become leaders in the community. In fact they will have to learn to create community. This is going beyond . . . *social responsibility*. Social responsibility is usually defined as doing *no harm* to others in the pursuit of one's own interest or of one's own task. The new pluralism requires what might be called *civic responsibility: giving to the community in the pursuit of one's own interest or of one's own task*.

There is no precedent in history for such civic responsibility among institutional leaders. But there are, fortunately, signs that the leaders of our institutions in all sectors are beginning to wake up to the need to become leaders beyond the walls.

> Peter F. Drucker and Joseph A. Maciariello, *Management: Revised Edition*, 2008, pp. 224–25.

- The forces driving the growth of large social sector organizations are the multiple needs of civic society that are not being met by family, government, or business. These are creating the *demands* for social sector organizations. These demands are not likely to abate as a result of the retirement of any one superstar leader. On the supply side, there are many very able, educated people who need outlets for their talents and are prepared to serve as volunteers and as social entrepreneurs to help meet the needs of civic society.

- Nonprofit organizations are becoming acutely aware of the importance of defining results in terms of their mission and their ability to effectively manage to fulfill their mission.

3. A SOCIETY OF PERFORMING ORGANIZATIONS

"By their fruits ye shall know them."

Society in all developed countries has become *a society of organizations* in which most, if not all, social tasks are being done in and by an organization. Organizations do not exist for their own sake. They are means: each society's organ for the discharge of one social task. The organization's goal is a specific contribution to individual and society. The test of its performance, unlike that of a biological organism, therefore, always lies outside itself. This means that we must know what "performance" means for this or that institution.

Each institution will be stronger the more clearly it defines its objectives. It will be more effective the more yardsticks and measurements [there are] against which its performance can be appraised. It will be more legitimate the more strictly it bases authority on justification by performance. "By their fruits ye shall know them"—this might well be the fundamental constitutional principle of the new pluralist society of institutions.

Peter F. Drucker, January 18, "Society of Performing Organizations," *The Daily Drucker*, 2004.

- Results are much more difficult to define for social sector organizations than for business or governmental organizations. And that is because the social sector institutions are involved in changing lives of individuals for the better. Results must be more than merely good intentions.

- There is a growing sense of awareness among the institutions in the social sector of the need for professional management as they grow in size, scope, and complexity.

4. A SOCIAL SECTOR ORGANIZATION NEEDS MANAGEMENT

Its [a non-profit institution's] "product" is neither a pair of shoes [business] nor an effective regulation [government]. Its product is a *changed human being*. The non-profit institutions are human-change agents. Their "product" is a cured patient, a child that learns, a young man or woman grown into a respecting adult; a changed human life altogether. Forty years ago, "management" was a very bad word in non-profit organizations. It meant "business" to them, and the one thing they were not was a business. . . .

[T]he non-profit institutions themselves [now] know they need management all the more because they do not have a conventional "bottom line."

> Peter F. Drucker, *Managing the Non-Profit Organization*:
> *Principles and Practices*, 1990, pp. xiv–xv.

III. Practicum-Prompts

As the examples in Cleveland and California illustrate, executive competence is considerable within business organizations. Consider lending your expertise as a member of an executive team in support of efforts to improve your city, as illustrated in the introduction.

If you are a business, what needs are you meeting in society as a part of your primary mission? If you are a governmental organization, how effective and efficient are you in carrying out your mission? If you are a social sector organization, how effective are you in changing lives for the good?

While giving priority to your primary mission, do you seek to identify and meet the management needs beyond the borders of your organization within the community for which you have competence? Have you considered mentoring leaders of social sector organizations in leadership and management effectiveness?

Have you considered financial donations to social sector organizations? Do you volunteer your time to public service organizations? Do you encourage institutional giving by your organization, including short-term executive sabbaticals to help solve problems in the community?

The First Job in Any Organization Is to Make Top Management Effective

Introduction

Peter Drucker often told of how, like every other innovator, he built on the work of others and then added the missing pieces. He understood the practice of management as a "configuration" requiring the integration of existing "knowledges" and the addition of missing knowledges into a whole. He describes it as synthesizing known pieces and *creating* missing pieces:[25]

My own success as an innovator in the management field
was based on a similar analysis in the early 1940s. Many
of the required pieces of knowledge were already available:
organization theory, for instance, but also quite a bit of
knowledge about managing work and worker. My analysis
showed, however, that these pieces were scattered and lodged
in half a dozen different disciplines. Then I found which
key knowledges were missing: purpose of a business; any
knowledge of the work and structure of top management;
what we now term "business policy" and "strategy"; objectives;
and so on. All of the missing knowledges, I decided could

be produced. But without such analysis, I could never have known what they were or what they were missing.

Note his emphasis on top management, because without effective top management you cannot sustain a spirit of performance, and entropic processes will set in at an organization and eventually destroy it. His work in the 1940s (1944–1946) at General Motors involved "an in-depth study of [Sloan and GM's] top management" (*Concept of the Corporation*, 1946, p. 120). Close behind in importance is a program for developing executive talent to fill open management positions.

One should beware of apparent kindness and protective paternalism by top management. These could be a disguise for tyrannical behavior. For example, a top executive who insists on making all major and a good number of minor decisions stunts the growth of subordinates since they are not given authority to act beyond their own narrow duties as specialists. They may be paid well and enjoy job security in their positions. They may even receive frequent bonuses and friendly advice on career development, making them useful to competitors, yet their growth into effective executives within the organization will be stymied unless they are given executive responsibility for decision making and are allowed to make and learn from their own mistakes. This kind of paternalism may be a mask for a lust for power and end up creating an empty shell of an organization—something that will become evident only when the top leader passes from the scene. By turning a blind eye to one of the primary tasks of management, he will have failed to develop people who can succeed him. So, the first task in designing and assessing an organization is the presence of an effective top management team with a strong spirit of performance.

I. Read

Increasingly, in the Next Society's corporation, top management will, in fact, be the company. This top management's responsibilities will cover the entire organization's direction, planning, strategy, values, and principles; its structure and [the] relationships between its various members; its alliances, partnerships, and joint ventures; and its research, design, and innovation. Establishing an organization's unique personality may be the most important task of top management in the Next Society's big organizations.

Establishing a new corporate persona calls for a change in the corporation's values. And that may well be the most important task for top management. In the half-century after the Second World War, the business corporation has brilliantly proven itself as an economic organization, as a creator of wealth and jobs. In the Next Society, the biggest challenge for the large company and especially for the multinational may be its social legitimacy—its values, its mission, its vision.

Peter F. Drucker, January 9, "The New Corporation's Persona," *The Daily Drucker*, 2004.

II. Reflect

- Top management is responsible for creating and for maintaining the spirit of the organization, which includes values, standards of conduct, and standards of quality.

1. MAKE TOP MANAGEMENT EFFECTIVE

Introduction
Peter Drucker urges Bob Buford to make sure the top management of his organization, as well as of those organizations he is working with, is effective.

Peter Drucker

I think that one of your big jobs is to make sure that the first job of these organizations is done. The first job is *to make top management effective.* That's not what organization books talk about but that's what it is, and you and Fred [Fred Smith, president of Leadership Network from 1984 to 1996] are a most effective top management . . . , partly individually and collectively. *You are growing with a firm foundation in the pastoral church, and in the spiritual, you are growing into a dimension of the future society, the future community, which has to have a spiritual foundation or it has nothing.* It has to have more than that, a community dimension, and you are beginning to grow into this, and at the same time you have tackled the restoration of, call it religious diversity, because we need both the large church and the small church, and they need each other. You have not finished but you have created the vital energy for the large pastoral church, and you know what the smaller churches need. The most important thing you know is that the smaller churches can survive and become effective. Not a hundred percent of them but you don't need a hundred percent. One never needs a hundred percent.

> Drucker-Buford Dialogue Project, Estes Park, Colorado, August 9, 1993.

2. THE BOTTLENECK IS AT THE HEAD OF THE BOTTLE

"The bottleneck is at the head of the bottle," goes the old saw. No business is likely to be better than its top management, or perform better than they do. A business—especially a large one—may coast for a little time on the vision and performance of an earlier top management. But this only defers payment—and usually for a much shorter period than is commonly believed. A business needs a central governing organ and a central organ of review and appraisal. On the quality of these two organs, which together [make up] top management, its performance, results, and spirit largely depend.

Peter F. Drucker, *The Practice of Management*, 1954, p. 161.

- Top management is responsible for designing the organizational structure and for making key appointments at the level right below top management. Candidates for succession to top management in the future are likely to come from this second tier of executives.

3. TOP MANAGEMENT IS CRITICAL TO SOCIETY'S WELFARE

Manager development has become a necessity not because top management may have been allowed to become old as a result of depression and war, but because the modern business enterprise has become a basic institution of our society. In any major institution—the Church, for instance, or the Army—the finding, developing, and proving out of leaders of tomorrow is an essential job to which the best men must give fully of their time and attention.

Peter F. Drucker, *The Practice of Management*, 1954, p. 190.

- The key activities of top management must be identified by those persons at the top who are able to see the whole scope of responsibilities of the organization. Once these key activities are identified, then responsibility for each of these activities must be assigned to a specific member of the top management team.

4. THE CEO IN THE NEW MILLENNIUM

The CEO in the new millennium has six specific tasks. They are:

(1) To define the meaningful outside of the organization.

(2) To think through what information regarding the outside is meaningful and needed for the organization, and then work on getting it into usable form.

(3) To decide what results are meaningful for the institution.

(4) To set priorities for the organization.

(5) To place people into key positions.

(6) To organize top management.

Peter F. Drucker and Joseph A. Maciariello, *Management: Revised Edition*, 2008, p. 468.

• A small professional staff should be responsible for managing information flow and maintaining unity among members of the top management team.

III. Practicum-Prompts

Appointments to top management set examples for the rest of the organization. What kind of example is the top management of your organization setting? Does the top management foster a strong spirit of performance?

Which people in your organization are responsible for maintaining values, standards of conduct, and standards of quality? How are they doing? Is the organization maintaining, advancing, or in decline with regard to these standards? If it is in decline, make sure the right people are well aware of that.

Is your organization preparing future leaders by giving significant responsibility and authority to lower-level executives? What has been the organization's track record of finding successors for key positions inside versus outside?

Organizational structure is a tool for accomplishing the mission of the organization. Alternative structures can be used to achieve the mission, but badly designed structures can hinder the development of people and the performance of the organization as a whole. Identify any structures within your organization that might be hindering growth and performance, and try to bring change to these toxic structures.

Control by Mission and Strategy, Not by Hierarchy

Introduction

I wrote the book *Lasting Value: Lessons from a Century of Agility at Lincoln Electric* (2000), in which I studied three manufacturing companies known for their productivity and incentive systems and overall enlightened approach to managing their employees. The primary company, Lincoln Electric, a welding company with head-quarters in Cleveland, Ohio, was then celebrating a century of successful operations.

Lincoln Electric was very slow to move into foreign operations while its competitors were aggressively operating in the United States. Early on it built plants in Canada and Australia, but it had no operations in South America, Europe, or Asia. As it tried to build manufacturing plants and establish distribution channels in these areas, it experienced one problem after another. Lincoln's management displayed a surprising lack of knowledge of how to adapt its world-class U.S. operations to the cultures of Japan, Germany, and the countries of South America. But Lincoln learned quickly. After experiencing substantial economic losses and incurring a very large amount of debt needed to finance its foreign expansion, it went public and reorganized, bringing in a team of top executives experienced in international operations. Lincoln rationalized its foreign operations, relying more on alliances and joint ventures than on command and control structures, and completely recovered from its initial missteps into global business.

After completing my work at Lincoln Electric, I was referred by its top executives to Worthington Industries of Columbus, Ohio, and to NUCOR of Charlotte, North Carolina. They believed Worthington and NUCOR had certain similarities in their culture and incentive systems to those in place at Lincoln Electric in Cleveland. I was interested in exploring these other examples to demonstrate that Lincoln, although exceptional, was not the only world-class American manufacturing company excelling in globally competitive industries.

Worthington is a processor of steel for use by various customers all over the world and is a leading manufacturer of pressurized propane cylinders. NUCOR invented the steel mini-mill in the United States and is one of America's great industrial success stories. All three companies now provide lessons on control by mission and strategy, not by hierarchical authority.

I. Read

We are increasingly moving towards multinational, transnational organizations that are held together by two factors: Control of mission and strategy [as opposed to hierarchical control], and enough people who know and trust each other. You [at World Vision International] are not multinational; you are transnational, and you are an example.

Let me give you another example. I have on my desk an unopened FedEx parcel from the Atlanta Coca-Cola company, who have been friends and clients of mine on and off for fifty or sixty years. . . . [It] is [about] an Argentinean service organization, started and run by a magnificent young woman who began the process of turning around key

Argentinean social institutions such as churches . . . [and] schools with money from Coca-Cola. With the total collapse of Argentina, I was quite sure they would have practically gone out of business. I had a phone call from the young woman who runs and invented it, and she said, *"We are not sure that we can continue our health care program. But we will continue our most successful, most important one, to turn around schools, because Coca-Cola Argentina has decided they will continue to finance it no matter what Atlanta says."*

Coca-Cola Atlanta is very unhappy about this. One of the questions: *How do we control our subsidiaries?* We are going to show a big loss in Argentina no matter what. The Argentineans simply say, *"This is the right time for us to be visible."* However, the people in Atlanta scream about quarterly earnings. Those people in solely owned subsidiaries tell them to go climb up a tree. They could care less about their quarterly earnings. Atlanta could order them, yet Atlanta is not going to order that.

The Argentinean management knows two things: First, *"They need us more than we need them."* They do not say so, but it is very clear. Secondly, *"Our job is to build Coca-Cola in Argentina. Our job is not to build Coca-Cola based on the New York Stock Exchange and we are being measured and judged in Argentina on what we do in Argentina. How that affects you in Atlanta is your business, not ours."* They made it very clear that they made their decisions based on what is good for Argentina Coca-Cola. When everybody else is eliminating charitable contributions, this is the right moment to double them. Nobody's results in Argentina are going to look good, so we might as well get something for our losses. That is, increasingly, the kind of reality, how to balance it? On the one hand, the Coke people in Atlanta own the money. The manufacturing of Coca-Cola is in the United States; but approximately 60 percent of their business is not. Therefore, from the point of view of Atlanta, the cost of money in this country, which is their share price, is the foremost consideration. The people who run the local affiliates have very heavy competition, both from Pepsi-Cola and from local bottlers. However, they are not a bit concerned about the share price in New York, and should not be.

> Peter F. Drucker, *Executive Summary: A Conversation with Peter Drucker on Leadership and Organizational Development*, 2002, p. 8.

II. Reflect

- Performance measures for foreign subsidiaries should be adapted to local political and economic realities.

1. GLOBAL ECONOMIC REALITIES AND POLITICAL SPLINTERING

National policies impose constraints on the strategy of the transnational enterprise. Pure economic realities prevail only in the global flow of money and information. Strategy has to be based upon the reality that within transnational enterprises, national politics still overrule economic reality. . . . To reconcile the separation of political and economic reality, the change leader must recognize that business growth and expansion in different parts of the world will increasingly have to be based on alliances.

> Peter F. Drucker, *Driving Change*, 2004.

- Lincoln now has more than forty manufacturing locations, including solely owned operations and joint ventures in twenty countries plus "a worldwide network of distributors and sales offices covering more than 160 countries."[26] This approach has allowed Lincoln to adjust to political realities in foreign countries. The economic reality is that Lincoln Electric is a world-class company invented in the United States! The political reality is that Lincoln has adapted its U.S. operations to each country's regulations and culture to become a global world-class company.

2. WHEN TO COMMAND AND WHEN TO PARTNER

Successful participants in joint ventures understand that one can't "command" one's partner. Working with a partner is essentially a marketing job, and that means asking questions: What are the other party's values? Objectives? Expectations? But of course there are times when command is critical to getting things done. The CEO of tomorrow will have to understand when to command and when to partner. This is not without precedent—J. P. Morgan built a partnership of twelve people, yet he still knew when to assume the role of leader—but it won't be effortless.

Peter F. Drucker, *Managing in the Next Society*, 2002, p. 86.

• Worthington operates eighty-two facilities in eleven countries and employs ten thousand people, slightly more than Lincoln. It also operates thirty-one joint ventures in the United States and fifteen outside the United States.[27] Worthington avoided Lincoln's problems by using joint ventures and alliances much earlier in its global expansion. Worthington normally controls manufacturing and quality but capitalizes on its partners' local knowledge and their marketing and distribution expertise.

3. "AS A CORPORATION MOVES TOWARDS A CONFEDERATION"

As the corporation moves towards a confederation or a syndicate, it will increasingly need a top management that is separate, powerful, and accountable. This top management's responsibilities will cover the entire organization's direction, planning, strategy, values, and principles; its structure and relationships among its various members; its alliances, partnerships, and joint ventures; and its research, design, and innovation.

Peter F. Drucker and Joseph A. Maciariello, *Management: Revised Edition*, 2008, p. 58.

• Trust-based relationships must replace command and control mechanisms as coordinating mechanisms. This will allow top management time to perform its duties.

4. NEW TOP MANAGEMENT OF MULTINATIONALS WILL HAVE TO BALANCE CONFLICTING DEMANDS OF CONSTITUENTS

Tomorrow's top management [of multinational and transnational organizations] is likely to be a distinct and separate organ; it will stand for the company. One of the most important jobs ahead for the top management of the big company of tomorrow, and especially for the multinational, will be to balance the conflicting demands on business being made by the need for both short-term and long-term results, and by the corporation's various constituencies: customers, shareholders (especially institutional investors such as pension funds), knowledge employees, and communities.

Peter F. Drucker, *The Next Society*, 2004.

• Observe in the example of Coca-Cola in Argentina the way local needs—to continue to assist in improving schools—were met with full knowledge that meeting them would hurt the short-term results of the parent corporation in Atlanta. Management in Argentina had to meet these short-term local needs to maintain the company's good citizenship there. So, here we see the limits on the actions of Coke in Atlanta to command those in the subsidiary in Argentina, where local knowledge was important in decision making.

- NUCOR is the largest steel mini-mill in the United States, and along with its wholly owned subsidiaries, the company's two hundred operating facilities make it the largest steel manufacturer in the United States. Much of its growth can be attributed to the "radical" decentralization shaped by founder Ken Iverson, whereby general managers of operating facilities are given high levels of autonomy. This autonomy is carried right down to production levels in the organization. NUCOR's employee teams enjoy significant autonomy to operate and innovate. Powerful compensation incentives similar to those in place at Lincoln Electric help motivate high productivity and quality at NUCOR. Burdensome command and control features are mostly absent.[28]

III. Practicum-Prompts

How does your organization manage its operations? Does it use formal command and control systems, or more relation-based informal steering and coordination?

What roles do strategy, mission, and values play in integrating the work of the various units of your organization? For example, do you set prices of goods and services flowing into these units from other parts of the company in such a way as to help these units succeed locally?

How much autonomy do the domestic and international units of your organization have in adjusting to local political and economic conditions? Is it sufficient to meet the local realities they face?

Does your organization have resilient trust networks that allow individuals to transfer information to and from one another? If not, how can trust be strengthened and made more resilient?

Week 15

Sustaining the Spirit of an Organization

Introduction

A primary objective of Drucker's work on management is to create organizations with a high spirit of performance. All organizations draw from the same pool of prospective employees. They employ common people. To make common people perform at an uncommon level, then, can be done only in what Drucker calls the "moral realm." Why? Because it requires that organizations overcome natural, ever-present entropic forces toward bureaucracy, deterioration, and decay.[29] And this requires one to submerge selfish interests to the welfare of the group.

After Rick Warren described how Saddleback Community Church grew to be very large, Drucker advised him of the need to introduce a *disturbing element* into his organization to sustain its spirit of performance. A disturbing element in an organization or in a profession is a person who seeks to change its culture and practices to prevent bureaucratic behavior from setting in.

Then Peter Drucker encouraged Rick Warren himself to become the disturbing element at Saddleback. A cellular church like Saddleback works as long as Rick, or somebody like him, supplies the outside energy, holds the values before the people, and sets the standards. These are all "conscience activities" that are necessary to sustain the spirit of an organization.

I. Read

What you describe [a very large and growing organization] implies having somebody like you in the organization who is the *disturbing element*. Someone who is always shaking things up. It must be somebody who is free enough from the day-to-day managing to do this. Usually nobody is ever free enough from day-to-day duties to have the energy and commitment to be a disturber inside a large organization. I don't remember how many thousands of members you have now but you have shown that a large congregation can work. But it only works because your church is composed, to a very large extent, of many smaller congregations [cells]. These groups come together to renew their commitment on Sundays. That works on one condition: that there is a Rick Warren. Or somebody like a Rick Warren who is the energy and the conscience and the example of the movement. Whoever that is will never be totally free of, and shouldn't be free of, all administrative duties. This is in part because otherwise you'll very soon lose the feel of it all, and in part because nobody can escape paperwork. But your primary work is not administrative but providing *energy and spirit*.

Drucker-Warren Dialogue, January 22, 2003.

II. Reflect

• An organization with the spirit of performance is one led by executives who are committed to *getting the right things done* (effectiveness) and *doing the right thing* (efficiency). These executives possess integrity of character; have a vision for the purpose of their organization; focus on opportunities; are change leaders; and follow essential tasks, responsibilities, and practices of management.

1. THE PURPOSE OF AN ORGANIZATION

The purpose of an organization is to "make common men do uncommon things." . . . It is the test of an organization that it make ordinary human beings perform better than they are capable of, that it bring out whatever strength there is in its members and use it to make all other members perform better and better. It is the test of an organization that it neutralize the weaknesses of its members.

> Peter F. Drucker, *The Practice of Management*, 1954, pp. 144–45.

• The disturbing element in an organization consists of one or more leaders who prod people to develop, improve, innovate, and sustain the spirit of the organization. They often disturb the status quo by pursuing destabilizing, systematic innovation, which is essential to achieving and sustaining a spirit of performance.

2. THE DISTURBING ELEMENT: THE ENTREPRENEUR

That only a minority of existing successful businesses are entrepreneurial and innovative is . . . seen as conclusive evidence that existing businesses quench the entrepreneurial spirit. But entrepreneurship is not "natural" [and] it is not "creative." It is work. Hence, the correct conclusion from the evidence is the opposite of the one commonly reached. That a substantial number of existing businesses, and among them a goodly number of fair-sized, big businesses, and very

big ones succeed as entrepreneurs and innovators indicates
that entrepreneurship and innovation can be achieved by any
business. But they must be constantly striven for. They can
be learned, but it requires effort. Entrepreneurial businesses
treat entrepreneurship as a duty. They are disciplined about
it . . . they work at it . . . they practice it.

> Peter F. Drucker, *Innovation and Entrepreneurship*, 1985, pp.
> 149–50.

• Those executives who provide the sustaining spirit for an organization are forever watchful for bureaucratic tendencies allowing
people to drift into repetitive routines and lose focus on primary
results.

3. THE SPIRIT OF PERFORMANCE

Spirit of performance in a human organization means that
its energy output is larger than the sum of the efforts put in.
To get out more than is being put in is possible only in the
moral sphere. But morality, to have any meaning at all, must
not be exhortation, sermon, or good intentions. *It must be
practices.* Specifically:

(1) The focus of the organization must be on *performance.*
The first requirement of the spirit of organization is high
performance standards, for the group as well as for each
individual.

(2) The focus of the organization must be on *opportunities*
rather than on problems.

(3) The decisions that affect *people*: their placement and their
pay, promotion, demotion, and severance, must express
the values and beliefs of the organization.

(4) Finally, in its people decisions, management must
demonstrate that it realizes that *integrity* is one absolute

requirement of a manager, the one quality that he has to bring with him and cannot be expected to acquire later on.

Peter F. Drucker, *Management: Tasks, Responsibilities, Practices*, 1973, 1974, pp. 455–56.

- People who have contributed to the organization for a long time but who no longer fit current and future demands create the most important conscience decisions an organization has to make. These people can't stay in their current positions without demoralizing the organization, yet if they are released abruptly that will have the same result. By asking, "What can they do?" you may find satisfactory solutions to these conscience decisions that satisfy almost everyone.

4. THE "CONSCIENCE" ACTIVITIES

"Conscience," many people will argue, is a very strong, in addition to being a rather strange, term. But it is the right term. The task of the conscience activities is not to help the organization do better what it is already doing. The task is to remind the organization all the time of what it should be doing and isn't doing. The task is to be uncomfortable, to hold up the ideal against the everyday reality, to defend the unpopular and to fight the expedient. This requires, however, self-discipline on the part of the conscience executive and acceptance of his competence and integrity on the part of the organization.

Peter F. Drucker, *Management: Tasks, Responsibilities, Practices*, 1973, 1974, p. 536.

III. Practicum-Prompts

Who provides the sustaining spirit for your organization? Who provides the disturbing element? If the answer is no one, how can you find people, and advise or assist in getting them started?

Do you help people in your organization grow by giving them significant responsibilities? What steps can you take to bring out the best in the people working in your organization?

Innovation is vital because it affects the long-term competitiveness and survival of your organization. Does your organization understand this? If not, what can you do to encourage disturbers or to become one yourself?

Are conscience decisions, especially those regarding people with long tenure in your organization, handled in a way that increases or decreases morale? If it's the latter, what can you do to change the way these decisions are made?

Navigating a
Society in Transition

Our Problems in the United States Are Social Problems

Introduction

Drucker's first major book, *The End of Economic Man*, was an analysis of fascism and why he thought fascism and communism would fail. Winston Churchill reviewed the book for the *London Times Literary Supplement* on May 27, 1939, before he became prime minister of England in 1940. Churchill said:

> Mr. Drucker is one of those writers to whom almost
> anything can be forgiven because he not only has a mind
> of his own, but has the gift of starting other minds along a
> stimulating line of thought. . . . [He has written] a book that
> successfully links the dictatorships which are outstanding in
> contemporary life with that absence of a working philosophy
> which is equally outstanding in contemporary thought.[30]

Drucker knew that economic man—a topic emphasized during the 1992 presidential campaign—was not a working philosophy of life that could sustain the country. So he looked for another, reaching back into American history for a potential solution to the malaise he thought was present in 1993.

He viewed the resurgence of the pastoral mega-church as a positive force for the development of society, and the work of Bob Buford as instrumental in rebuilding American society.

I. Read

Peter Drucker

I'm going to make myself very unpopular in two weeks in Aspen at the seminar where I am the keynote speaker; by saying we have no economic problems. We have only social problems. But we have those in spades. This morning when I woke up at three in the morning, you have no idea, I had to pray very hard to get over that despair, and I haven't gotten over it yet. Yes, I know, the very fact that we are conscious of it is probably the only optimistic thing.

Bob Buford

Why have you not written about this topic?

Peter Drucker

Because I am not called! You [Bob Buford] see the healthy energies in the individuals. It needs leadership. It needs example, it needs vision, and it needs direction. . . . You have that tremendous vision. Look, this is an eschatological vision; it's not a rational one. The modern society, precisely because of its pathology, has an opportunity to establish— don't call it sainthood; it's a difficult word—but to establish creaturehood for the ordinary individual. You saw it in a church context, and in this country it is the most important one because if this country does not survive as a Judeo-Christian civilization it won't survive at all.

Drucker-Buford Dialogue Project, Estes Park, Colorado, August 10, 1993.

II. Reflect

- During the 1992 presidential campaign, Clinton's strategist James Carville coined a slogan: "It's the economy, stupid!" The public seemed to believe it and Clinton won. Drucker disagreed and thought our growing social problems were more significant than our economic problems.

1. GROWING SOCIAL NEEDS

Social needs will grow in two areas. They will grow, first, in what has traditionally been considered *charity*: helping the poor, the disabled, the helpless, the victims. And they will grow even faster in respect to services that aim at *changing the community* and at *changing people*. In a transition period, the number of people in need always grows. . . . Even in the most settled and stable societies people will be left behind in the shift to knowledge work. It takes a generation or two before a society and its population catch up with radical changes in the composition of the work force and in the demands for skills and knowledge. It takes some time—the best part of a generation, judging by historical experience—before the productivity of service workers can be raised sufficiently to provide them with a "middle-class" standard of living.

Peter F. Drucker, *Post-Capitalist Society*, 1993, p. 168.

- Government social programs often have unintended negative consequences. Certain social sector organizations, such as The Salvation Army, Alcoholics Anonymous, and Prison Fellowship, can often have better outcomes in the areas where they specialize.

- Alternative solutions can work. In inner cities, church-run schools—especially those run by certain orders such as the

Jesuits—often outperform public schools, when we adjust for so-cioeconomic status plus numerous other variables.[31]

2. SOCIAL PROBLEMS DEFY GOVERNMENT SOLUTION

None of the U.S. programs of the last forty years in which we tried to tackle a social problem through government action has produced significant results. But independent non-profit agencies *have* had impressive results. Public schools in inner cities—for example, New York, Detroit, and Chicago—have been going downhill at an alarming rate. Church-run schools (especially those in Roman Catholic dioceses) have had startling successes—in the same communities, and with children from similar broken families and of similar racial and ethnic groups. The only successes in fighting alcoholism and drug abuse (very substantial ones) have been achieved by such independent organizations as Alcoholics Anonymous, The Salvation Army, and the Samaritans.

Peter F. Drucker, *Post-Capitalist Society*, 1993, p. 170.

• Drucker regards religion as necessary to support the American republic. In this respect he is merely echoing the sentiments of the second president of the United States, John Adams (1735–1826), quoted below. Drucker concludes that America will not survive if it loses its foundational values. Note: *This may not be so for other societies that have structured their social sectors differently.*

• "We have no government armed with power capable of contend-ing with human passions unbridled by morality and religion. Avarice, ambition, revenge, or gallantry, would break the stron-gest cords of our Constitution as a whale goes through a net. Our Constitution was made only for a moral and religious people. It is wholly inadequate to the government of any other." This quote from John Adams is on the fifth formatted page of "The Moral Basis of a Free Society," Hoover Institution, Stanford University, November 1, 1997.

3. CHURCHES STILL PLAY A LARGE ROLE IN AMERICA'S SOCIAL SECTOR

Citizenship in and through the social sector is not a panacea for the ills of post-capitalist society and post-capitalist polity, but it may be a prerequisite for tackling these ills. It reinforces the civic responsibility that is the mark of citizenship, and the civic pride that is the mark of community. . . . Different societies and different countries will surely structure the social sector differently. In Western Europe, for instance, the churches are unlikely to play the key role that they play in still largely Christian America. . . . But every developed country needs an autonomous, self-governing social sector of community organizations—to provide the requisite community services, but above all to restore the bonds of community and a sense of active citizenship. Historically, community was fate. In the post-capitalist society community has to become commitment.

Peter F. Drucker, *Post-Capitalist Society*, 1993, p. 177.

III. Practicum-Prompts

Do you believe that we in the United States have social problems that dominate our economic problems? What contribution can you make to help turn society in a more wholesome direction? Are you afraid of criticism? Or do you consider criticism a fair price to pay to do what you know must be done?

Nonprofit institutions and pastoral churches both have missions to change lives for the better. Moreover, it was Drucker's view that in the United States "there is a very strong correlation between success in community opportunities and community problems and religious faith—Christian faith."[32] This is supported by the work of Putnam and Campbell (see below). As we help others in our civic and religious involvements we live out the Judeo-Christian commandment to "love thy neighbor." How can you make yourself useful and effective in helping to solve a social problem of our society?

Extensive empirical evidence compiled by Harvard sociologist Robert D. Putnam and Notre Dame political scientist David E. Campbell has confirmed the correlation between religious affiliation and involvement in religious activities that Drucker asserts for the United States. They find: "People who have more friends in general are much more likely than social isolates to give, volunteer, and take part in civic life. In that sense, friends in general have a powerful effect on civic involvement, partly because friends are likely to ask. However, while religious people do have more friends overall than nonreligious people, this difference in general sociability is much too small to explain the substantial religious edge on generosity, neighborliness, and civic engagement."[33] Do you find their observations to be true of you and your friends?

How can you leverage your social and religious involvements to increase your involvement in civic life?

Week 17

Rough Period of Transition Ahead for America

Introduction

Near the end of his life Drucker turned pessimistic as he looked at the problems confronting the United States and other civilized nations of the world. First there is the turbulence caused by the shift in the balance of power away from the United States. The rise of China and India as economic powers and the rise of China as a military power, coupled with the new economic trading blocs in South America, the European Union, and China, are altering the economic and military landscapes. In addition, major problems such as terrorism and environmental pollution are global and can be solved only by effective cooperation among a stable coalition of governments. This is going to change the landscape for citizens and organizations in the United States. It will involve new economic, military, and security issues that will have to be addressed by individuals, organizations, and the U.S. government, along with an effective coalition of governments.

This transition is already upon us. Our challenge is to recognize it as a transition and begin to develop solutions at every level.

I. Read

Tom Ashbrook

There's a lot of unease today over where the world is headed. What's your sense of the direction in which the world is moving?

Peter Drucker

Well, I think anybody who is not uneasy about the direction in which the world is moving is blind and deaf. The belief in progress, which we inherited from the eighteenth century, is gone. The belief in a western-dominated world is going. The emerging powers—China and India—are by no stretch of the imagination western nor will they westernize themselves the way Japan did 150 years ago. We don't understand this new world. We don't know the extent to which the EU will become a union or remain a loose confederation.

We don't understand the way MERCOSUR [the Latin American EU] is going. We are in a period of transition as fundamental as the eighteenth century before the Napoleonic Wars. We know this much. The world is not going to be dominated by any one great power. For Americans that's going to be a very difficult thing to accept. Most of us still see a world—the world of 1960—in which America was the only great power, and the only functioning economy. Today the EU is bigger. China is trying to build a free-trade zone that will be bigger than America as both producer and consumer. So we Americans will have to learn that it is going to be a very different world and a world in which *different values* must coexist. It will have western production and western competitiveness, and it will be held together by information, not by power. That is the direction the world is going. It will be a rough period of transition for the next thirty years or so.

"Management Guru Peter Drucker," WBUR for National Public Radio, December 8, 2004.

II. Reflect

• In a period of turbulence like the one we are going through, trying to create our own future is better than trying to predict the outcome of all these global forces. Nevertheless, while trying to create our own future, we must be sure to follow closely and face the new realities described by Drucker and illustrated in this entry.

1. THE CHANGE LEADER

"The most effective way to manage change successfully is to create it."

One cannot manage change. One can only be ahead of it. In a period of upheavals, such as the one we are living in, change is the norm. To be sure, it is painful and risky, and above all it requires a great deal of very hard work. But unless it is seen as the task of the organization to *lead change*, the organization will not survive. In a period of rapid structural change, the only ones who survive are the *change leaders*. A change leader sees change as an opportunity. A change leader looks for change, knows how to find the right changes and knows how to make them effective both outside the organization and inside it. To make the future is highly risky. It is less risky, however, than not to try to make it. A goodly proportion of those attempting to will surely not succeed. But, practically, no one else will.

Peter F. Drucker, March 1, "The Change Leader," *The Daily Drucker*, 2004.

- Information technology now permits knowledge to be accessed worldwide, almost instantly. Information about the outside environments—industrial; national, including regulatory; and international—may be the most important information executives need to prosper, especially during turbulent periods. But enterprises must not only collect these data but also organize the information they need and choose from the numerous tools available those that fit the needs of the organization. The categories of information that are among the most important to track are those pertaining to the various environments in which organizations operate. Here information categories include prices and quality of competitive products and substitutes; technologies that can affect processes and products; innovation pipelines of the competition; and regulations that affect them in the countries where they operate.

2. TURBULENCE: THREAT OR OPPORTUNITY

"When it rains manna from heaven, some people put up an umbrella. Others reach for a big spoon."

The manager will have to look at her task and ask, "What must I do to be prepared for danger, for opportunities, and above all for change?" First, this is a time to make sure that your organization is lean and can move fast. So this is a time when one systematically abandons and sloughs off unjustifiable products and activities—and sees to it that the really important tasks are adequately supported. Second,

she will have to work on the most expensive of resources—
time—particularly in areas where it is people's *only* resource,
as it is for highly paid, important groups like research
workers, technical service staffs, and all managers. And
one must set goals for productivity improvement. Third,
managers must learn to manage growth and to distinguish
among kinds of growth. If productivity of your combined
resources goes up with growth, it is healthy growth. Fourth,
the development of people will be far more crucial in the
years ahead.

The demands on the manager are therefore going to be
steadily increasing. But so are the opportunities. Whether
the demands are threats or opportunities will depend on
your competence. You will do well to work on your own
management competence.

> Peter F. Drucker, March 8, "Turbulence: Threat or
> Opportunity," *The Daily Drucker*, 2004.

• The coalition of sovereign nations assembled by President George
H. W. Bush in 1991 to reverse Iraq's invasion of Kuwait may be
the precise model we need going forward to control nuclear pro-
liferation, transnational terrorism, and environmental degrada-
tion. These are clearly areas that cannot be left to market forces
or to any one sovereign nation.

3. TRANSNATIONAL NEEDS: THE ENVIRONMENT AND TERRORISM

There is a growing need for truly transnational
institutions. . . . These institutions can . . . make decisions
and take actions in a wide range of areas, cutting through
the barrier of sovereignty and directly controlling citizens
and organizations within a nation-state. . . . The first is the
environment. Local action is necessary to prevent destructive
pollution. But the biggest threat to the environment is not

local pollution. . . . The greatest threat is damage to the human habitat, to the atmosphere, to the tropical forests which are the earth's lungs, to the earth's oceans, to its water supply, and to the air—the very environment on which all humanity depends. . . . Second only to the environment is the growing need for transnational action and institutions to abort the return of private armies and stamp out terrorism. The military invasion of Iraq in the winter and spring of 1991 may have been a starting point. . . . [F]or the first time in recorded history, practically all nation-states acted together to put down an act of terrorism—for this is what the Iraqi invasion of Kuwait represented.

Peter F. Drucker, *Post-Capitalist Society*, 1993, pp. 145–46.

III. Practicum-Prompts

How will the challenges and changes identified by Drucker, which are affecting America, influence you? How will they affect your organization?

Can you anticipate where the greatest changes and challenges to your organization are likely to come from during the next five years? Have you developed alternative strategies to prosper from these changes and challenges if and when they do occur?

What steps are you taking to improve your competencies for managing during these turbulent times?

Is your organization lean? Can it move fast in response to change?

Do you have a program of systematic abandonment to rid yourself of unproductive items?

Are your most talented people applied to your most promising, new opportunities?

What steps are you taking to develop your people on a continuous basis?

A Major Period of Transition for Society and Individuals

Introduction

During his campaign for the presidency of the United States in 1980, Ronald Reagan made a campaign appearance in front of the Honnold Library of the Claremont Colleges. A two-term governor of California, he was no stranger to Claremont, having visited the colleges in a number of capacities before 1980.

A large number of students gathered at the campaign event, mostly to jeer the Republican nominee. Reagan let them go on for a time and then broke out into a memorable address that stilled the crowd. He agreed that he had attended college at a much earlier time in U.S. history and was of a different generation. During his time in college, he recalled, students did not have access to televisions, computers, or other forms of entertainment and laborsaving devices, nor were they witnesses to space exploration, the U.S.-Soviet space race, and Neil Armstrong's walk on the moon in 1969. These conveniences and achievements had not been even imagined when he went to college. He then paused, and said, "My generation didn't have these; *we invented them.*" A hush came over the students and he then proceeded to deliver his remarks uninterrupted.

I. Read

I think we are in the midst of a very major transition in which the new—not just new structures, new organizations, but fundamentally new concepts, new ways of seeing the world, new ways of relating as individuals, as organizations, and as countries—will have to be developed. I've tried to relate where we are in terms of historical parallels, and I found two kinds of markers. In 1506, about ten years before the Protestant Reformation, Leonardo da Vinci moved to France, and a nephew wrote him, and said, "Dear Uncle, Tell me what was the world like when you were born?" He was fifty years old at the time. And Leonardo wrote back and said, "Dear nephew, Nobody who was not born before 1460 can possibly understand what the world was like when I was born."

Now, in November 1992, we have already reached the point where if we tried to explain to one of our intelligent seventeen- or eighteen-year-olds what the world was like before World War II, would she be willing to believe that there was a world before television? And surely there could have never been a world without rubber bands. If you are an eighty-year-old, you know we had a world without rubber bands but it is hard to imagine. We also had a world without television, and so on and so forth.

Probably for an eight-year-old even more than for the eighteen-year-old, a world without computers is very hard to imagine. It's a different world and these are just the externals. I think we are in a period in which there is enormous uncertainty and danger. In the last election some of my friends who were very active in the Bush campaign came to me and said, "Explain to us, the economy is doing all right, it is doing better than any other"—which happens to be true—"and yet people are so worried. Why?" And I said, "Well, they are a little more intelligent than you are."

It's uncertainty, it's the feeling that the ground under your feet is shaking and that you don't know whether to step down or whether to go right through or not. That is what is bothering people. It has very little to do with economic statistics; it has to do with the feeling. . . . The things you measure are not meaningful anymore.

There is nothing more frightening, and I don't think I convinced them on that position. That makes it a very dangerous time because it is one in which demagogues flourish. And it's a very exciting time because it is also a time in which what individuals do, what small and large organizations do, what countries and governments do, really matters. So I think this is a very dangerous, a very upsetting, and a very exciting period.

> Peter F. Drucker, address to Advisory Board of the Peter F. Drucker Nonprofit Foundation, November 8, 1992.

II. Reflect

- Maintaining the values and institutions that have endured the test of time is important to help navigate the tumultuous changes we are now experiencing in the economy and in society.

1. THE TRANSFORMATION

Every few hundred years in Western history there occurs a sharp transformation. We cross what in an earlier book [*The New Realities*, Chapter 1, 1989] I called a "divide." Within a few short decades, society rearranges itself—its worldview; its basic values; its social and political structure; its arts; its key institutions. Fifty years later, there is a new world. And the people born then cannot even imagine the world in which their grandparents lived and into which their own parents were born. We are currently living through just such a transformation. It is creating the post-capitalist society.

Peter F. Drucker, *Post-Capitalist Society*, 1993.

• A serious interest in one or more social sector organizations is helpful in navigating the competitive pressures of the knowledge society and the transition we are now going through.

2. PRICE OF SUCCESS IN THE KNOWLEDGE SOCIETY

"The fear of failure has already permeated the knowledge society."

The upward mobility of the knowledge society comes at a high price: the psychological pressures and emotional traumas of the rat race. There can be winners only if there are losers. This was not true of earlier societies.

Japanese youngsters suffer [from] sleep deprivation because they spend their evenings at a crammer to help them pass their exams. Otherwise they will not get into the prestige university of their choice, and thus into a good job. Other countries, such as America, Britain and France, are also allowing their schools to become viciously competitive. That this has happened over such a short time—no more than 30 or 40 years—indicates how much the fear of failure has already permeated the knowledge society. Given this competitive struggle, a growing number of highly successful knowledge workers—business managers, university teachers, museum directors, doctors—"plateau" in their 40s. If their work is all they have, they are in trouble. Knowledge workers therefore need to develop some serious outside interest.

Peter F. Drucker, *Managing in the Next Society*, 2002, pp. 262–63.

3. THE ONE DECISIVE RESOURCE OF A BUSINESS IS KNOWLEDGE

Neither results nor resources exist inside the business. Both exist outside. . . . Results depend not on anybody within the business or on anything within the control of the business. They depend on somebody outside. It is always somebody outside who decides whether the efforts of a business become economic results or whether the efforts of the business become so much waste and scrap. The same is true of the one and only distinct resource of any business: knowledge. Other resources, money or physical equipment, for instance, do not confer any distinction. What does make a business distinct and what is its peculiar resource is its ability to use knowledge of all kinds—from scientific and technical knowledge to social, economic and managerial knowledge. It is only in respect to knowledge that a business can be distinct, can therefore produce something that has a value in the marketplace. Yet knowledge is not a business resource; it is a universal social resource. It cannot be kept secret for any length of time. "What one man has done, another man can always do again" is old and profound wisdom. The one decisive resource, therefore, is as much outside the business as are business results. Indeed, a business can be defined as a process that converts an outside resource, namely knowledge, into outside results, namely economic values.

Peter F. Drucker, *Managing for Results*, 1964, p. 5.

• An organization uses knowledge of all types—technological, social, economic, moral, and human—to produce goods and services through people at work in order to deliver economic value to customers. Thus management is clearly more than technique; it is a liberal art.

• The immediate need of young people is to acquire marketable skills—thus the need to emphasize technique in education.

Yet the task of executives, especially important during this period of transition, is to integrate knowledge under their jurisdiction, while retaining their own specialty. To be effective in managing they must know a fair amount about themselves and others.

4. MANAGEMENT AND THE LIBERAL ARTS

"Management is a liberal art."

Management is what tradition used to call a liberal art—"liberal" because it deals with the fundamentals of knowledge; self-knowledge, wisdom, and leadership; "art" because it deals with practice and application. Managers draw upon all of the knowledges and insights of the humanities and social sciences—on psychology and philosophy, on economics and history, on the physical sciences and ethics. But they have to focus this knowledge on effectiveness and results—on healing a sick patient, teaching a student, building a bridge, designing and selling a "user-friendly" software program.

Peter F. Drucker, *The New Realities*, 1989, p. 231.

- The advent of the knowledge society is one of the factors contributing to income inequality and uncertainty in the United States. It is creating winners and losers, opportunities and dangers. Continuous learning and education are prerequisites to competing and to succeeding in the knowledge economy. The transition, therefore, is indeed both exciting and upsetting.

- Here is Drucker's advice, recorded in an interview with T. George Harris, about our need to take responsibility for managing our careers and not to depend on any organization to do it for us.

5. TAKE RESPONSIBILITY FOR YOUR CAREER

The stepladder is gone, and there's not even the implied structure of an industry's rope ladder. It's more like vines, and you bring your own machete. You don't know what you'll be doing next, or whether you'll work in a private office or one big amphitheater or even out of your home. You have to take responsibility for knowing yourself, so you can find the right jobs as you develop and as your family becomes a factor in your values and choices.

T. George Harris, "The Post-Capitalist Executive: An Interview with Peter F. Drucker," *Harvard Business Review*, May 1993, pp. 114–22.

III. Practicum-Prompts

We usually do very well when performing activities that we enjoy and that fully utilize our strengths. Continue to apply and develop your strengths in areas that you find motivating. Stay abreast of new developments in your field through a systematic program of continuous education.

Develop a noncompetitive outside interest in which you can make a contribution to the mission of a social sector organization and develop your talents in the process. Understanding the mission and values of a social sector organization can give you "fresh eyes" for the people and tasks in your primary occupation.

Take control of your career while developing your own human capital. Your working career is likely to outlast the life of the organization in which you currently serve, so be eager to stay but prepared to move on when conditions warrant that.

Knowledge is becoming more specialized. As knowledge continues to splinter, try to understand the knowledge areas of your colleagues and figure out how to communicate what you do in your knowledge area that impinges on their work and how what they do impinges on your work. This is the information that you should communicate to your colleagues. A warning: this is tougher than it sounds because each field tends to develop its own jargon that often is understandable only by people in the field. As a result, you must work at simplifying your expertise so that an intelligent knowledge worker in another area can understand it. Ask your colleagues on whom you depend for information to do the same thing for you.

Week 19

Seeing the Future That Has Already Happened

Social and Demographic Changes Emerging in the United States

Introduction

Peter Drucker and Bob Buford convened two separate meetings, on January 29, 1991, and June 15, 1991. The purpose of these two meetings was to identify and capitalize on *social and demographic changes* that were emerging in the United States. Tom Patterson, a strategic planning consultant with a history of working with Peter Drucker, Rick Warren, and Bob Buford asked Drucker to describe the emerging trends in the United States.

This is an exercise in "seeing the future that has already happened." As such, the exercise is an application of a portion of the methodology Drucker applied as a social ecologist. Drucker used this methodology often in teaching, consulting, and writing. Both the methodology and the specific trends Drucker identified are useful for establishing premises for strategic planning, which was the purpose of these two meetings.

Drucker first summarized expected results of the meetings and then began identifying demographic trends that are likely to affect all organizations in the United States, not just pastoral churches.

I. Read

I take it that the end result of these meetings is a planning guide for organizations, which I think is not only an excellent idea but also a badly needed one. The guides I know of are reacting rather than acting, which is what one does if one grows very fast.

One of the places to start is always the only place, the place one can count on and one doesn't have to have opinions on. These are *demographics*, and if you look out ten to fifteen years—and I think that probably [this] is as far as one can look with demographics—there is going to be a substantial increase in the number of people who, in the last twenty or thirty years, have not been very close to the church.

I think if you look at an opportunity, or for a ministry of pastoral churches to young adults who are as a lot moving to urban and suburban areas, they are as confused as one is at that age. They need—call it awareness; that's the best word. The second thing you can say is that it is going to be a racially heterogeneous group. The fastest growth has not been in African-Americans, where the growth has been very limited, but in the *Latinos and Asian populations in this area* [Southern California], *and in the nation as a whole, and I think the tensions are going to be quite great.* The next thing you can say demographically is: the group that has been the main mover in the pastoral churches is going to be *substantially older.* Those are, I think, *certainties.* You can feel that this is going to be a turbulent time worldwide.

Drucker-Buford-Warren-Patterson Dialogues, January 29, 1991, and June 15, 1991.

II. Reflect

- Identifying emerging trends is different from trying to forecast the future. The former lacks the precision of a forecast and concentrates on directions and patterns. A social ecologist attempts to discern patterns from emerging trends, and separates fads from real changes. Thus the work of the social ecologist is very different from that of the futurist, who tries to predict the future, absent concrete evidence.

- Executives can capitalize on emerging trends and use them to create a new future for their organizations, thus providing a competitive advantage in times of rapid change. This is a proactive, not a reactive, response.

1. IDENTIFYING THE FUTURE

"The important thing is to identify the 'future that has already happened.'"

Futurists always measure their batting average by how many things they have predicted come true. They never count how many of the important things that came true they did not predict. Everything the forecaster predicts may come to pass. Yet he may not have seen the most meaningful of the emergent realities, or, worse still, may not have paid attention to them. There is no way to avoid this irrelevancy in forecasting, for the important and distinctive are always the result of changes in *values, perception, and goals*, that is in things that one can divine but not forecast.

But the more important work of the executive is to identify the changes that have already happened. The important challenge in society, [the] economy, [and] politics is to exploit the changes that have already occurred and to use them as opportunities. The important thing is to identify the "future that has already happened"—and to develop a methodology for perceiving and analyzing these changes. A good deal of this methodology is incorporated in my 1985 book *Innovation and Entrepreneurship,* which shows how one systematically looks to the changes in society, in demographics, in meaning, in science and technology as opportunities to make the future.

> Peter F. Drucker, January 2, "Identifying the Future," *The Daily Drucker,* 2004.

- The methodology that Drucker refers to consists of searching for seven "windows" of opportunity for innovation and pursuing one or more of them as strategies of innovation. The seven sources are (1) unexpected success or failure, (2) incongruities, (3) process need, (4) a change in industry or market structure, (5) demographics, (6) changes in perception, and (7) new knowledge. This is the subject of chapters 3–9 of Drucker's 1985 book *Innovation and Entrepreneurship.* The methodology Drucker employed involved searching for these sources of innovative opportunity and extrapolating from changes that had already occurred. In this way, he was able to identify "the future that had already happened," changes that had already occurred but were not yet fully recognized. In his 1992 introduction (p. x) to the Transaction edition of his 1969 book, *The Age of Discontinuity,* Drucker says: "Every one of the book's assertions was brand-new when the book came out, and quite contrary to the received wisdom of the times. Yet readers alike said at once, 'Of course,' and have [said] so ever since. This is the response social analysis aims at, the response that validates it. . . . Every book of social analysis that has stood the test of time—whether the works of Max Weber or those of Thorstein Veblen—had that quality of being both brand-new and 'of course.'"

• Demographic trends are among the most predictable and useful, because age distributions affecting future spending patterns (e.g., family formations affecting the purchase of homes and other durable goods) can be projected on the basis of current age distributions.

2. DEMOGRAPHIC CHANGES HAVE THE MOST PREDICTABLE CONSEQUENCES

Of all external changes, demographics—defined as changes in population, its size, age structure, composition, employment, educational status, and income—are the clearest. They are unambiguous. They have the most predictable consequences. They have major impact on what will be bought, by whom, and in what quantities. They also have known and almost certain lead times. . . . All people reaching retirement age in 2030 in developed countries are already in the labor force, and in most cases in the occupational group in which they will stay until they retire or die.

Peter F. Drucker, *Innovation and Entrepreneurship*, 1985, p. 88.

• The social ecologist, in describing the future that has already happened, should do so with such clarity that readers interpret it as "common sense." The aim of the social ecologist is action, and for there to be action there must be understanding by those in a position to act on their findings.

3. SOCIAL ISSUES DOMINATE IN THE NEXT TWENTY TO THIRTY YEARS: INTERVIEW BY JAMES DALY, EDITOR IN CHIEF OF *BUSINESS 2.0* MAGAZINE.

Daly: One of the seminal books you wrote was *The Age of Discontinuity*. If you were to revisit that today, in this age of accelerated change, what would you write?

Drucker: I would put much more emphasis on demographics. . . . In the last forty or fifty years economics was dominant. In the next twenty or thirty years, social issues will be dominant. The rapidly growing aging population and the rapidly shrinking younger population means there will be social problems.

> Reprinted in Peter F. Drucker, *Managing in the Next Society*, 2002, pp. 72–73.

• Drucker's book *Concept of the Corporation* (1946) has been widely recognized as having established management as a discipline. Its findings were taken from a two-year study of the policies and structures of General Motors. Drucker acknowledges, in his introduction to the 1990 edition of Alfred P. Sloan's book *My Years with General Motors* (1963, 1990), that Sloan "was proud, and deservedly so, to have been the first to work out systematic organization in a big company, planning and strategy, measurements, the principle of decentralization—in short, basic concepts of a discipline of management." Drucker looked, found new knowledge, and innovated by defining in 1946, and then in 1954 with *The Practice of Management*, the discipline and practice of management that were largely in place already at General Motors and General Electric, two companies with which he consulted, and that illustrate the points of the next reading: "Practice comes first" and "Theory organizes the new realities."

4. PRACTICE COMES FIRST

"Theory organizes the new realities; it rarely creates them."

Decision-makers—in government, in the universities, in business, in the labor unions, in churches—need to factor into their present decisions the *future that has already happened.* For this they need to know what events have already occurred that do not fit into their present-day assumptions, and thereby create new realities.

Intellectuals and scholars tend to believe that ideas come first which then lead to new political, social, economic, psychological realities. This does happen but it is the exception. As a rule, theory does not precede practice. Its role is to structure and codify already proven practice. Its role is to convert the isolated and "atypical" from exception to "rule" and "system," and therefore into something that can be learned and taught, and above all, into something that can be generally applied. Theory organizes the new realities; it rarely creates them.

Peter F. Drucker, *The New Realities*, Preface to the Reissue, 2003, pp. ix–x.

III. Practicum-Prompts

Drucker saw discontinuous and radical changes in the environment that would create challenges and opportunities for organizations. These changes are now upon us. What opportunities have they created for your organization? What opportunities have they created for you?

A substantial increase in young adults who have come to maturity after the new millennium is one of these changes—this group is often referred to as the millennials. The main movers in organizations are going to be substantially older, often baby boomers, those born right after World War II. How are these generational differences going to affect your organization?

The period we are now going through is, as Drucker predicted, one of worldwide turbulence. Unless you can turn some of these changes into opportunities, you and your organization may become vulnerable to this turbulence. What steps are you taking to turn this turbulence to your advantage?

As Drucker discusses in his book *Innovation and Entrepreneurship*, look for sources of opportunity for innovation in your organization. Look for "the future that has already happened" and turn it into an opportunity for innovation. If you do this, you can become a change leader and make competition irrelevant for you and for your organization.

Seeing the Future That Has Already Happened

Turmoil in Education

Introduction

I had the good fortune to meet Nobel laureate Kenneth G. Wilson and his colleague Constance Barsky during the summer of 2009. After Wilson left Cornell University in 1988 he became very interested in applying Drucker's work on systematic innovation to education. He spent twenty years, from 1988 to 2008, at The Ohio State University conducting research on a paradigm shift in learning theory applied to education. Ken's book *Redesigning Education* (Teachers College Press, New York, 1994), written with Bennett Davis, calls for a process of systematic innovation in our nation's schools.

Marie Clay worked with the faculty of The Ohio State University during the 1980s. Her book *Reading Recovery: Guidelines for Teachers in Training* (1993) has had an enormous impact on education, selling more than eight million copies. This book helps in training new trainers and teachers in the program at a very rapid rate, thus increasing our capacity to use Reading Recovery. Ken saw Reading Recovery as an example of an "unexpected success," one of the seven sources of opportunities for innovation in Drucker's book *Innovation and Entrepreneurship* (1985). Ken participated with Marie Clay in extending Reading Recovery across North America and the world.

But Ken became discouraged with the educational establishment in the United States, which he thought was impeding the spread of Reading Recovery by engaging in recurring "reading wars" while cutting support for proven educational programs.

It was through my association with Wilson and Barsky that I understood how Drucker's idea of "focus on strength" was at the heart of individual remediation: the central idea in Reading Recovery. In the midst of Drucker's gloom about our educational system in the United States, I saw a glimmer of light, and this entry describes that light. I went on to write a case study, "Drucker's Ideas for School Reform," based on the work of Wilson and Barsky at The Ohio State University.[34]

I. Read

The second thing I think you can be quite sure of is that a lot of things which we—not just in this country, but in the developed world—have been treating by patching, from the inner-city schools to health care, are going to get "out of control."

I think one has to accept it, no matter whether you like it or not. By the end of this period, it's predictable that all the things we are now trying to do will be just as ineffectual as the things we have been doing the last ten years to patch it, and we will have to accept the fact that no matter how [unsatisfactory] we believe the traditional system was, with its narrow focus on learning a few key skills, it is one that worked within its limits.

And you know when you have lost your way in the mountains you don't try to be clever. You try to go back to the last place where you knew you were on the right path; and I think you will see, it will probably come by vouchers, which means very large church-related schools, not an organizational, public school, necessarily.[35]

So, I think you will see turmoil in education because it clearly doesn't work.

Drucker-Buford-Warren-Patterson Dialogues, January 29, 1991, and June 15, 1991.

II. Reflect

- We have tried to patch up a primary and secondary school system—with No Child Left Behind, Race to the Top, Common Core, etc. But these programs are not producing the results we need as a nation to be competitive in the global economy. According to data compiled by the Intelligence Unit of *The Economist* in September 2012, the United States ranks seventeenth in cognitive skills (reading, math, and science) and educational attainment (literacy and graduation rates) among thirty-nine countries plus Hong Kong, the Special Administrative Region of the People's Republic of China, which ranks third on this list of educational attainment.[36]

- "Perhaps the time has come for an entrepreneur to start schools based on what we know about learning, rather than on the old wives' tales about it that have been handed down through the ages."[37]

1. EDUCATION MUST INCLUDE THE DISCIPLINE OF LEARNING

"Literacy" traditionally means subject knowledge, for example, the ability to do multiplication or a little knowledge of American history. But the knowledge society needs process knowledge—something the schools have rarely even tried to teach. *In the knowledge society, people have to learn how to learn.* Indeed, in the knowledge society subjects may matter less than the students' capacity to continue learning and their motivation to do so. Knowledge society requires lifelong learning. For this, we need a *discipline of learning.*

Peter F. Drucker, *Management: Revised Edition*, 2008, pp. 154–55.

• Reading Recovery is a program developed to bring at-risk first-graders up to grade level in reading and to maintain grade level standards in subsequent years. Reading is of course the basic skill required in lifelong learning.[38]

2. WE KNOW HOW TO TEACH THE DISCIPLINE OF LEARNING

Actually, we do know what to do [to create the discipline of learning]. In fact, for hundreds of years, if not thousands of years, we have been creating both the motivation for continuing to learn and the needed discipline. The good teachers of artists do it; the good coaches of athletes do it; so do the good "mentors" in business organizations of which we hear so much these days in the literature of management development. They lead their students to achievements so great that it surprises the achiever and creates excitement and motivation—especially the motivation for rigorous, disciplined, persistent work and practice that continued learning requires.

Peter F. Drucker, *Management: Revised Edition*, 2008, p. 155.

• Marie Clay focused her attention on individualized instruction based on an assessment of the reading status of individual students and on each student's strengths. She found that children had different problems in learning how to read and had different patterns of learning. Teachers have to learn how to "unlock" these patterns in order for their students to achieve grade level status and to maintain that status in subsequent years of school-

ing. Reading Recovery provides a proven example of how to accomplish this.

3. ACHIEVEMENT IS ADDICTIVE

[A]chievement does not mean doing a little less poorly
what one is not particularly good at. The achievement that
motivates is doing exceptionally well what one is already
good at. Achievement has to be based on the student's
strengths—as has been known for millennia. . . . In fact,
finding the student's strengths and focusing them on achievement is
the best definition of the goal of teaching. It is the definition
in the "Dialogue on the Teacher" by one of the greatest
teachers of the Western tradition, Saint Augustine of Hippo
(354–430).

Peter F. Drucker, *Post-Capitalist Society*, 1993, p. 184.

III. Practicum-Prompts

Kenneth Wilson and Constance Barsky met with Drucker shortly
before Drucker's death. Ken and Constance were interested in fur-
thering their innovative work on primary and secondary education
and sought Drucker's advice. After talking with Constance and Ken
about innovation in education for a short time, Drucker turned his
attention to Ken, asking him numerous questions about his work in
physics, and this consumed a good part of the meeting. Drucker, a
genius, was a humble man. He learned from his associates and students. He was a very successful lifelong learner, and he provides an
example of humility that we would do well to follow in our pursuit
of knowledge. Develop a plan for lifelong learning.

We know from all the research on Reading Recovery, and from
an abundance of other research, that we all learn differently. But
many if not most schools and colleges are organized on the assumption that there is one right way to learn. There is not. If you are to

make rapid progress as a lifelong learner, give attention to determining just how you do learn most effectively. You might start by answering this question: "Do I learn most effectively by reading or by listening?"

Figure out how your children or other family members learn. Make sure they are aware that learning, to be most effective, should be individualized—otherwise it can be torture.

Reading Recovery is really a mentoring process. Does your organization use mentors? Are they effective in leading people to outstanding levels of achievement and motivation? What have you learned from this entry that might make you and your organization better mentors of others?

Maintaining Your Organization Through Change

Continuity and Change

Introduction

A remarkable meeting between Rick Warren and Peter Drucker took place on January 22, 2003, after the publication of Warren's best-selling book, *The Purpose Driven Life* (2002). It was a period of rapid growth both for Saddleback Community Church and for other satellite purpose-driven churches inspired by Warren's book and the program *40 Days of Purpose*. Warren consulted with Drucker to explore questions of leadership development and organization structure caused by this rapid growth.

This entry describes principles involved in dealing with organization and management problems of rapid growth. These principles include the need for innovation and change; for preventing the natural tendencies of organizations to become bureaucratic; for transmitting core values; and for carrying on conscience activities, that is, those activities concerned with maintaining standards and values.

These principles should be implemented in a way that will perpetuate the mission and values of an organization and provide continuity, while also facilitating change.

I. Read

Rick Warren

Peter, years ago you taught me that the structure of rapidly growing organizations must continually keep changing. Nothing works forever. Our purposes never change—but our methods and tactics must constantly change. It is amazing how quickly a successful organization can deteriorate into mediocrity.

Peter Drucker

Yes, that's right. An organization needs something new every so often, and yet at the same time it also needs *continuity*. The mission or purpose remains the same, so you need people that are committed to the mission, but sometimes you also need to make radical *changes*. For example, early Methodism was a radical innovation because [the Methodists] allowed women to serve as lay ministers. That was very different from the Church of England, where women were supposed to keep their mouths shut and their purses open. So when Methodism first began to grow [it] attracted many lower-class women. But after [it] had grown to be a mass movement [the Methodists] wanted to become respectable and they stopped using women lay ministers. What annoyed the traditionalist[s] was the strength of these women ministers. So, they eventually stopped using women and within twenty years of that decision they became a denominational bureaucracy.

Rick, I can't predict your future. I can only say that you will successfully create new problems.

Drucker-Warren Dialogue, January 22, 2003.

II. Reflect

- Peter Drucker sternly corrected me when I once suggested that continuity and change are opposites. He yelled, "No! They are a continuum!" I later found out that this unusual response reflected the centrality of these concepts in his work on organizations and society. The themes of continuity and change permeate all of his work and actually began with his very first published monograph, *Friedrich Julius Stahl: His Conservative Theory of the State*, published in German in 1933.[39] Stahl, an ecclesiastical lawyer of the mid-nineteenth century, tried to create a society of institutions for Germany that would sustain a balance between institutions that provided *continuity* and those designed to foster *change*. The Lutheran Church was one of the institutions Stahl relied on for continuity; another was government. Economic institutions and universities were designed to facilitate change. Stahl's attempt to create a functioning society of institutions in Germany survived until World War I.
- If an organization does not *change*, it may stagnate and die, thus losing *continuity*. In order to achieve continuity, therefore, an organization must be designed to change. That continuity and change are a continuum, and not opposites, may at first seem counterintuitive to you, as it once did to me.

1. BALANCE, CONTINUITY, AND CHANGE

"Precisely because change is a constant, the foundations have to be extra strong."

Change and continuity are thus poles rather than opposites. The more an institution is organized to be a change leader, the more it will need to establish continuity internally and externally, the more it will need to *balance* rapid change and continuity. . . . One way is to make *partnership in change*

the basis of *continuing relationships*. . . . Balancing change
and continuity requires continuous work on information.
Nothing disrupts continuity and corrupts relationships
more than poor or unreliable information. It has to become
routine for any enterprise to ask at any change, even the most
minor one: "Who needs to be informed of this?" And this
will become more and more important as more enterprises
come to rely on people working together without actually
working together—that is, on people using the technologies
of information. . . . Above all, there is need for continuity
in respect to the fundamentals of the enterprise: its mission,
its values, its definition of performance and results. Precisely
because change is a constant in the change leader's enterprise,
the foundations have to be extra strong.

Finally, the balance between change and continuity has
to be built into compensation, recognition and rewards. We
will have to learn, similarly, that an organization will have
to reward continuity—by considering, for instance, people
who deliver continuing improvement to be as valuable to the
organization, and as deserving of recognition and reward, as
the genuine innovator.

> Peter F. Drucker, *Management Challenges for the 21st Century*,
> 1999, pp. 90–92.

- A constant stream of incremental improvements will lead to substantial change over time. An organization should therefore seek and reward continuous improvement activities.

- To maintain continuity while changing rapidly requires continuous work on communications with all major stakeholders including employees and suppliers. Executives must ask, "Who must be informed of these changes?" The more an organization changes, the more it will require its employees and suppliers to become partners in change.

- The larger an organization, the more time it may require to change direction. A plan must be put into place and followed closely.

2. ORGANIZATIONAL AGILITY

"Fleas can jump many times their own height but not elephants."

Large organizations cannot be versatile. A large organization is effective through its mass rather than through its agility. Mass enables the organization to put to work a great many more kinds of knowledge and skill than could possibly be combined in any one person or small group. But mass is also a limitation. An organization, no matter what it would like to do, can only do a small number of tasks at any one time. This is not something that better organization or "effective communications" can cure. The law of organization is concentration.

Yet [a] modern organization must be capable of change. Indeed it must be capable of initiating change, that is, innovation. It must be able to move scarce and expensive resources of knowledge from areas of low productivity and nonresults to opportunities for achievement and contribution. This, however, requires the ability to stop doing what wastes resources.

Peter F. Drucker, *The Age of Discontinuity*, 1969, pp. 192–93.

- Change in organizations may take two forms: creating new wealth through innovation, and creating new wealth by moving resources from low to high productivity. Moving resources from areas of low productivity to areas of high productivity requires executives to abandon certain activities, products, and processes.

- Ongoing competition will result in changes in the economic structure of an industry. This process of creative destruction described by Joseph Schumpeter[40] requires change, continuous improvement, and innovation in order to ensure the survival of an organization: "It is what capitalism consists in and what every capitalist concern has got to live with." The process is more rapid during turbulent times. An organization that is bureaucratic and slow to change is likely to be a casualty of creative destruction.

3. MANAGING IN TURBULENT TIMES

There is one overall text on which this book preaches. It is *"Don't be clever, be conscientious."*

Predicting the future can only get you into trouble.
The task is to manage what there is and to work to create what could and should be. There are no miracle cures . . . no quick fixes. Indeed the book asks what work *must* be done. The controlling word is "must." Executives are not in control of the universe any more than other mortals are. But executives are accountable for the survival of the organization in their keeping, for its ability to perform, for its results.

Peter F. Drucker, *Managing in Turbulent Times*, 1980, p. 4.

III. Practicum-Prompts

The future of your organization will not be like the past or present. Change is inevitable although its direction may be difficult to predict. Your task then is not to predict the future but to go to work to create new products, processes, and services that will serve customers in the future. Do you have policies in place that permit people to create a "new" future?

The greater the changes faced by your organization, the stronger your values will have to be. Are your values strong enough to maintain organizational cohesiveness during periods of rapid change?

The more your organization relies on people working together who are not co-located, the more you must make sure these people are fully informed of any changes that will affect them. Do you provide for a constant flow of information to key people inside and outside your organization?

It is risky to become a change leader and to try to make the future. But it is more risky for you and your organization to leave yourselves open to being overcome by competition. How do you and your organization plan to proceed in light of these realities?

Systematic Abandonment and Innovation

Introduction

Each of the three sectors of society has difficulty abandoning obsolete products, services, policies, and processes.

Government often uses fiscal policy to introduce new programs in order to stimulate the economy. These programs tend to gather the support of strong lobbyists representing industrial, environmental, public policy, and community service organizations to maintain or expand them. As a result, government programs at the federal level tend to stay in place, even if the original purpose of these programs no longer exists. The inability to abandon existing programs reduces the resources available to fund new initiatives that are necessary if the United States is to remain competitive as a nation.

The social sector is engaged in doing good. Often the institutions in this sector attempt to *maximize* the delivery of services (for example, they try to "totally eliminate poverty") rather than to *optimize* according to their mission and resources. In other cases, such institutions have fulfilled their original and unique mission. But rather than declare victory and disband, these victors sometimes adopt a new mission that may duplicate the missions of other worthy institutions. For example, the March of Dimes was founded in 1938 by President Franklin D. Roosevelt to develop a cure for polio and to provide aid to victims. With the development of the Salk vaccine in 1955 and the Sabin oral vaccine in 1962, polio has been almost totally eradicated in developed countries and essentially eradicated worldwide.

The original mission of the March of Dimes has been magnificently fulfilled. But rather than disband, the organization began to search for another mission. In 1958, it found one. Its new mission is to "help moms have full-term pregnancies and research the problems that threaten the health of babies." While this is a very important mission, there were already numerous other centers in the United States pursuing it. There are so many that for the past three years, *U.S. News & World Report* has provided a ranking of the top fifty pediatric hospitals for neonatology.[41] One wonders if the March of Dimes is still necessary.

Business is different because it is disciplined by profit and loss. Yet programs in business also develop supporters, who often resist attempts to defund pet projects. Continued investments in these projects are often referred to as "investments in managerial ego." They may survive as long as the enterprise is profitable even though, like some programs in government and the social sector, they no longer serve their intended purpose.

Given the difficulties associated with abandonment in government, a workable proposal has been put forward by Robert N. Anthony. Anthony was a professor of management control at the Harvard Business School, and comptroller of the Department of Defense under Secretary of Defense Robert McNamara, while on leave from Harvard from 1965 to 1968. His proposal, published in a *Wall Street Journal* editorial, is to hire "outside experts to go into an agency and examine its reason for being, its methods of operations, and its costs."[42] This is good advice for all levels of government as well as for organizations in both the social and the private sectors.

I. Read

Abandonment of the old is particularly important for
the nonprofit service organization because it believes, and

must believe, in the righteousness of its cause. That makes innovation very difficult because the first key to innovation is the willingness to abandon the old so that you free yourself for the new. There is an old proverb in medicine that if you can't eliminate you drown in your own waste products, and very fast. That's true of every organization, and yet if you believe in a cause, [elimination is] difficult to do in a nonprofit.

The ultimate goal of the organization may be forever; the means, however, are short term. Let me give you an example. I am working with a friend who is the vicar of one of our major Catholic archdioceses, which has a tremendous shortage of Catholic priests. And here are the schools of the diocese that have more kids than ever but not one of them is a Catholic.

So you have to think through the purpose of the organization. I'm arguing with him because he really wants to close the schools. They don't add to salvation. I said, But look, the Bible says, "The greatest of these is charity," and we are kind of struggling through the decision. But it's a very serious question about *contribution*.

I'm quite willing to say to him, Take the diocese out of hospitals. You make no contribution, it's not needed, we now have numerous good hospitals. A hundred and fifty years ago a Catholic hospital was the only hospital in this country. Today it's not, and if it's gone it's a pity perhaps but we will survive, and so one looks at abandonment decisions by keeping one's priorities open, and then by organizing systematically to look for new opportunities to practice systematic abandonment and innovation.

We know how to abandon programs, and the nonprofit organization needs abandonment as much as a business organization. I've been through this with three service community organizations: two in the health field, and one in community service. All three of them practice systematic innovation. The two in the health field have regained momentum on the American Heart Association by looking at the enormous advances in cardiovascular medicine, and by becoming education institutions where their original focus was basically raising money for poor people who didn't have money for health care. The third one redirected itself from traditional education into the continuing professional education of already highly educated people, and gained vitality, enthusiasm, and effectiveness. But if you wait for luck, or a brain wave, or for what's so popular in today in books, entrepreneurship, where you go down the street and suddenly the idea hits you, you are going to wait a very long time. You'd better organize yourself to look for the changes inside and outside the organization as close to an opportunity as possible. We know how to do it.[43]

Peter Drucker–David Hubbard Dialogue, February 22, 1988.

II. Reflect

- In the passage above Drucker is arguing that the chief vicar of the diocese should drop the Catholic hospitals and keep the Catholic schools. The diocese has *competence* in both, but the pressing *need* is for high-performing schools among the poor. Drucker shifted the basis of the argument with the chief vicar from advancing the religious mission of the diocese to advancing the mission of charity—each *a virtue* of the Catholic Church—in order to arbitrate between two important criteria: *competence* and *need*.

1. THE PRACTICE OF ABANDONMENT

"If we did not do this already, would we go into it now? If the answer is no, 'What do we do now?'"

The question has to be asked—and asked seriously—"If we did not do this already, would we, knowing what we know, go into it now?" If the answer is no, the reaction must be "What do we do now?"

In three cases the right action is always outright abandonment. Abandonment is the right action if a product, service, market, or process "still has a few years of life." It is these dying products, services, or processes that always demand the greatest care and the greatest efforts. They tie down the most productive and ablest people. But equally a product, service, market, or process should be abandoned if the only argument for keeping it is: It is "fully written off." For *management* purposes there are no "costless assets." There are only "sunk costs." The third case where abandonment is the right policy—and the most important one—is the old or declining product, service, market, or process for the sake of maintaining which, the *new* and growing product, service, or process is being stunted or neglected.

> Peter F. Drucker, *Management Challenges for the 21st Century*, 1999, pp. 74–75.

• Abandonment of any program is difficult for a nonprofit organization because of the strong belief in the righteousness of its cause. It is sometimes difficult for a for-profit organization to abandon a program because the program may represent an investment by the people who introduced it and who nursed it along. Beware of commitment to ego as an excuse for maintaining the status quo.

2. EXAMPLE OF A SYSTEMATIC ABANDONMENT PROCESS

In one fairly big company offering outsourcing services in most developed countries, the first Monday of every month is set aside for an abandonment meeting at every management level from top management to the supervisors in each area. Each of these sessions examines one part of the business. . . . In the course of a year three to four major decisions are likely to be made on the "what" of the company services and perhaps twice as many decisions to change the "how." But also each year three to five ideas for *new things* to do come out of these sessions.

> Peter F. Drucker, *Management Challenges for the 21st Century*, 1999, p. 79.

• Developing a process of systematic abandonment, and making it a regular part of the culture of an organization, is one of the most effective ways to eliminate the old and make room for the new.

3. KNOWING THAT AN EXISTING PRODUCT WILL BE ABANDONED IN THE NEAR FUTURE AND RESOURCES FREED UP MAY HELP TO CONCENTRATE YOUR MIND ON INNOVATION

Sometimes abandonment is not the answer, and may not even be possible. But then at least one limits further efforts and makes sure that productive resources of men and money are no longer devoured by yesterday. This is the right thing to do in any event to maintain the health of the organization: every organism needs to eliminate its waste products or else it poisons itself. It is, however, an absolute necessity if an enterprise is to be capable of innovation and is to be receptive to it. "Nothing so powerfully concentrates a man's mind on innovation as the knowledge that the present product or service will be abandoned within the forseeable future."

> Peter F. Drucker, *Innovation and Entrepreneurship*, 1985, pp. 151–52.

III. Practicum-Prompts

When forced to choose between two competent programs, keep the one that makes the more significant contribution to the mission of the organization and to society.

Does your organization practice systematic abandonment? If not, identify the forces at work in your organization right now impeding the abandonment process. How can you remove these impediments?

Do you measure the percentage of annual sales and profits derived from new products and services? If not, why not? Begin by assessing the effectiveness of your innovation pipeline. It will create the right kind of pressures for instituting a program of systematic abandonment.

Have you ever asked Drucker's tough question "If we did not do this already, would we go into it now?" about a current product, service, or process? Have you acted on the answer? This question can be incorporated into a process of systematic abandonment in your organization.

Using the Mission Statement to Create Unity in the Organization

Introduction

Developing a mission statement that is widely shared and used effectively provides a number of benefits to an organization. It creates unity of action and motivation and answers the question "What are results?" Answering this question is especially difficult.

Many mission statements are simply mottoes and do not influence the actions of participants. What a waste of an opportunity to develop a useful management tool. A mission statement can be used to effectively allocate the time, talents, and resources of all the people in an organization.

A good mission statement can create unity of effort and prevent the organization from going out of alignment, especially during periods of rapid change. It can be used as a recruiting, appraisal, and retention tool to ensure that those in an organization are focused on doing the right thing.

Creating a culture wherein constructive dissent is tolerated in defining and solving problems will go a long way toward helping to develop effective mission statements. Constructive dissent stimulates the imagination of the dissenter and of other parties to a decision. Dissent should be focused, as much as humanly possible, on "What is right?" and not on "Who is right?" One should not underestimate how difficult this is to do.

In summary, a mission statement that has been thoroughly vetted, agreed on, and revised as conditions change provides an integrating device for the entire organization. It is tough work to prepare one but once prepared, the statement can be referred to frequently for guidance on decisions and behavior.

I. Read

Peter Drucker

The mission statement is your tool to force—and I use quite intentionally a nonpermissive word—to force your people to think through, "What is my objective? What is my goal? And what does it mean for me to contribute?" If you don't use it that way, you deprive yourself of your best communications tool and of your best development tool, but you also get a person who, like the bank teller, sees paperwork as being what he is paid to do, [and] treats customers gathered around his window as the factor limiting his success!

Drucker's favorite mission statement:
Your job is not selling, it is buying

Julius Rosenberg at Sears in about 1917 shocked his merchants by saying, Your job is not selling, but buying. I have learned that the only merchants that do well are merchants who see themselves as buyers, and not sellers. If the merchandise is not right, there is nothing you can do anyhow. All right, you can do very well in next week's clearance sale, but that's the end of it.

Then Rosenberg asked each of his store managers, What

does it mean for you? One of the store managers said, You know, it's not enough to have the merchandise. You have to know how to display it, and above all you have to explain to customers how to use it. The success of Sears in the Depression was phenomenal. They prospered when everyone else collapsed.

Peter Drucker–David Hubbard Dialogue, February 22, 1988.

II. Reflect

- Asking each of his store managers, "Now, what does this mean for you?" helped Rosenberg to integrate their efforts into the overall mission of Sears.
- "Doing the right thing" is seeing the whole of the organization's mission as one's personal mission.
- "Workmanship" is an example of "doing things right," and it is essential. But even more essential is "doing the right thing," which is what the third freestone mason (below) did.

1. WORK MUST BE RELATED TO THE NEEDS OF THE WHOLE

There is that very old story, a Chinese story, of three freestone masons, who were asked what they were doing, and one said, Don't you see? I'm chipping stones. And the other said, I'm making building blocks; and the third said, I'm building a cathedral. That's [what makes] the difference . . . seeing yourself as contributing to the overall mission and then developing one's objectives to do so. The point of this is that the third stonemason also probably—certainly—did the best job chipping stones because they had to fit. They were essential to a great undertaking. So you start out with the mission statement, and then you basically use it to challenge yourself and your people. You ask the question of everyone,

"What are objectives for you that follow from and support the mission?"

> Peter Drucker–David Hubbard Dialogue, February 28, 1988.

2. WORKMANSHIP

It is the second man [in the story above] who is a problem. Workmanship is essential; without it no work can flourish; in fact, an organization demoralizes if it does not demand of its members the most scrupulous workmanship they are capable of. But there is always a danger that the true workman, the true professional, will believe that he is accomplishing something when in effect he is just polishing stones or collecting footnotes. Workmanship must be encouraged in the business enterprise. But it must always be related to the needs of the whole.

> Peter F. Drucker, *The Practice of Management*, 1954, p. 123.

• Developing a mission statement to actually guide the work of an organization is a high-stakes decision that deserves care and constructive conflict.

3. USE DISSENT TO ACHIEVE UNITY AND COMMITMENT

Recently the Foundation for Nonprofit Management, which [was] started eleven years ago by a few of my friends and they named it after me, was having a board meeting. My wife, who sits on the board, was very unhappy. "Do we have to again think through our Mission Statement? And are we going to spend the whole of the second day on it?" Unsuccessfully, I tried to convince her that the purpose is not to rewrite the Mission Statement. The purpose is to

create unity. We are bringing in half a dozen new people who
have not worked for us before. Yes, we are going to change
this word or that word in the Mission Statement, and we are
going to fight over this for three hours or more. My wife,
quite rightly, sees no point to it. I do not think she accepted
the fact that the Mission Statement [i.e., the document itself]
does not matter; it is that the new people, and even the old
people, are being forced to think through the mission. These
discussions about whether the word should be "should" or
"would" in the Mission Statement are the ways to create
unity [by getting people to think through the mission].

> Peter F. Drucker, *Executive Summary: A Conversation with
> Peter Drucker on Leadership and Organizational Development,*
> 2002, p. 9.

• The assumptions embedded in any mission statement must fit
reality. You should often examine your mission statement. Otherwise your organization's activities may become obsolete. By
encouraging constructive dissent you can prevent organizational
obsolescence.

4. THE NEED FOR DISSENT

Emotions always run high over any decision in which the
organization is at risk if that decision fails, or [over] one that
is not easily reversible. The smart thing is to treat this as
constructive dissent and as a key to mutual understanding.

If you can bring dissent and disagreement to a common
understanding of what the decision is all about, you create
unity in action, and in all things trust. And trust requires
that dissent come out into the open, and that it be seen as
disagreement.

This is particularly important for non-profit institutions,
which have a greater propensity for internal conflict than

businesses precisely because everybody is committed to a common, good cause. Disagreement isn't a matter of your opinion versus mine, it is your good faith versus mine. Non-profit institutions have to be particularly careful not to become riddled by feuds and distrust. Disagreements must be brought out into the open and taken seriously.

> Peter F. Drucker, *Managing the Non-Profit Organization*, 1990, p. 124.

5. COMMITMENT TO THE MISSION

When you violate the values of an institution, you are likely to do a poor job. . . . A mission is not, in that sense, impersonal. I have never seen anything being done well unless people were committed.

All of us know the story of the Edsel automobile. Everybody thinks the Edsel failed because Ford did not do its homework. In fact, it was the best engineered, the best researched, the best everything car. There was only one thing wrong with it: nobody in the Ford Motor Company believed in it. It was contrived. It was designed on the basis of research and not on the basis of commitment. And so when it got into a little bit of trouble, nobody supported the child. I'm not saying it could have been a success. But, without that personal commitment, it certainly never could be. . . . So, you need three things [for a good mission statement]: opportunities; competence; and commitment. Every mission statement has to reflect all three or it will fall down on its ultimate goal, its ultimate purpose and final test. It will not mobilize the human resources of the organization for getting the right things done.

> Peter F. Drucker, *Managing the Non-Profit Organization*, 1990, p. 7.

III. Practicum-Prompts

Is your organization successful in achieving top-down and bottom-up commitment to the mission? If so, how is it achieved? If not, how can it be achieved?

Identify people in your organization whose attitude represents the three stonecutters. Do you have any in category one or two? How can you gain both workmanship and contribution to the mission from these people? Will incentives work? Will positive appraisals work?

Organize dissent for a specific decision under your responsibility. Choose people to bring into the discussion who you believe are likely to bring different points of view to the decision.

Make sure you focus on what is right, not on who is right, when making the decision. Work toward establishing a culture in which this approach to problem solving is *routine and respected* for making important decisions.

If after vigorous debate, a decision is made on your mission statement, and then actual events do not meet expectations in the mission statement, ask yourself if the contents of the debate contain possible answers as to why results do not meet expectations. Try to arrive at a revised mission statement that more accurately reflects the environment and your organization's competence and commitment to achieving the mission.

Week 24

A Primer on Market Research of Noncustomers

Introduction

One of Drucker's major contributions was his insistence that "[marketing] is the distinguishing, the unique function of a business" (*The Practice of Management*, 1954, p. 37). Moreover "marketing is so basic that it is not just enough to have a strong sales department and entrust marketing to it. Marketing is not only much broader than selling; it is not a specialized activity at all. It encompasses the entire business. It is the whole business seen from the point of view of its final result, that is, from the customer's point of view. Concern and responsibility for marketing must therefore permeate all areas of the enterprise" (p. 38).

Bill Hybels was an early practitioner of Drucker's approach to effective marketing, in the social sector. Hybels applied marketing research concepts advocated by Drucker to develop the first large pastoral church in 1975.[44] Drucker interviewed Hybels in 1988, on topics including his approach to market research of noncustomers.

Given the advanced state of Bill Hybels's work at the time, I have called a portion of the interview "A Primer on Market Research of Noncustomers." In my summary of the interview the topic of each of

Drucker's four key questions is followed by his summary of Hybels's response. Drucker's overall summation of the interview appears at the end of section I. The complete 5,000-word interview transcript is in Volume 2 of the Drucker Nonprofit Tape Series (1988). This is a wide-ranging interview between Drucker and Hybels on the history and management of Willow Creek Community Church, including the central role of market research. From the full transcript, I have chosen (and edited) Hybels's novel contributions to market research.

The principles used by Hybels for assessing customer value are among those Drucker wrote and taught about for decades and remain useful to leaders in all sectors of society because they make the convincing case that all the activities of an organization should be viewed from the marketing perspective. Chapter 6, "The Customer Is the Business," in Drucker's *Managing for Results* (1964) is perhaps the best treatment of this subject ever written.

I. Read

[Bill Hybels went door-to-door asking people if they attended church. If they did, he thanked them and left. If not, he asked why they didn't, since he was in a geographical region where church attendance is relatively high. He then compiled a list of reasons why people in the wealthy suburbs of Chicago did not attend church. Drucker called these people "nonchurchgoers." Drucker then rephrased and summarized Hybels's answers systematically to make them most useful to a broad audience.]

Peter Drucker

(1) You ask nonchurchgoers, "Why are you not attending a church?"

You, Bill, basically reacted to a new opportunity in South Barrington, Illinois. You went out and researched the people who should be customers, but weren't. Now that is one of the most important things to say. *We don't ask.* So you asked and listened. And heard [people say], "These churches always say, 'We need your money,' and [don't] say, 'You need us?'"

(2) You asked, "What is *value* to nonchurchgoers?"

Bill, if you do this successfully, you don't have to ask for money. We need to tell people this is what we do for you and these are the results. We are so tired of being told of the needs of churches. First, there is no end of them [that is, no end to the needs of churches], absolutely none, and all of us have limited resources, both of time and of money, and we have to allocate them to [get] results. I think that is one of the most important things we can learn from you—not to talk about our needs—*we need what you need.*

(3) You then asked yourself, "How do we provide a relevant church experience for those people who are nonchurchgoers?"

[From the answers he received from nonchurchgoers, Hybels decided to design a church around their needs and to apply a strict test for meeting these "felt needs" of nonchurchgoers in an excellent way, and on a priority basis, before moving on to offer other ministries. He concentrated his efforts on preaching, for example, until additional resources were available to offer additional ministries.]

Peter Drucker

Bill, you concentrate on what you do best; you concentrate on what the market really needs and responds to; and you strive for excellence before you branch out because far too many entrepreneurial adventures immediately see all those market opportunities and start sprinkling themselves and they don't have the resources to make it first rate, and so they start cutting corners, they start getting by, and in no time at all, they've lost all [of] what the market people call "product differentiation." You can't tell them apart. And you avoided it.

[Hybels was well aware that he had to attract volunteers by offering them nonmonetary rewards for their service.

Drucker, in his article "What Business Can Learn from Nonprofits" (*Harvard Business Review*, July–August 1989), offers advice from nonprofits to business for attracting and motivating knowledge workers. It is similar to the process nonprofits follow in recruiting volunteers.]

Peter Drucker

(4) You offer new ministries when quality lay leadership is available. You make professionals out of the laity through training and feedback.

So basically from the beginning, Bill, *you were committed to making professionals out of the laity.* The only differences being that they're not ordained and that they're not being paid, and they don't work full-time, but you make the same demands on them for excellence [by providing training and feedback on performance].

Bill, let me try to put together the things you have told me. First, you based your strategy on very extensive, in-depth market research of the people who should be customers but weren't. And then [you] not only got a sense of the need, but also a pretty good list of potential customers who would respond. And then you really worked hard at giving them the one product they really needed, and you kept, at first, very close to this, and moved into other areas only when you had the human resources—the people to do it with very great attention to training people, to supervising them, and to building quality into programs.

Peter Drucker–Bill Hybels Dialogue, 1988.

Author's Note: Peter Drucker was a frequent contributor to *The Economist*. In its obituary in the print edition, "Special Report: Peter Drucker—Trusting the Teacher in the Grey-Flannel Suit" (November 17, 2005), the editors make special mention of Drucker's influence on Bill Hybels:

One perhaps unexpected example of Druckerism is the modern mega-church movement. He suggested to evangelical pastors that they create a more customer-friendly environment (hold back on the overt religious symbolism and provide plenty of facilities). Bill Hybels, the pastor of the 17,000-strong Willow Creek Community Church in South Barrington, Illinois, has a quotation from Mr. Drucker hanging outside his office: "What is our business? Who is our customer? What does the customer consider value?"

Mr. Drucker went further than just applying business techniques to managing voluntary organisations. He believed that such entities have many lessons to teach business corporations. They are often much better at engaging the enthusiasm of their volunteers—and they are also better at turning their "customers" into "marketers" for their organisation. These days, business organisations have as much to learn from churches as churches have to learn from them.[45]

II. Reflect

- Churches are not alone in believing that they supply just what the customer needs without finding out what the customer really needs.

1. "THE CUSTOMER RARELY BUYS WHAT A BUSINESS THINKS IT SELLS HIM"

Here, first, are the marketing realities that are most likely to be encountered:

What the people in the business think they know about customer and market is more likely to be wrong than right. There is only one person who really knows: the customer. Only by asking the customer, by watching him, by trying to understand his behavior can one find out who he is, what he does, how he buys, how he uses what he buys, what he expects, what he values, and so on.

The customer rarely buys what the business thinks it sells him. One reason for this is, of course, that nobody pays for a "product." What is paid for is satisfactions. But nobody can make or supply satisfactions as such—at best, only the means to attaining them can be sold and delivered.

Peter F. Drucker, *Managing for Results*, 1964, p. 94.

• It is a mistake to assume that a prospective customer is irrational if he or she is not enthusiastic about a producer's logic. Rather, it is the producer's duty to determine what the customer will find valuable.

2. WHY DOES IT SEEM THAT CUSTOMERS SOMETIMES BEHAVE IRRATIONALLY?

The customers have to be assumed to be rational. But their rationality is not necessarily that of the manufacturer; it is that of their own situation. To assume—as has lately become fashionable—that customers are irrational is as dangerous a mistake as it is to assume that the customer's rationality is the same as that of the manufacturer or supplier—or that it should be. . . .

It is the manufacturer's or supplier's job to find out why the customer behaves in what seems to be an irrational manner. It is his job either to adapt himself to the customer's rationality or to try to change it. But he must first understand and respect it.

Peter F. Drucker, *Managing for Results*, 1964, pp. 96–97.

• Noncustomers can be converted to customers if they are first asked, "What do you consider value?"—and if this question is followed by a serious attempt to provide the value desired by the noncustomers.

3. HOW CAN WE SERVE NONCUSTOMERS?

Who is the noncustomer, the person who does not buy
our products even though he or she is (or might be) in
the market? And can we find out why the person is a
noncustomer? . . . What product or service would fulfill the
satisfaction areas of real importance—both those we now
serve and those we might serve?

Peter F. Drucker, *Managing for Results*, 1964, pp. 101, 103.

• We can learn a lot about how to motivate knowledge workers by
understanding how to motivate volunteers. They do not receive
a paycheck but provide their services for the reward of the service itself—"the reward of service is more service."[46] Satisfaction
comes from successfully applying one's expertise to a worthwhile
purpose.

4. MANAGING KNOWLEDGE WORKERS

"The management of people is a marketing job."

The key to maintaining leadership in the economy and
the technology that are emerging is likely to be the social
position of the knowledge professionals and social acceptance
of their values. Today, however, we are trying to straddle
the fence—to maintain the traditional mind-set, in which
capital is the key resource and the financier is the boss,
while bribing knowledge workers to be content to remain
employees by giving them bonuses and stock options. But
this, if it can work at all, can only work as long as the
emerging industries enjoy a stock-market boom, as did the
Internet companies.

The management of knowledge workers is a "marketing
job." And in marketing one does not begin with the

question: "What do we want?" One begins with the
question: "What does the other party want? What are its
values? What are its goals? What does it consider results?"
What motivates knowledge workers is what motivates
volunteers. Volunteers have to get *more* satisfaction from their
work than paid employees, precisely because they don't get a
paycheck. They need, above all, challenges.

> Peter F. Drucker, May 1, "Managing Knowledge Workers,"
> *The Daily Drucker*, 2004.

III. Practicum-Prompts

Ask your customers, "What do you consider value in the products
and services we provide you?" Are your findings consistent with
your preconceived notions?

Have you determined what your noncustomers consider value?

Do you treat your noncustomers' buying behavior as irrational?
Reconsider this in light of what noncustomers actually do consider
value. How can you convert at least a segment of your noncustomers
into customers?

Consider what truly motivates the knowledge workers in your
organization. Appeal to the full range of their motivations, not
merely to financial remuneration.

Phase Changes as Organizations Grow and Change

Introduction

As an organization grows it can lose its vitality by focusing on the needs of those inside the organization rather than on customers. This often happens, for example, in star-driven organizations that have experienced phenomenal growth under the leadership of their entrepreneur-founder. At some point there is a need for a "phase change" in management: the founder either has to become an executive or bring in someone else to run the organization.

For example, Wilson Greatbatch, a Cornell-educated biomedical engineer at the University of Buffalo, along with several other researchers, studied the relationship between a heartbeat and electrical pulsation. Greatbatch was hoping that by using electrical stimulation he could return an irregular heartbeat to normal. He was working on a device to monitor heart sounds when he accidentally placed the wrong resistor in the device. The new resistor was a hundred times more powerful than the old one and emitted a rhythm that mimicked a heartbeat. This unlocked the mystery he had been trying to solve for many years and led in 1960 to the implantation of the Chardack-Greatbatch cardiac pacemaker at Millard Fillmore Hospital in Buffalo, New York.

Almost immediately, Greatbatch licensed the pacemaker technology to Medtronic, a medical device company with headquarters in Minneapolis, allowing the pacemaker to be brought to market quickly and on a large scale. He has described the license agreement and his subsequent relationship with Medtronic:

> The license agreement was a very tight one. I assumed
> design control for all Medtronic implantable pacemakers.
> I signed every drawing, every change, and had to approve
> every procurement source. . . . Quality control reported
> directly to me for ten years. I sat on the board of directors. I
> had major (and noisy) input into all company affairs, selling
> pacemakers, and particularly on the dropping of unprofitable
> lines like cardiac monitors and AC defibrillators. Medtronic
> had been in a precarious financial situation in 1960, but
> substantially recovered within two years and became number
> one in pacemakers.[47]

In 1970, Greatbatch left Medtronic and formed his own company, Wilson Greatbatch Ltd. (WGL), in Clarence, New York, just outside Buffalo. This company developed the first lithium-iodine battery for pacemakers, replacing the original power source, the mercury-zinc battery. The lithium-iodine battery extended the life of the implantable pacemaker from months to decades. The new battery is now the gold standard power supply and is used in 90 percent of all pacemakers.

The final phase change in Greatbatch's career took place in 1995, when he turned the operations of WGL over to his son Warren, a University of Rochester MBA. Wilson realized that his real calling, as well as his real interest and expertise, was as a researcher and inventor—a role he continued until his death in 2011. He had rightly concluded that the company needed professional executive management, which he was not able to provide. This decision served him and the company very well.[48]

I. Read

From where I sit, I've seen any number of businesses where a star has built a business and has no successor, doesn't perpetuate himself or herself, and it becomes a bureaucracy. In my experience with both profit and nonprofit organizations, there are really two problems. One is that the founder refuses to accept the fact that the organization is different. And the other one is that [founders] reject, almost fear, any capable successor. And those are the same whether you deal with a business or whether you deal with a church or whether you deal with a university. There are not any great differences.

In my own work, whether with business or with nonbusiness, I find . . . the need for the person who built the organization to face up to the fact that it's no longer the same organization and that *he has to change his behavior.* He has to have the willingness *to work on having somebody else succeed him and take over his child.*

> Drucker-Buford-Warren-Patterson Dialogues, January 29, 1991, and June 15, 1991.

II. Reflect

- As executives change their role from *entrepreneur to executive,* they should continue to do some professional work so as not to lose touch with the organization, its people, and its processes.
- Andy Grove, a personal friend of Peter Drucker, helped Robert Noyce and Gordon Moore found Intel Corporation in 1968. In 1986, Drucker asked Grove about his experience as an innovator

and his transition to executive. In Reading 1 I have reproduced
the portion of the interview in which Grove discusses his transition from innovator to executive, which, at the time of the interview, was seventeen years after the start of the new venture.

1. ANDY GROVE OF INTEL: ENTREPRENEUR TURNED EXECUTIVE

Andy Grove

The content of what I do now is substantially different.
Seventeen years ago I was buying equipment myself, running
experiments, and reducing the data. I was one step away from
silicon wafers and stuff like that at the time. Today I am
many steps away from that. Today, I deal with abstractions
but still with people. People have been a constant. . . . I went
through a gradual process. Things became more complex.
You go into a new company with everything in your head.
I went through a gradual realization; a shifting of tasks
took place gradually. The picture of my own role emerged
relatively early. I was the organizer and taskmaster. People in
the initial group almost immediately gravitated to roles that
fit them. The team built itself up almost. Roles that were
needed gravitated to appropriate team members. If you don't
think through the roles of the key people very early you build
up tribes and power struggles in the organization that in the
early stages [have] to be deadly. New people, subordinates,
had a different way of operating than me. I had some real
conflict with those individuals. They were not reaching for
roles and colliding with the initial group but had a different
way of operating. [They insisted] that their way of operating
prevail and [tried] to exert power with the others, [and as
a result] we were led to a power struggle: a struggle that
resulted in our wasting substantial emotional energy. It was
a very early introduction to the responsibilities that I had to

deal with, responsibilities I did not want to deal with but had no choice [about].

The initial group was very willing to make changes with a little bit of friction and a little bit of debate. Most of us had hungry minds, the mind of a student, and the notion of getting into a new area had more attraction than imposing your views in an old area. And for the same reason we did not resist going out to the customer. My role was not so much as "going out" [but] rather as being "major domo" for people "coming in." And that started relatively early. Here is a self-respecting semiconductor device person [me] setting up tools for representatives of major corporations whose biggest concerns at that time were not technical but had to do with the viability of Intel as a company. I started doing this work almost immediately. Our industry had promised all kinds of things that it had not delivered upon. So, we had a very skeptical customer base. So, we adopted as a corporate logo *Intel Delivers*.

> Peter F. Drucker and Joseph A. Maciariello, *Management Cases: Revised Edition*, 2009, pp. 185–86.

- Problems of leadership *transition* and *succession* are common and they are often difficult problems to solve. Members of the board of directors who have had experience solving these problems are a great asset to an organization.

- It is not uncommon to see organizations lose their vitality as they grow and age; this loss can be fatal, especially during periods of rapid changes in the environment and in the behavior of their customers.

2. MANAGEMENT AS A "CHANGE OF PHASE"

The change from a business that the owner-entrepreneur can run with "helpers" to a business that requires a management is what the physicists call a *change of phase*, such as the change from water to ice. It is an abrupt change from one state of matter, from one fundamental structure, to another. Sloan's example shows that it can be made within one and the same organization. But Sloan's restructuring of GM also shows that the job can be done only if *basic concepts, basic principles, and individual vision are changed* radically.

Henry Ford wanted no managers [see Reading 3]. The result was that he misdirected managers, set up their jobs improperly, created a spirit of suspicion and frustration, disorganized his company, and stunted or broke management people. The only choice managers have in these areas is therefore whether management jobs will be done well or badly. But the jobs themselves will exist, because there is an enterprise to be managed. And whether the jobs are done right or not will determine largely whether the enterprise will survive and prosper or decline and ultimately fall.

> Peter F. Drucker and Joseph A. Maciariello, *Management: Revised Edition*, 2008, p. 238.

- As organizations grow and develop, there is the tendency to look inward, not to recognize that as an organization changes in size, load, and complexity there is a need for executives to change their role from *entrepreneur to executive.*

3. THE RISE, DECLINE, AND REBIRTH OF FORD—A CONTROLLED EXPERIMENT IN MISMANAGEMENT

Henry Ford, starting with nothing in 1905, had fifteen years later built the world's largest and most profitable manufacturing enterprise. The Ford Motor Company, in the early [1920s], dominated and almost monopolized the American automobile market and held a leadership position in most of the other important automobile markets of the world. In addition, it had amassed, out of profits, cash reserves of a billion dollars or so.

Yet only a few years later, by 1927, this seemingly impregnable business empire was [a] shambles. Having lost its leadership position and barely a poor third in the market, it lost money almost every year for twenty years or so, and remained unable to compete vigorously right through World War II. In 1944 the founder's grandson, Henry Ford II, then only twenty-six years old and without training or experience, took over, ousted two years later his grandfather's cronies in a palace coup, brought in a totally new management team, and saved the company.

It is not commonly realized that this dramatic story is far more than a story of personal success and failure. It is, above all, what one might call a *controlled experiment in mismanagement*.

The first Ford failed because of his firm belief that a business did not need managers and management. All it needed, he believed, was the owner-entrepreneur with his "helpers." The only difference between Ford and most of his contemporaries in business was that, as in everything he did, Henry Ford stuck uncompromisingly to his convictions. He applied them strictly, firing or sidelining any one of his "helpers," no matter how able, who dared act as a "manager," make a decision, or take action without orders from Ford. The way he applied his theory can only be described as a test, one that ended up by fully disproving Ford's theory.

In fact, what makes the Ford story unique and important is that Ford *could* test the hypothesis. This was possible in part because he lived so long and in part because he had a billion dollars to back his convictions. Ford's failure was not the result of personality or temperament. It was first and foremost the result of his refusal to accept managers and management as necessary, as a necessity based on task and function rather than in "delegation" from the "boss."

Peter F. Drucker and Joseph A. Maciariello, *Management: Revised Edition*, 2008, pp. 235–36.

• Controlled experiments in executive management are difficult to plan. Henry Ford provides us with a rare controlled experiment in executive mismanagement. He tested the hypothesis that as an organization grows, it does not need professional management. Instead, it can be successfully run by a boss with helpers, not managers. His experiment failed and we can all learn from his mistakes.

III. Practicum-Prompts

Are you facing a change in phase in your career? Are you preparing a successor?

Are there people you can consult who have successfully navigated a similar change?

Does your organization have formal programs in place for both individual managers and the management group?

How can you and your organization use the experience of Andy Grove?

What can you and your organization learn from the experiences of Wilson Greatbatch and Henry Ford?

Structuring Your Organization

Centralization, Confederation, and Decentralization

Introduction

This week's entry deals with general issues of organization with historical roots in government. Examples of centralization, confederation, and decentralization are found in various forms of government, and they have direct application to the management of organizations in all sectors.[49]

The American colonies were organized by the British primarily to promote British mercantile interests. The king of England appointed governors of the colonies, and most important decisions were made by the king. This is an example of a *centralized* or *unitary* form of organization where most of the autonomy and authority rests at the top.

In response to a number of laws imposing taxes on them, the colonies established the Continental Congress in 1774 to coordinate their opposition to British rule. Each of the colonies operated under the jurisdiction of its own constitution. The congress adopted articles of association on October 20, 1774, and began the process of attempting to gain independence from Great Britain. It endorsed the Declaration of Independence on July 4, 1776. The Continental Congress became the national government. The government of the thirteen colonies through the period of the Declaration and the Revolutionary War was a *confederation* operating under the Articles of Confederation with maximum autonomy granted to the colonies but with central coordinating functions carried out by the Continental Congress.

The Constitutional Convention then met in 1787 to address the problems created by a weak central government. The Constitution of the United States was ratified in 1789, establishing a federal system of government with an executive, a congress, and a judiciary. All powers not specifically delegated to the federal government were granted to the states and to the people by the Tenth Amendment to the Constitution. The system of government established by the U.S. Constitution is often designated as *federal decentralization*.

I. Read

In a wide-ranging interview with Tom Ashbrook on December 8, 2004, Drucker indicated that the world would be moving toward nonwestern political and cultural systems but that it would be based on western economics and therefore the trend would be toward knowledge-based organizations.

Tom Ashbrook

What's your sense of the direction in which the world is moving?

Peter Drucker

We know this much. . . . It will have western production and western competitiveness, and it will be held together *by information, not by power.* That is the direction the world is going.

"Management Guru Peter Drucker," WBUR for National Public Radio, December 8, 2004.

As the corporation moves towards a confederation or a syndicate, it will increasingly need a top management that is separate, powerful, and accountable. This top management's responsibilities will cover the entire organization's direction, planning, strategy, values, and principles; its structure and relationships among its various members; its alliances, partnerships, and joint ventures; and its research, design, and innovation. Top management will have to take charge of the management of the two resources common to all units of the organization: *key people* and *money*. It will represent the corporation to the outside world and maintain relationships with governments, the public, the media, and organized labor.

> Peter F. Drucker and Joseph A. Maciariello, *Management: Revised Edition*, 2008, p. 58.

II. Reflect

- "I just know that the more control there is, the less growth there is. The great lesson of the twentieth century is that central planning doesn't work" Rick Warren (Drucker-Warren Dialogue, January 22, 2003).

1. CENTRAL PLANNING DOESN'T WORK: "LEADERSHIP AND ORGANIZATION FOR RAPIDLY GROWING CHURCHES"

Rick Warren

Our plan is not only to decentralize our congregation off campus through small groups, but also on campus by holding multiple worship services in multiple buildings at multiple times. *We feel this will allow for exponential growth.* Our model is the movie theater Cineplex—that offers different venues, styles, and times on the same campus. I don't like the arena/stadium-sized church buildings for several reasons. First, the larger the service, the more the attenders become passive spectators. Second, history shows that the next generation never fills the giant temples built by the previous generation. Spurgeon's Tabernacle in London is now one fourth the size it was in its heyday. Third, it's wasteful stewardship to build a 7,000-seat building that can only be filled once a week and sits empty the rest of the week.

I have a staff pastor that I send out to visit other purpose-driven churches in the field and report to me. I'm always thinking about who we're *not* reaching. The staff and lay ministers care for the people we've already reached.

Peter Drucker

That's what I mean when I say you need that staff pastor who is available to allow you to think through these things. For such a system not to become bureaucratic it needs one person who does what you are doing, and is reasonably free from managing what is becoming your big system—but is not isolated from it. In our little church, the husband and wife are both ordained ministers. He is director and she is assistant director but she is the spirit of it because she is free pretty much from administrative duties and can visit and talk with a work group or a Bible study group. Wednesday evening is our small group evening and each week she sits in on one of our forty groups. She affirms them, but she is also the quality control in which she can say to a group that the host doesn't measure up and they have to do something about it.

Now, in your case, within ten years, you'll have 50,000 to 60,000 members. That won't work like a small church. You must have the freedom to maintain the spontaneity of your church. That is your role. And decentralization is the wrong word for what you are doing. *Decentralization* implies a sense of rules that the units operate under. What we are actually talking about is a *confederation*. You want these churches to be independent units but carry the spirit, right? That's a confederation.

Drucker-Warren Dialogue, January 22, 2003.

2. GENERAL MOTORS: AN EXAMPLE OF FEDERAL DECENTRALIZATION

General Motors could not function as a holding company with the divisions organized like independent companies under loose financial control [a confederation]. Central management not only has to know even minor details of divisional management but the top officials have to exercise the power, the prestige, and the influence of real bosses. On the other hand General Motors could not function as a centralized organization in which all decisions are made on the top, and in which the divisional managers are but little more than plant superintendents. Divisional managers too must have the authority and standing of real bosses.

Hence General Motors has become *an essay in federalism—on the whole, an exceedingly successful one.* It attempts to combine the greatest corporate unity through local self-government and vice versa [local self-government through corporate unity]. This is the aim of General Motors' policy of decentralization.

Peter F. Drucker, *Concept of the Corporation*, 1946, pp. 45–46.

• A unit of a confederation is independent, but it operates under loose direction from the parent organization. A confederation is held together by values, strategy, and information.

3. THE TOYOTA WAY: AN EXAMPLE OF A CONFEDERATION

The second example of a corporation as a confederation goes exactly the other way [from General Motors]. Toyota, which since the 1980s has been the most successful automotive company and is now the largest, is restructuring itself around its core competency—manufacturing. It is moving away from having multiple suppliers of parts and accessories to having one or two everywhere. At the same time it uses its manufacturing competence to manage these suppliers. They remain *independent companies* [emphasis mine] but they are basically part of Toyota in terms of management [a confederation].

Peter F. Drucker, *Management: Revised Edition*, 2008, p. 57.

III. Practicum-Prompts

Is the growth of your organization limited by tight controls? How can the latent energy of the people in your organization be released?

Explore the use of confederations in your organization to stimulate both imagination and growth.

Is there any one person in your organization who is responsible for maintaining spontaneity and growth? If not, should there be?

Is your organization held together by information or by power? If it is held together by power, will this limit your growth?

The Networked Organization

A Model for the Twenty-First Century

Introduction

Peter Drucker discusses the nature of network organizations and the prerequisites for making this organizational form effective within society and within specific organizations. It is a very demanding organizational form but one that is increasingly required by the organizations of our society. An application of the network is then discussed by Rick Warren and Peter Drucker as the new organizational form at Saddleback.

A networked organization is one that operates within a system of interdependent organizations for the purpose of achieving objectives that are agreeable to partner organizations. In our published research examining the behavior of twenty-three interorganizational networks managed by Texas Instruments, Karen Higgins identified seven variables that were present in the highest-performing networks.[50]

Leading complex network organizations requires the development of *trust* and *shared values* among leaders of participating organizations. Leaders of member organizations in a network must possess *integrity* and live up to the *commitments* made when the network is formed.

Leaders must *align the goals* among members of participating organizations; this alignment in turn requires *continuous communication* and good working relationships. Finally, procedures must be in place to *resolve conflicts* within and between member organizations. Because not all conflicts can be resolved, procedures for removing nonconforming organizations from the network must be established at the outset.

I. Read

"THE DEVELOPED COUNTRIES ARE MOVING FAST TOWARD A NETWORK SOCIETY"

For well over a hundred years all developed countries were moving steadily toward an employee society of organizations. Now developed countries, with the United States in the lead, are moving fast toward a Network Society in respect to the relationship between organizations and individuals who work for them, and in respect to the relationships between different organizations.

Most adults in the U.S. labor force do work for an organization. But increasingly they are not employees of that organization. They are contractors, part-timers, temporaries. And relations between organizations are changing just as fast as the relations between organizations and the people who work for them. The most visible example is "outsourcing," in which a company, a hospital, or a government agency turns over an entire activity to an independent firm that specializes in that kind of work. Even more important may be the trend toward alliances. Individual professionals and executives will have to learn that they must take responsibility for placing themselves. This means above all [that] they must know their strengths and look upon themselves as "products" that have to be marketed.

> Peter F. Drucker, May 2, "The Network Society," *The Daily Drucker*, 2004.

II. Reflect

• Drucker asked participants in an alumni seminar what to call this new organization and its society. At first they said, "Call it free form." But then they reconsidered and said, "Call it the network society."

1. THE DEMANDS MADE BY PARTNERSHIPS AND ALLIANCES

Equally novel are the demands partnerships and alliances make on managing a business and its relationships. Executives are used to *command*. They are used to think through what they want and then to get acceptance of it by subordinates. Even Japanese "consensuses management" is a way to get acceptance by the organization of whatever the higher-ups have decided should be done—and so is the much touted "participative management." But in a partnership—whether with an outsourcing contractor, a joint-venture partner, or a company in which one holds a minority stake—one cannot command. One can only gain *trust*. Specifically that means that one must not start out with the question, "What do we want to do?" The right questions are, "What are their objectives? Their values? Their ways of doing things?" Again: these are marketing relationships, and in marketing one starts out with the customer rather than with one's own product.

> Peter F. Drucker, *Managing in a Time of Great Change*, 1995, p. 72.

- Networked organizations are extremely demanding to manage, and rely on developing and maintaining strong personal relationships among partners of the association. Command authority does not work in managing a network.

2. SYSTEMS ORGANIZATION: INTEGRATE DIVERSITY OF CULTURE, VALUES, AND SKILLS INTO UNITY OF ACTION

Systems organization is an extension of the team design principle. But instead of the team consisting of individuals, the systems organization builds the team out of a wide variety of different organizations. They may be government agencies, private businesses, universities and individual researchers, and organizations inside and outside the parent organization. . . . What organizations that use the systems structure have in common is a need to integrate diversity of culture, values, [and] skills into unity of action. . . . The requirements for the systems structure to work at all are extremely stringent. It demands absolute clarity of objectives. . . . Another requirement is a demand for universal communications responsibility. Every member of the systems structure, but especially every member of every one of the managing groups, has to make sure that mission, objective, and strategies are fully understood by everyone, and that doubts, questions, and ideas of every member are heard, listened to, respected, thought through, understood, and resolved. . . . It needs clear goals, high self-discipline throughout the structure, and a top management that takes personal responsibility for relationships and communications.

> Peter F. Drucker and Joseph A. Maciariello, *Management: Revised Edition*, 2008, pp. 452, 453.

- Rick Warren sees his purpose-driven strategy as network-oriented, not command-oriented. The values or purposes are the strategy that holds these organizations together. Rick's job is to carry out conscience activities and to maintain values—to "infect" these churches with the purpose-driven chip.

3. THE NETWORKED CHURCH

Proper organizational form for Saddleback was the main subject of the final consultation between Rick Warren and Peter Drucker on May 27, 2004. Drucker opened the conversation by noting previous correspondence in which Warren told Drucker that he was trying to avoid becoming a denomination. Warren and Drucker had previously considered the denominational form for Saddleback and purpose-driven churches but Warren developed strong arguments against the idea, preferring the network form, which has many of the characteristics of a confederation. Drucker has written quite a bit about network organizations, and as we see in this exchange Warren has internalized the requirements for this organization form.

Peter Drucker

Implicit in your approach is that the emphasis on denominations, which is perhaps of the fifteenth or sixteenth century, has become obsolete and you are disregarding them. First, if you ask that neighbor of ours who is a very faithful Roman Catholic, apart from his belief in the pope, he probably knows nothing about the denomination. And the pope is very far away from him. I think I once told you of the American Catholic bishop who said to me, "You don't understand. We don't have a Roman Catholic Church in America. We have a Protestant church from the Irish denomination." Second, your emphasis is that the congregation is the church, not the denomination. And yet there is a need to maintain the values throughout the network—that is basically your job.

Rick Warren

Denominations are old wineskins. My model for the twenty-first-century church is that of the networked church. It's not about control as in a denomination. It's about sharing *common values*. I try to embody the values. I try to communicate the values. I am injecting the values into these different churches. The reason why I fought the title "denomination," why I didn't want to be called a denomination, is [that] then I would be in competition with all of these other groups, that is, Lutheran, Catholic, Baptist, and Pentecostal denominations. I wanted people to be able to keep their denominational label but change the inside.

I explain the networked concept by comparing it to a computer store that sells all major brands of computers. If I go into the computer store I see all these different computers with different brand names, Apple, IBM, Dell, H-P, etc. They're different sizes, they're different shapes, they even run different programs, but in every computer there is an Intel chip: it's the processor that makes the computer run. I don't care whether the label of the church says Lutheran, Baptist, Presbyterian, Catholic, whatever. I don't care about the size of the church, the color of the church—whether it's black, Hispanic, or Asian, or whatever. Purpose-driven is the operating system of the twenty-first-century church. Purpose-driven is the Intel chip. It's the processor that teaches the church to move people into membership, build them up to maturity, train them for ministry, and send them out on mission.

Drucker-Warren Dialogue, May 27, 2004.

III. Practicum-Prompts

The network concept has many uses between organizations. But it also has uses within organizations through internal markets and micro profit centers. How can you use the network concept?

Why are you and your organization attractive partners for a networked organization? Make a list of reasons.

What steps are you taking to learn how to manage your organization and to market yourself in this network society?

E-commerce is widely used in our network society to carry out and to coordinate transactions among organizations. Amazon provides ample proof that we can sell what we can distribute, and not merely what we can manufacture. This ability to transact using the Internet contributes to our ability to work well within the network society of organizations. Is your business closer to Amazon.com or to the local bookstore? If the latter, determine how you can use e-commerce to fight back.

Managing Your Members

Managing the Superstar

Introduction

Star performers present unique opportunities and challenges for executives. On one hand performance can be attained only through the strengths of people, and the purpose of organization is to make people productive. So star performers enhance the ability of the organization to attain its goals, and this effect is very desirable. Helping each person to focus on his or her strengths will enhance the performance of the entire organization.

But there are challenges in managing star performers. "Where there are peaks, there are valleys." [51] Star performers must be managed carefully lest they damage the spirit of the organization by their behavior and demands. Yet it is very important that the contribution of star performers to the organization be secured and recognized, even if it takes extraordinary effort by executives to minimize the negative effects. The goal is to use the performance of stars not only to promote their objectives but, by their positive example, to raise standards of performance of others and to help others become star performers.

In the world of knowledge work, the contributions of star performers are often greater than those of the executives to whom they report. It should not be unusual, therefore, for star performers to receive salaries and bonuses that exceed those of executives to whom they report simply because their contribution to direct results, performance, values and people development, may be greater. This is often the norm in professional athletics, where, for example, salaries of professional players exceed those of their managers.

I. Read

THE SUPERSTAR SYNDROME

Remember:

Stars are expensive. I always have to remind [their managers] that the Bible says, "You shall not muzzle an ox while it is treading out the grain" [Deuteronomy 25:4]. Let it thresh the corn [and reap rewards accordingly]!

Stars are one-sided. As you are building stars, stars are one-sided. It is a constant fight with the stars; because every star wants to do something he or she does not perform well. If they are stars, their range is very narrow and their temperament is narrow. Actually, it is more a matter of temperament than of range.

Stars, almost without exception, are very unbalanced. World Vision will have to face this problem. For instance, here is a woman in Santa Barbara who has never seen a female client. She has never seen a retired person, and Santa Barbara is full of retirees. She has only seen small businesspeople—the drugstore owner who owns a drugstore or two; the food-store owners, who are not rich but have $50,000 a year to invest— and she handles them all. They all buy equities; they should not, but they do. It is their money and they are grown-ups. On the other hand, 80 percent of the Santa Barbara market is not covered, and I have had a hell of a time convincing them [her and the firm] that they should put two more brokers in Santa Barbara to go after the market. It has been difficult convincing her because she views this as a threat.

World Vision will have very much the same problem. When you start, your graduates will develop what they are. Partly what they are good at, what they are passionate about, but also where they are successful [in performing]. This is not a matter of central government, but of the organization.

> Peter F. Drucker, *Executive Summary: A Conversation with Peter Drucker on Leadership and Organizational Development,* 2002, p. 15.

II. Reflect

- Superstars tend to be jaded, yet their contributions to an organization can be enormous. They do present executives with unique problems. Executives need to learn how to manage superstars and their strengths without poisoning the spirit of the organization. This usually means overlooking behavior that is borderline inexcusable or at least trying to minimize the collateral damage of this behavior to the rest of the organization.

1. SUBORDINATES ARE PAID TO PERFORM

Effective executives know that their subordinates are paid to perform and not to please their superiors. They know that it does not matter how many tantrums a prima donna throws as long as she brings in the customers. The opera manager is paid after all for putting up with the prima donna's tantrums if that is her way to achieve excellence in performance. It does not matter whether a first-rate teacher or a brilliant scholar is pleasant to the dean or amiable in the faculty meeting. The dean is paid for enabling the first-rate scholar to do his work effectively—and if this involves unpleasantness in the administrative routine, it is still cheap at the price.

> Peter F. Drucker, *The Effective Executive,* 1967, p. 73.

- Organizations provide us with the opportunity to make strengths productive and weaknesses irrelevant. The idea is to neutralize the weaknesses of one person with the strengths of others.

- An executive cannot avoid weaknesses in people, and often the greater the strengths the greater the weaknesses. The question is always, What can this person do? His deficiencies must become subordinate to his strengths.

2. CONCENTRATE ON TURNING PEOPLE OF HIGH COMPETENCE INTO STAR PERFORMERS

One should waste as little effort as possible on improving areas of low competence. Concentration should be on areas of high competence and high skill. It takes far more energy and far more work to improve from incompetence to low mediocrity than it takes to improve from first-rate performance to excellence. And yet most people—and equally most teachers and most organizations—try to concentrate on making incompetent performers into mediocre ones. The time, energy, and resources should instead go into making a competent person into a star performer.

> Peter F. Drucker and Joseph A. Maciariello, *Management: Revised Edition*, 2008, pp. 483–84.

- Superstars can be managed to lift the performance of members of the entire organization. This can be done by highlighting the performance example they set and by making them accessible to colleagues who need their help.

3. FEATURE STAR PERFORMERS TO RAISE THE PERFORMANCE CAPACITY OF THE ORGANIZATION

Standards should be very high and goals should be ambitious. Yet they should be attainable. Indeed, they should be attained, at least by the star performers of the institution. . . . But one also needs to use the star performers to raise the sights, the vision, the expectations, and the performance capacity of the entire organization. *One features performers.* The best way— and the way that conveys the most recognition and builds the most pride—is to use star performers as the teachers of their colleagues. . . . Nothing makes as much impact on a sales force as to have a successful salesman stand up before his peers and tell them, "This is what has worked for me." And it does even more for the star performer. There is no sweeter recognition. . . . And it is the function of any organization to make human strengths effective in performance and to neutralize human weaknesses. This is its ultimate test.

> Peter F. Drucker, *Managing the Non-Profit Organization,*
> 1990, p. 119.

• General Ulysses S. Grant was caught by surprise at Shiloh in western Tennessee on April 6, 1862, by generals Johnston and Beauregard. The Battle of Shiloh lasted two days. Total casualties were approximately 23,000 men: 13,000 Union and 10,000 Confederate. After receiving reinforcements, Grant did prevail on April 7, but the sloppy assessment of the threat and the cost in lives brought demands on President Lincoln for Grant's removal. Lincoln went to Grant's defense, stating, "I can't spare this man—he fights." Thus we see Lincoln correctly identifying what Grant could do, despite his limitations. Lincoln proved correct in his assessment of Grant's strengths, which were needed to win the war, even at an awful cost in lives. For Lincoln, Grant's deficiencies became subordinate to his strengths.[52]

III. Practicum-Prompts

Does your organization have a number of superstar performers?

Are the superstars in your organization managed to take full benefit of their strengths while minimizing their weaknesses? Or are they mismanaged and hampering the spirit of performance in your organization?

If your superstars are being mismanaged, how can your executives maximize the superstars' contributions to the organization while minimizing negative consequences to what the organization stands for?

Do you and your organization keep superstars where their strengths remain productive? Do you protect them against their blatant weaknesses and errors?

A Second Chance for Failures

Introduction

People decisions—hiring, promotion, and dismissal—are the most important decisions an organization makes. Adhering to the right procedure in picking people should improve the rate of successful placements. The right procedure involves:

(1) Thinking through the job assignment.
(2) Interviewing a number of people for the job.
(3) Looking at what each candidate has done well in the past.
(4) Discussing a candidate's performance with those with whom he or she has previously worked.
(5) Being very clear about the specific assignment to the candidate selected, to the point of having the candidate repeat the description of the assignment to the executive.

These procedures should help reduce failed placements. Nevertheless, failures still occur, and the executive who made the promotion decision is responsible for making things right for both the organization and the individual who has failed.

This can be done without too much difficulty for an internal promotion if at the outset the selected candidate is offered a right of return to his or her previous position. However, the executive responsible should try to find out what went wrong.

A common cause of failure involves promotion from a staff position to one that requires significant executive and decision-making responsibility. Good staff people may be brilliant at analysis and make significant contributions to the organization, but they may be poor executives because they do not have the temperament to make tough decisions. These people should be removed because temperaments don't change.

There is a potential problem in identifying failures, especially when people are moved from staff to line positions. In these cases it is important to obtain multiple opinions to eliminate potential bias. General Dwight D. Eisenhower, the thirty-fourth president of the United States, illustrates the problem. In the 1930s, he served in the Philippines as "assistant military adviser" to General Douglas MacArthur, then Army Chief of Staff. The two had very different styles. MacArthur made disparaging remarks about Eisenhower. Near the end of World War II, MacArthur was quoted as saying, "He was the best company clerk I ever had,"[53] hardly an endorsement of Eisenhower's actual potential. MacArthur did not think Eisenhower possessed executive and command capabilities even though he was highly regarded as a military strategist. MacArthur was dead wrong, and it is fortunate for the world that his assessment was overruled by his own superiors, whose second opinion illustrates the dangers of relying on a sole opinion in making assessments of failure and the need for a second chance. Eisenhower was certainly no failure—but he was one in the view of MacArthur.

Eisenhower later became a five-star general in the U.S. Army during World War II. Army Chief of Staff General George Marshall, one of the best judges of talent in the military, chose him over "400 senior officers"[54] to serve as supreme commander of the Allied forces in Europe, leading the invasion of Normandy.

When failure occurs after people are appointed from staff to line positions, the person who failed should be given a second chance in another position and offered the training necessary to succeed.

While hard data are not available there are enough success stories to recommend this course of action. This entry deals with providing people who have failed a second chance to succeed.

I. Read

When people do poorly on their first assignment, will they do well in their second? I have learned to measure the success rate of people on their second assignment [or the casualty rate of those placed in retraining].

Your casualty rate is going to be high if your demands are high. If your demands are not high, you damage your organization. Mediocre results can destroy the spirit of an organization.

The success rate in the second assignment, after failure in the first, is the best measure of the way we prepare people. If you have a 60 percent success rate in the second assignment, then you have prepared and selected these people well. The "second chance" job success rate, therefore, is a good indication of the soundness of your training.

A third measure of people in our school for failures is, How many are you willing to use as your teachers in your school for failures? Make it a practice to bring those graduates who have been on a job three or four years [in the second assignment] back to allow them to teach others.

> Peter F. Drucker, *Executive Summary: A Conversation with Peter Drucker on Leadership and Organizational Development,* 2002, p. iv.

II. Reflect

- The Peter Principle (an observation by Laurence J. Peter) asserts that a person who keeps getting promoted eventually reaches his or her level of incompetence. The Peter Principle is invalid. It is an excuse for the mistakes made by executives in promoting people to positions for which they are unqualified. Their past experiences and assessments of strengths required for the new position are not accurately taken into account in making the promotion.

- Organizations that offer people a second chance along with appropriate training for the new position achieve good success rates for people in second assignments.

1. WHAT IS THE RIGHT JOB FOR PEOPLE WHO PERFORM POORLY?

Just because a person doesn't perform in the job he or she was put in doesn't mean that that person is a bad worker whom the company should let go. It only means that he or she is in the wrong job. What, then, is the right job . . . ? Of the people who get a second chance in a job that fits their strengths—the job they should have been put into in the first place—a very high percentage perform well. Few managers believe that.

Peter F. Drucker and Joseph A. Maciariello, *Management: Revised Edition*, 2008, pp. 311–12.

2. CARE

In each country in which CARE (Cooperative for American Relief Everywhere) works, it has a country representative—usually a young man or woman only a couple of years out of college. They are carefully trained and prepared, and yet they are on their own in that foreign country—say Cambodia or Kenya—and so the failure rate was very high.

For many years, when [it] came across a nonperformer, CARE brought him or her back home, said, "Thank you," and then let him or her go. But [it] simply didn't get enough good people to fill all the country slots. And so with tremendous misgivings and with a great deal of opposition from within the organization, *CARE put some of these first-rate failures into a second job as a country representative.* And to everybody's tremendous surprise, the great majority of these people succeeded—indeed, quite a few became star performers.

Peter F. Drucker and Joseph A. Maciariello, *Management: Revised Edition*, 2008, pp. 311–12.

• Some of the best trainers for those people given a second chance are the people who have successfully made the transition in the past.

3. THE SALVATION ARMY

In an interview with James Osborne, a forty-year veteran with The Salvation Army, and the Southern U.S. Territorial Commander in Atlanta, Georgia, Peter Drucker asked, "What do you do with people who consistently don't perform?" Osborne replied, "We point out weaknesses and try to do everything we can to have them improve, send them to additional courses, give them very close supervision. If none of that is successful we place them on probation and say, Unless you measure up, your services are no longer required." Drucker continued, "And how many to whom you give a second chance make it? The great majority?" "Well, I wish I could say that all of them made it," Osborne said, "but it runs about 60 percent."

Adapted from Drucker's 1988 interview with James Osborne.

• The right job for people who fail repeatedly may be in another organization.

4. EMPHASIS SHOULD BE ON PERFORMANCE

People given a second chance usually come through. If people
try, give them a second chance. If people try again and they
still do not perform, they may be in the wrong spot. Then
one asks: Where should he or she be? Perhaps in another
position in the organization—or perhaps elsewhere, in another
organization. But if a person does not try at all, encourage him
or her as soon as possible to go to work for the competition.

> Peter F. Drucker, *Managing the Non-Profit Organization*:
> *Principles and Practices*, 1990, p. 183.

III. Practicum-Prompts

What is the casualty rate of people in the first assignment in your organization? Are these people given a second chance? If not, why not?

If you and your organization give people a second chance, do they
receive adequate training for the new assignment?

Do you measure the casualty rate of people who are retrained
and given a second chance in your organization and fail?

Your casualty rate is going to be high for people who are given
a second chance unless you lower your performance standards. And
if your demands are not kept high, you will damage your organization. Mediocre results can destroy the spirit of an organization. You
should not tolerate mediocre performance if people fail after they
are given a second chance.

A third measure is how many second-chance people you are subsequently willing to use to retrain others. Make it a practice to
bring back those who have been on a second job three or four years
to allow them to train others who have failed, thus establishing a
successful "school for failures."

If it is obvious that a person does not fit in your organization,
can you help that person find a position in another organization for
which he is better suited?

What Kind of Organizations Does America Need to Strengthen Society?

Introduction

Peter Drucker's work in management aims to create and sustain a society of functioning organizations in which individuals find meaningful existence and purpose while also contributing to the common good. Each institution in our pluralistic society of organizations has a role to play, and each sector must perform according to its mission if our society is to thrive. The purpose of this entry is to describe the specifications for the kind of organizations America needs.

In his attempt to deal with society's problems, Drucker emphasized that leaders should be more concerned with serving the mission of their organization, serving its customers, and developing its people than with the "glitz" of rank and power. Unlike his friend Robert Greenleaf, who did work on "servant leadership," Drucker was not a "moralist" or a preacher. Rather, he was a pragmatist and a teacher who extolled results. "Bob," he said, "was always out to change the individual, to make him or her into a better person. I was interested in making people *do* the right things, in their actions and behavior. Bob was interested in motives; I was interested in consequences." [55]

As a teacher, Drucker taught many aspects of servant leadership. His mentor Alfred Sloan taught him that leaders were the servants of the institution that employed them. And he shared the teachings of his longtime friend Max DePree, former CEO and chairman of Herman Miller, that people in organizations should be treated as a debt owed and as a responsibility of the executive. Treating people as a debt owed can be explained using the language of the balance sheet, where assets are listed on the left side and liabilities and debts are listed on the right side and balanced against each other to determine net worth. As the number of people managed increases, the responsibilities or debts of the leader increase.

How is the leader to accomplish this for his or her organization? First, leaders discharge their debt by acting as servants to the mission of the organization they serve and to its people. Service provides the basis for the *legitimacy* of power and authority, a topic that looms large in Drucker's writings. Next, leaders should seek to provide *social status* to members of the organization. This simply means that each individual should be recognized as fulfilling an important role in the mission of the organization; such recognition gives the individual *status* within the group. Finally, the individual should be treated in accordance with the basic ideals of the society in which the organization operates. This provides the individual with *function*. In other words there should be a functional relationship between what the individual does at the workplace and the working philosophy of the society of which the organization is a part. How does this functional relationship work? In the United States our working philosophy or ethos is often stated in terms of the second paragraph of the Declaration of Independence: "We hold these Truths to be self-evident, that all Men are created equal, that they are endowed by their Creator with certain unalienable Rights, that among these are Life, Liberty, and the Pursuit of Happiness."

Bringing these rights down to the level of the organization, Drucker translated them as the right to *freedom* within the bounds of *responsibility*, the right *to equal opportunity*, and the right to be treated with the *dignity* accorded to all human beings in the Declaration. These rights create *purpose and meaning* for the individual at the workplace, and a functional relationship between the individual at work and society's basic beliefs.

A concrete example will help to clarify these terms and their relationship among individuals, organization, and society. After playing for two years in the Negro league, Jackie Robinson became the first African-American to play professional baseball in the major leagues. There were many great baseball players in the Negro league, but it wasn't until Robinson was chosen by Branch Rickey, president of the Brooklyn Dodgers, that an African-American became a member of major league baseball. Rickey, knowing the talent of Robinson, wanted to both help the Dodgers win a pennant and break the color line in professional baseball. He chose Robinson not only because he was a great all-around athlete and baseball player at UCLA, but also because he was a person of strong character who could "turn the other cheek" when insults and physical threats were going to come his way. He was given "status" commensurate with his abilities and accorded freedom or liberty promised to all citizens in the Declaration. Thus he had a "functional relationship" with the ideals of the United States. Furthermore, the leadership of the Dodgers was exhibiting "legitimate authority" by making a decision that was in accordance with the founding documents of our nation. Status, function, and legitimacy of authority are each illustrated in the Jackie Robinson–Branch Rickey story, which exemplifies Drucker's notion of the ingredients necessary for a functioning society of organizations.

Finally, as a society of organizations, we need institutions that provide for continuity and those that provide for change. Drucker was worried about the direction of American society and its institutions in the midst of the rapid changes we are experiencing. The "conserving" institutions, including government, the Supreme Court, religious institutions, and the family, are intended to *preserve continuity* with the past. The conserving institutions are to be contrasted with the destabilizing institutions such as businesses and universities, which are designed to promote *change*. In a period of very rapid change, conserving institutions must provide the values that hold society together. Thus the importance Drucker assigned to the role of the church, synagogue, and mosque in society.

Each institution requires legitimacy of authority in leadership, and status and function for individuals.

I. Read

Unless power is legitimate there can be no social order. A functioning society must always be capable of organizing the actual reality in a social order. It must master the material world, the actual reality in a social order. It must master the material world, make it meaningful and comprehensible for the individual; and it must establish legitimate social and political power. No society can function unless it gives the individual member social status and function, and unless the decisive social power is legitimate power. The former establishes the basic frame of social life: the purpose and meaning of society. The latter shapes the space within the frame: it makes society concrete and creates its institutions. If the individual is not given social status and function, there can be no society but only a mass of social atoms flying through space without aim or purpose. And unless power is legitimate there can be no social fabric; there is only a social vacuum held together by mere slavery or inertia.

Peter F. Drucker, January 31, "A Functioning Society," *The Daily Drucker*, 2004.

II. Reflect

- Legitimate authority in leadership requires taking responsibility for the stewardship of the human, financial, and physical resources of an organization and performing the duties that advance an organization's mission.

1. SOCIAL STATUS AND FUNCTION

Social status and function of the individual is the equation of
the relationship between the group and individual member.
It symbolizes the integration of the individual with the
group, and that of the group with the individual. It expresses
the individual purpose in terms of society [social function],
and the social purpose in terms of the individual [individual
status]. It thus makes comprehensible and rational individual
existence from the point of view of the group, and group
existence from that of the individual.

For the individual there is no society unless he has
social status and function. Society is only meaningful if its
purpose, its aims, its ideas and ideals make sense in terms of
the individual's purposes, aims, ideas and ideals. There must
be a definite functional relationship between individual life
and group life.

Peter F. Drucker, *A Functioning Society*, 2003, Prologue, p. xvii.

- With the ever-changing demands on individuals during this
time of turmoil, religious organizations and related social sector
organizations offer individuals opportunities for rebuilding and
stabilizing their status and function within society.

2. THE CHURCH IN AMERICA IS THE ONE ORGANIZATION AROUND WHICH SOCIETY COULD BE REBUILT

You [Bob Buford] have created an agency for the
repositioning and revitalization of the American Protestant
churches, churches that are respectful of the denominations
but that are nondenominational. And fundamentally you
started out with the assumption that the church in America
is the one organization around which society could be
rebuilt. I'm not saying it will be. One can only hope and

pray for that, but it can be, and it has proved its ability. That's what the pastoral churches have proved, and they are growing. And you have helped to create the center of the focal point for the healthy and growing part.

I took a look at Schaller's book [Lyle E. Schaller, author and church consultant, Fuller Seminary emeritus]. I think he brings out that the church is the effective dynamic force in the community and in everyday life, and not just Sunday [from] ten to twelve, and he makes it very clear that this definition is not the mega-church but it's a church of substantial size, not the small congregations. The small churches are withdrawn from this world. They are not having any impact on society. They are the way in which the individual escapes society, and responsibility. They are a very different world [from] the larger churches. They may be hungry and in need but there is also a great deal of defeatism. The danger is exceedingly great that one becomes problem-focused when working with these smaller churches.

Drucker-Buford Dialogue, Estes Park, Colorado, August 9, 1993.

- Membership in a church or social sector organization provides individuals with opportunities to find meaning and purpose in their lives.

- The modern trend toward teaching "mindfulness" in business and business schools[56] is recognition of the benefits of meditation to organizations and employees to reduce stress and to obtain other favorable results, such as increased productivity and creativity in the workplace.

3. WORK AND HUMAN NATURE

Management always lives, works, and practices in and for an institution, which is a human community held together by the bond that, next to the tie of the family, is the most powerful human bond: the work bond. And precisely because the object of management is a human community held together by the work bond for a common purpose, management always deals with the Nature of Man, and (as all of us with any practical experience learned) with Good and Evil as well. I have learned more theology as a practicing management consultant than I did when I taught religion.

> Peter F. Drucker, "Teaching the Work of Management," 1988, pp. 2–5.

III. Practicum-Prompts

Does your organization provide dignity, freedom, and equal opportunity to each of its members, thus promoting American ideals? How does it seek to provide these positive attributes?

"Management by Objectives and Self-Control" is the managerial philosophy developed by Drucker in the early 1950s to provide individuals with freedom and autonomy in their work while simultaneously requiring them to take responsibility for results as negotiated with their superiors. How does your organization provide autonomy while simultaneously requiring accountability for results?

Drucker believed that abuse of power was the besetting sin of leaders in an organization and that it could be overcome only by imposing various checks and balances on them. Are checks and balances in place in your organization to control abuses of power? How well do these checks and balances function? Is power legitimate in your organization? Does it seek to serve the mission of the organization and the welfare of its constituents?

What specific contributions are you and your organization making to become a dynamic force for good and for change in your community? What kind of encouragement or preparations do you need to become a force for change and for good?

The Succession Decision

Week 31

The Succession Decision

Maintaining the Spirit of the Organization

Introduction

The succession to the top position of an organization is a difficult decision and indeed, according to Drucker, sometimes a "desperate gamble" (*Management: Tasks, Responsibilities, Practices*, 1973, p. 618). And past performance in a range of lower-level positions is no guarantee of success in the top position.

One of the best examples comes from American political history. James Buchanan, fifteenth president of the United States, was a graduate of Dickinson College and served five terms as a congressman and two terms as a United States senator from Pennsylvania. He also served as minister to Russia and to Great Britain. Before assuming the presidency in 1856, he was the seventeenth secretary of state, under President Polk. His background and experience would seem to have prepared him well for the presidency. Yet historians and political scientists consider Buchanan among the worst of our presidents.

Abraham Lincoln, Buchanan's successor, on the other hand, was self-educated and served a number of terms in the Illinois state legislature and one term as a congressman from Illinois. He was twice defeated in his bid for the U.S. Senate. Yet historians and political scientists consider Lincoln among the best of our presidents, if not the best. Buchanan had significant, relevant national and international experience and failed; Lincoln had very little national and international experience and succeeded. Expectations of those observers skilled in the nuances of presidential politics predicted precisely the opposite outcome, but events proved them wrong. Had those skilled observers asked, "What is going to be the biggest challenge over the next few years?" they might not have underestimated Lincoln as badly as they did. Those closest to him in Illinois, including one of his powerful political opponents, Senator Stephen Douglas, certainly did not underestimate Lincoln's ability, nor did Lincoln's friends who worked so hard for his election.

What no one could have known is just how much this man could grow in character and competence as he tried to solve one problem after another in extraordinary times that lasted from his first day in office until his death.

I. Read

I would not say that I am an expert on the topic, but I got into political science and political theory when I was eighteen, and I was really intrigued by the succession problem: "How does one manage to maintain or preserve the wisdom, the counsel, and the example of a founder and yet not have him kill off his successor?"

I sat down the other day with an old friend, Derek Bok, who is now president of Harvard.[57] He was on a leave of absence; formerly [he was] dean of Harvard Law School. He leads an operation in which, in the best years of the leading American universities, almost every strong president came from the outside, not from the inside. This is partly because strong people very rarely encourage strength in their subordinates, and partly because of the very strength of these leaders. They continue to exercise influence over the governance of the institution for many years after their departure—like the way Alfred Sloan influenced the governance of General Motors after he left.

Stanford University has in many ways since its inception in 1891 been the best-run university of the lot. A president who comes from the outside and a provost who comes from the inside run it.

In some ways you need the [former chief executive] today when people live so long, and when the founder is at his peak in many ways, at his very best, at the time of succession. Ambition is burned out so he is no longer self-seeking; he has the experience; and in many cases he has a quiet, and a certain transcendental, quality, and yet that is the time when he needs to move out.

How does one maintain a role for [former chief executives] or balance this? You can go to one extreme or another. At the General Electric Company the former chief executives are not allowed on the premises—to the point where a few years ago they wanted to celebrate the twenty-fifth anniversary of the GE Management Institute, and at the last minute they canceled [the celebration] because somebody pointed out that they had two choices, or three. One was to tell the former chief executives, including the one who founded [the institute], that they wouldn't be welcome. The other was to break the rule, and the third [was] to move the celebration out of the GE Management Institute. So they canceled it; now that's going a little far, and I would have broken the rule for a dinner party. Then there is the other extreme, where the founder is around like the grin of the Cheshire cat.

So the question is, "How does one make the founder productive?" How does one give the founder a meaningful sphere of influence where he has to contribute, and still become effective, without really discouraging the organizational spirit? Charles V of Spain abdicated [in 1556] and went to a monastery [to make way] for his son [Philip II], and we have the letters—and his poor son, because the old man had nothing to do but sit quietly there and write letters; he interfered with every detail, always piously protesting that he was totally happy, and his only concern was the hereafter. Thousands of letters, every day, but how do you prevent that?

The succession decision should focus on the maintenance of the spirit that keeps an institution alive. Solutions have to fit the specific organization and maintain its spirit of performance.

Drucker-Buford Dialogue, February 24, 1987.

II. Reflect

- Derek Bok was a successful president of Harvard University during his twenty years of distinguished service in that position. He was an internal candidate, having previously served as dean of Harvard's Law School. Lawrence Summers, former U.S. secretary of the treasury, succeeded Derek Bok. His six-year tenure, 2001 to 2006, was marred by controversy and ended in a no-confidence vote by the Harvard faculty. Unlike Bok, Summers was an external candidate. In this specific succession decision, the performance of the internal candidate was superior to that of the external candidate. The difference may lie in Summers's inability to maintain the spirit of the institution.

1. "THE SPIRIT OF AN ORGANIZATION IS CREATED FROM THE TOP"

The proof of the sincerity and seriousness of a management is uncompromising emphasis on integrity of character. This, above all, has to be symbolized in management's "people" decisions. For it is character through which leadership is exercised; it is character that sets the example and is imitated. Character is not something one can fool people about. The people with whom a person works, and especially subordinates, know in a few weeks whether he or she has integrity or not. They may forgive a person a great deal: incompetence, ignorance, insecurity, or bad manners. But they will not forgive lack of integrity in that person. *Nor will they forgive higher management for choosing him* [emphasis mine].

This is particularly true of the people at the head of an enterprise. For the spirit of an organization is created from the top. If an organization is great in spirit, it is because the spirit of its top people is great. If it decays, it does so because the top rots; as the proverb has it, "Fish die from the head down." No one should ever be appointed to a senior position unless top management is willing to have his or her character serve as the model for subordinates.

> Peter F. Drucker, *Management: Tasks, Responsibilities, Practices*, 1973, 1974, pp. 462–63.

- J. Kermit Campbell was the first person from outside to become chief executive officer of Herman Miller, in 1992. He succeeded Max DePree, who remained chairman of the board of directors until he reached the board's mandatory retirement age, seventy, in 1995. Campbell was relieved of his duties in 1995 after a difficult period within Herman Miller, characterized by numerous changes and disruptions, including major changes in personnel, some of which were contrary to the company's historic values and threatened its spirit. Campbell was succeeded by Mike Volkema, who served as CEO from 1995 to 2004. Volkema, an internal candidate, was mentored by Max DePree and reverted back to Herman Miller's historical values, including an emphasis on the importance of people, but changed some of the company's practices, including the promise of lifetime employment. Clearly, Volkema returned to the long-held values and spirit of Herman Miller.[58]

2. THE TONE OF THE BODY

Max DePree: There is one further element [in what the leader owes]: the way in which you judge the quality of leadership by what I would call the tone of the body, not by the charisma of the leader, not by how much publicity the company gets, or any of that stuff. How well does the body adjust to change? How well does the body deal with conflict? How well does the body meet the needs of the constituency or customers, whatever it is? That in the end, is the way you judge the quality of the leadership.

Peter Drucker: Would you include in your tone of the body also what happens when the leader passes off the scene?

Max Depree: Succession is one of the key responsibilities of leadership.

> Peter F. Drucker, *Managing the Non-Profit Organization*,
> 1990, pp. 43–44.

- In the cases of both Herman Miller and Harvard we see that the spirit of the institution was disrupted in undesirable ways by new CEOs. At Herman Miller Max DePree, Campbell's predecessor, remained chairman of the board. At Harvard, Bok returned to a faculty position and later served as interim president from July 1, 2006, to June 30, 2007, after Lawrence Summers resigned. Lincoln's choice of Ulysses Grant as general in chief to succeed Henry Halleck, on the other hand, proved decisive in developing a strong spirit and winning the Civil War. Despite his personal weaknesses Grant implemented the strategy that Lincoln believed would win the war. There were enormous casualties on both sides, but Lincoln knew that the arithmetic, men, and matériel favored the Union. General Grant implemented Lincoln's strategy of striking at multiple positions simultaneously— something other Union generals were either unable or unwilling to do—and was able to win big battles against General Lee. As a result, the spirit of the Union Army soared.

3. PICK SUCCESSORS BASED UPON THEIR STRENGTH, NOT TO MINIMIZE WEAKNESSES

President Lincoln [a teetotaler], when told that General Grant, his new commander-in-chief, was fond of the bottle said: "If I knew his brand, I'd send a barrel or so to some other generals." After a childhood on the Kentucky and Illinois [Indiana] frontier, Lincoln assuredly knew all about the bottle and its dangers. But of all Union generals, Grant's appointment was the turning point of the Civil War. It was an effective appointment because Lincoln chose his general for his tested ability to win battles and not for his sobriety, that is, [not] for the absence of a weakness.

Peter F. Drucker, *The Effective Executive*, 1967, p. 71.

- Our examples do not make an argument for either internal or external candidates. But they do illustrate that the succession decision is a gamble, and that it helps when newly appointed CEOs of organizations seek to maintain or restore the spirit of the institution while using their unique strengths to change in-effective practices and meet pressing challenges.

4. "WHERE THERE ARE PEAKS THERE ARE VALLEYS"

Whoever tries to pick a man or staff an organization to avoid weakness will end up at best with mediocrity. The idea that there are "well-rounded" people, people who have only strengths and no weaknesses (whether the term used is the "whole man," the "mature personality," the "well-adjusted personality," or the "generalist") is a prescription for mediocrity if not for incompetence. Strong people always have strong weaknesses too. Where there are peaks there are valleys. And no one is strong in many areas. Measured against the universe of human knowledge, experience, and abilities, even the greatest genius would have to be rated a total failure. There is no such thing as a "good man." Good for what? is the question.

Peter F. Drucker, *The Effective Executive*, 1967, p. 72.

III. Practicum-Prompts

What has been the track record of succession decisions in your organization? If the record has been a good one, what accounts for it? If the record has been mediocre or poor, what accounts for that?

Would you describe your organization as one possessing a high spirit of performance? What accounts for the high spirit?

If your organization cannot be characterized as high performing, what can you do to improve its spirit? What recommendations can you make to others who may be in a better position to influence the spirit of the organization?

As the example of Ulysses S. Grant illustrates, individuals with weaknesses often have extraordinary strengths on which distinguished careers can be built. Does your organization look for all-around strengths in its appointments to top management? Or does it, like Lincoln, look for people who possess the strengths needed for the demands confronting the organization, recognizing that such people may, and often do, have significant weaknesses?

Planning for Succession in Organizations

Introduction

Succession to top management is a high-risk decision for all organizations. The best way to plan for succession is to have a systematic program of development in place, and to have available a slate of qualified people for all significant managerial positions so that when a position becomes vacant, human resources can scan the list and recommend to decision makers multiple qualified candidates from whom a successor can be chosen.

Having the ability to test a number of people in highly responsible positions before making a decision is one of the safest approaches to succession. Yet even in this case, a successful charismatic leader is very hard to replace, so one must be sure that the person chosen has his or her own set of strengths to bring to the top position. The candidate selected, while knowing and respecting the traditions of the past, will be well served to be his or her own person and not try to duplicate the predecessor's style and approach. First of all, the predecessor no doubt made some mistakes that were not challenged but will now have to be corrected. Second, no two people are alike, and trying to clone a successor to match the predecessor is bound to fail.

The ability to obtain the advice of a very experienced board of directors is invaluable in making decisions about succession. The directors are able not only to bring their own past experiences to bear on the decision but also to draw on the experiences of colleagues in other organizations—organizations that have made good choices as well as those that have not. Designating certain board members as coaches and sounding boards for newly appointed chief executive officers is also very helpful.

I. Read

Rick Warren was invited to participate in a Pew Research Center Forum on Religion and Public Life held on November 13, 2009, in Washington, D.C. Leadership succession at Saddleback Community Church was one of a number of subjects discussed. Warren explained that it was his intention to devote forty years as senior pastor of the church and then turn over the leadership to a younger group. Warren had served for thirty years at the time of the forum and was asked to elaborate upon his plans for succession.

Rick Warren

I knew that with me being 10 years out, I wanted a successful transition. So we did at Saddleback Church something that I don't know any other church has ever done, almost a year and a half ago. We lowered the age of the leadership body in our church by 16 years in one week. We had a group of pastors who have been with me pretty much since the start that we call our elders. Most of us are in our 50s, mid-50s, and we have led the church all these years. All along we've been mentoring the next generation, which is what I'm doing. I'm spending the rest of my life mentoring the next generation. We had a group of young guys who were in their 30s and a couple reaching 40, and in one week we turned over the leadership. We moved all of the guys out of leadership who were in, including me—I'm just a teaching pastor—and we moved these guys in their

30-somethings into the leadership, which we call the PMT, the Pastors' Management Team, and we turned over the leadership of a mega-church to . . . nine guys. . . . They're all young guys who are running this enormous mega-church and we're doing other stuff. So the transition is already being made right now.

Warren was asked still later if he knew who his successor would be. He answered, "I don't know. But I will tell you this: Peter Drucker, my mentor, said you should never choose your successor. I believe that because typically what you'll do is you'll choose a person like yourself, and what the organization usually needs is the exact opposite of what you were, at that point. Do you know what I'm saying?"

> Rick Warren, Pew Research, Religion and Public Life,
> "The Future of Evangelicals: A Conversation with Pastor
> Rick Warren," November 13, 2009.

II. Reflect

- "There is no success without a successor" is Rick Warren's paraphrase of Drucker's point about the importance of developing successors for the well-being of any organization.

1. SUCCESSION IS KEY TO AN ORGANIZATION'S SUCCESS

An organization that is not capable of perpetuating itself has failed. An organization therefore has to provide today the men and women who run it tomorrow. It has to renew its human capital. It should steadily upgrade its human resources.

An organization [that] just perpetuates today's level of vision, excellence, and accomplishments has lost the capacity to adapt. And since the one and only thing certain in human affairs is change, it will not be capable of survival in a changed tomorrow.

> Peter F. Drucker and Joseph A. Maciariello, *The Effective Executive in Action*, 2006, p. 48.

- "Level 5 leaders set up their successors for even greater success in the next generation, whereas, egocentric Level 4 leaders often set up their successors for failure" (Jim Collins, *Good to Great: Why Some Companies Make the Leap . . . and Others Don't*, 2001, p. 39).

- "Elevate HR [human resources] to a position of power and primacy in the organization, and make sure HR people have the special qualities to help managers build leaders and careers. In fact, the best HR types are pastors and parents in the same package" (Jack Welch, *Winning,* 2005, p. 98).

- In 2005, to commemorate the fifteenth anniversary of the Leader to Leader Institute, the successor to the Peter F. Drucker Foundation for Nonprofit Management (1990 to 2003), a special journal issue of *Leader to Leader, Shine a Light*, was published. For the opening article, the editors asked me to interview Peter Drucker on concerns facing all nonprofit organizations in the United States. The portion of the interview devoted to management succession in nonprofit organizations appears in Reading 2.

2. PETER DRUCKER ON SUCCESSION DECISIONS IN NONPROFIT ORGANIZATIONS

Joseph Maciariello

Peter, many executives of major nonprofits will be retiring [soon]. . . . Little seems to have been done to groom successors, the pipeline of leaders seems sparse. Isn't this a very serious problem?

Peter Drucker

One of the major challenges in institutions as you point out will be in leadership changes and we are not as prepared in the social sector for succession as we are in business. We are at the stage now that business was when we began executive development in business.

The present nonprofit executives came into management about the time of the Vietnam War, when they were in their thirties. And now they are moving out. And few nonprofit organizations have prepared their successors. . . .

It's going to be rough. Very few of these people have thought through the succession questions: "What kind of people do we need to succeed us? What kind of background should they have? How do we train them? How do we test them? How do we screen them?" The way we pick them now is to have the board get on the telephone and ask various people, "Do you know somebody?" . . . The questions I ask nonprofit organizations looking for successors are "What are results in the job? What competencies do you need? What experiences do you need?"

Joseph Maciariello

Peter, doesn't this succession problem also create real opportunities?

Peter Drucker

It does indeed! There is part of the social sector that is not volunteer and the succession crisis creates leadership opportunities. And for the part that is volunteer it creates opportunities for parallel careers.

Here is the fellow from business who at age 43 has become a comptroller of a small division of a large company. Basically, he has reached his terminal job. Only one of 40 comptrollers will become the chief financial officer of the company. He may make it from a small division to a large division of a large company. But he is in his terminal job. His opportunities for leadership, for growth and for stimulation are in the social sector. Either as a second career or as a parallel career.

The social sector is full of leadership challenges creating new opportunities for first, second and parallel careers.

Joseph A. Maciariello, "Managing for Results, Planning for Succession: An Interview with Peter F. Drucker," *Shine a Light*, 2005, pp. 15–19.

• A founder of an organization is not necessarily the best person to choose his or her successor. The danger is that a successor will be chosen who most nearly resembles the founder. No two people have the same strengths, so a look-alike successor may not be able to supply the vision to chart a course that makes sense for the new environment and problems likely to face the organization. The successor also may be facing and correcting the errors of the founder early in his or her tenure.

3. THE SUCCESSION PROCESS AT LINCOLN ELECTRIC DURING ITS 120-YEAR HISTORY

The Lincoln Electric Company, headquartered in Cleveland, Ohio, is a global leader in welding supplies and equipment with manufacturing and joint venture operations in over 160 countries. John C. Lincoln founded the company in 1895 as a motor business and patented a process for arc welding. John Lincoln officially served as President of Lincoln Electric from 1895–1929 and Chairman until his death in 1954. As his brother James F. Lincoln became more involved in the business, John began to pursue other business interests. James joined the company in 1907 and became General Manager in 1914, assuming the titles of Vice-President and General Manager until 1929, when he was formally named President of the company.

What is noteworthy about succession to the top at
Lincoln Electric is how orderly it has been. In its 120-year
history, it has had only eight CEOs including the current
CEO, Christopher Mapes, who assumed the position at the
beginning of 2013. Each of the three CEOs who succeeded
James Lincoln, William Irrgang (1972), George Willis
(1986), and Donald Hastings (1992), had direct connections
with James Lincoln and with the legendary values (most
notably its application of the Golden Rule to employees
and customers) and high performing spirit of the company.
Irrgang, a brilliant engineer who joined the company in
1928, succeeded James Lincoln upon Lincoln's death. He
was reluctant to expand outside of the United States, but
did maintain existing operations in Canada and Australia.
Irrgang's reluctance to expand globally occurred at a time
when foreign competitors were entering the U.S. market.

James Lincoln recruited both George Willis and Donald
Hastings from the Harvard Business School and personally
mentored them. Willis became President under Irrgang
in 1972 and CEO in 1986 with Hastings serving as his
President. Willis embarked on a major global expansion
of the company in 1986. He and others at the company
believed that because of Lincoln's superior status in the
United States it could expand rapidly into Europe, Asia, and
South America. Rapid foreign expansion turned out not to
be so easily accomplished [see the discussion of Lincoln's
foreign expansion in the Week 14 entry].

The Company stumbled badly in its global expansion
because it moved very fast and did not ask the succession
question: "What problems are Willis and Hastings likely to
face as they enter each new country?" Had they asked these
questions they would have known that the extraordinary
culture and management systems developed by Lincoln
in the United States would not work in Germany, Japan
and South America for reasons having to do with very

specific local culture and business practices in each of these countries. The result was that the company had to absorb large losses in its foreign operations. It took on huge amounts of debt putting the entire company at risk.

When Hastings became CEO in 1992, he brought in Anthony Massaro, a top executive from Westinghouse, who was an expert in rationalizing global operations. Massaro worked closely with Hastings to restructure Lincoln's foreign operations. As an outsider, Massaro did not understand or appreciate the Lincoln culture and management systems. Nevertheless, his contributions were very significant and the Board of Directors appointed him CEO in 1996. As a result the culture and spirit of the company began to change. The company he came from was very different from Lincoln Electric and was not nearly as competitive. Few companies were.

Had the company asked the key succession question: "What problems and opportunities are we likely to face as we expand globally?" it would not have appointed Willis to the top job in 1986 or it would have taken time to learn about the specific conditions in each country and how to adapt its operations to local conditions. With the shift to outside leadership, the company's historic culture began to atrophy and continued to do so for approximately a decade.

Massaro retired in 2004 and John M. Stropki was named President and Chief Executive Officer. Stropki, who retired at the end of 2012, spent his entire career at Lincoln Electric and as CEO restored the culture and spirit of performance that was mostly lost during the Massaro era. Here is an excerpt from the company's August 20, 2013, press announcement on the occasion of Stropki's retirement:[59] "During his tenure he ultimately positioned Lincoln to be the clear leader in the industry, significantly increased shareholder value, and did so while staying true to Lincoln's mission and values."

In summary, Lincoln has been one of America's most competitive manufacturing companies for 120 years. But it almost lost it all as a result of not asking key succession questions prior to expanding its global expansion. Fortunately, the operations of Lincoln Electric in Cleveland were able to carry practically the whole financial load until Lincoln could regain its bearings and transform itself into a global, world-class company.

> Joseph A. Maciariello, *Lasting Value: Lessons from a Century of Agility at Lincoln Electric*, 2000, pp. 36–38.

- Authority in the structure of the Calvary Chapel movement has been highly personal and based on giftedness and competence during the tenure of Chuck Smith, the founding pastor. The primary focus is on the pastoral office, similar to what we see in highly decentralized corporations. The lead church of the movement is the Costa Mesa, California, church, which Smith pastored. Its governance is congregational in form. Yet Chuck Smith had considerable charismatic authority. He was involved in the selection of pastors and churches that were allowed to associate with Calvary (e.g., those that had naming rights) and also in managing Calvary's assets such as its Bible colleges and network of radio stations. The movement flourished under Smith primarily as a result of his example and through his teachings. He was also a wise steward of the resources entrusted to him and to the movement. His new management structure, described below, was put into place in time to succeed him.

- Succeeding the charismatic, founding pastor of one of the world's largest church movements is especially challenging. Reading 4 contains Drucker's wisdom on succession planning for Calvary Chapel Association of churches, a worldwide organization. A number of Drucker's recommendations apply to succession decisions in large organizations in all sectors of society.

4. DRUCKER ASSISTS A FOUNDING LEADER TO ESTABLISH SUCCESSION PLANS

Peter Drucker: The likes of you do not retire. You should ask the question, "What is it I can do to make the best contribution to the church?" Think fifteen years out, not three to four. You are still a young man.

It is certain—not probable, certain—that when you are gone there will be changes. Nobody can succeed to a charismatic role. And then I think you know it as well as I do, maybe much better, that one way to go is to institutionalize, and it's an easier way to go because institutionalization makes possible—not certain, but possible—survival and continuation beyond charisma. With sixteen hundred churches worldwide, or two thousand or whatever it is, a certain amount of institutionalization is probably necessary for the movement to survive.

Let me say, the main benefit of institutionalization is that it allows an organization or an entity to survive mediocre leadership, and mediocre leadership happens to be the rule, not the exception. What you have done cannot be perpetuated, cannot be handed on. This is very much the known.

Institutionalization Makes Possible Two Things

Institutionalization makes possible continuation despite mediocre leadership, and it gives the emerging leader a legitimate place. It isn't that the office makes the man, but the office enables the man. I don't know your convictions, whether you think what you have built, which is a very big enterprise with close to two thousand churches, should and could be perpetuated. But if you believe it should be perpetuated, a minimum institutional structure would be required, not as a matter of succession to you, but because the good Lord bestows these gifts [which you have], and nobody else can do it.

Find the Leaders

So make it your business, I respectfully suggest, to find
the leaders, but you probably already know these people.
Whenever you meet them individually don't make it
a conference or a group affair, or [a] seminar. This is
something where you say, "Jim, I need your opinion. I
need you to think through your responsibility for the
perpetuation of the movement." When it comes to your
church in Orange County that's one issue. When it comes to
the movement it's another.

I'm not saying it's preferable, but it is quite conceivable
that you may find to your great surprise that of those forty
or fifty people, a large number see the successor not in
Orange County, but they see one of their own members
standing out. Or it may very well be that they come to you
and say, When you are no longer the head of the movement,
we think there should be a small but clearly defined
designated group, an executive committee that is available
to work with the sixteen hundred pastors we have plus the
thousand pastors we train [in our various Bible colleges].
This executive committee can handle one of the big churches
in your movement that gets into trouble.

> Peter Drucker–Chuck Smith–Chuck Fromm Consultation,
> December 3, 2003, Claremont, California.

• Institutionalizing the Leadership Structure at Calvary Chapel.
Chuck Smith died on Thursday, October 3, 2013. He had served
as pastor of Calvary Chapel Costa Mesa, California, from 1965
until his death. "In 2012, he established a 21-member leadership
council to oversee the Calvary Church Association, a fellowship
of some 1,600 like-minded congregations in the United States
and abroad."[60] The domestic and international regional structure
is extensive and well developed. The names and photos of those
people serving on the leadership council and those holding re-

gional offices in the United States and around the world can be found at the website of Calvary Chapel Association.[61]

5. SLOAN ON CHOOSING HIS SUCCESSOR

"[You] think I should be a good judge of people. Believe me, there's no such person. There are only people who make people decisions right, and that means slowly, and people who make people decisions wrong and then repent at leisure. We do make few mistakes, not because we're good judges of people but because we're conscientious. And," he emphasized, "the first rule is an old one: 'Never let a man nominate his own successor; then you get a carbon copy and they're always weak.'"

"What about your own succession, Mr. Sloan?" I asked. It had been publicly announced that he would step down from the chief executive office with the ending of the war. "I asked the executive committee of the board to make that decision," he said. "I did not tell them whom I would recommend, although they wanted to know. I told them I would tell them were they to pick someone whom I thought unqualified.

> Peter F. Drucker, *Adventures of a Bystander*, 1978, 1994, p. 281.

III. Practicum-Prompts

Does your organization ask these key questions when making a choice to fill the top position?—"What important issues are likely to face the organization in the future?" "Who is best prepared by experience and education to deal with these issues?"

Do you have a clear path of succession within the top executive ranks of your organization? Is your organization tolerant of diversity and strength in its executive group? Does your organization grant significant autonomy to executives to facilitate their development to positions in top management?

Does your organization have a strong executive development plan supported by an effective human resources organization?

Does your organization pay attention to age distribution among its high-ranking leaders at or near the top? Would the system of lowering the age distribution in the leadership group of Saddleback Community Church work in your organization?

Both Alfred Sloan and Peter Drucker advised against using the current CEO to choose his or her successor. What is the rationale for this advice and does your organization follow it? Should your organization follow it?

When the CEO of your organization retires, is he or she allowed to remain on the board of directors? Does this work for the good of the organization or is it counterproductive? What policies should your organizations adopt regarding involvement of retired CEOs?

Lessons from the Social Sector on the Power of Purpose

Week 33

Mission

Introduction

Peter Drucker, after reluctantly agreeing to lend his name to the Peter F. Drucker Foundation for Nonprofit Management, took on the task of writing both a preamble and a mission statement for the foundation. These guided its activities from its inception in 1990 until it was reorganized as the Leader to Leader Institute and then reorganized again on January 1, 2012, as the Frances Hesselbein Leadership Institute. The preamble is the only one I have seen for a social sector organization and no doubt reflects Drucker's respect for constitutionalism and federalism.[62] I believe this exercise and the follow-up work he did with his friend David A. Jones, cofounder, chairman, and CEO of Humana Inc., are important for understanding Drucker's vision for the social sector and the work that needs to be done to improve the leadership and management in the entire sector.

To understand the purpose of his preamble for the Drucker Foundation we can look at the Preamble to the U.S. Constitution. Its purpose is to define the rationale underlying the Constitution, which provides the structures, policies, and principles for running our federal and state governments. Drucker's rationale for the foundation was to develop the social sector as a vehicle to express the values he held for democratic societies. These values include commitment to individual responsibility; the building of community; promoting charity as a vehicle for individuals to give voice to their basic value commitments; and promoting volunteerism for accomplishing the mission of social sector institutions. He lent his name to this foundation because of its promise of accomplishing these values.

I. Read

The Preamble provides the Social Ecology (or human and social environment) within which the Foundation will operate. Notice, the Foundation is involved in living the commandment "love thy neighbor"; they build community and develop responsibility; they offer opportunities for self-fulfillment and citizenship; and they provide opportunities to volunteer one's service on behalf of our fellow citizens. The Preamble provides the basic intent for the Drucker Foundation, not the specifics of what the foundation is to do. The specifics are contained in the Mission Statement.

Preamble for the Peter F. Drucker Foundation for Nonprofit Management

This foundation is dedicated to the proposition that the nonprofit institutions, the churches in the community services, the hospitals and the health care associations, the Red Cross, the Girl Scouts, the Boy Scouts, and many, many more, are the most important institutions of a free America. They live the commandment "love thy neighbor," they represent our commitment to individual responsibility. They build community, and in an increasingly depersonalized society they offer millions of men and women opportunities for service, and contribution for self-fulfillment, and growth as volunteers. Unlike the business of the for-profit sector the nonprofit institutions do not supply. Unlike government they do not control; their goal is to change lives. The role of the

foundation is not to supply energy to nonprofit institutions. The role is to release energy, and to direct it. And because Peter F. Drucker as writer, teacher, and advisor has given service to nonprofit institutions, and has helped them attain effectiveness, the foundation for nonprofit excellence is proud to bear his name, and grateful for his willingness to take an active part in its work.

Mission Statement for the Peter F. Drucker Foundation for Nonprofit Management

The Peter F. Drucker Nonprofit Foundation intends to focus on helping nonprofit institutions to formulate, to think through, and focus on their mission and objectives; to help them focus on the ultimate customer, the recipient of their service and the volunteers; to make available to them the methods of nonprofit management; to provide a reference service of methods or materials, and of resources; and to bring to them experienced and successful men and women desirous to devote themselves to nonprofit work.

> Peter F. Drucker drafted this Preamble and Mission Statement during meetings in 1989 after his eightieth birthday celebration in November 1989. These meetings involved Peter Drucker, Doris Drucker, Bob Buford, Frances Hesselbein, and Richard Shubert, former head of the American Red Cross.

II. Reflect

- "A great many nonprofits have not yet developed professional management"—(Peter F. Drucker (Joseph A. Maciariello, "Managing for Results, Planning for Succession," *Shine a Light*, 2005, p. 17).
- A good mission statement is short and focuses the attention of each member of the organization on how his or her activities fit

into the overall mission of the organization. The statement tells each member what the organization is about and what it intends to do.

1. NEED FOR PROFESSIONAL MANAGEMENT IN THE SOCIAL SECTOR

One priority area [for the Foundation]—maybe the top one judging from the responses we have been getting—is the development of ways in which a non-profit organization (and especially one of the smaller ones) can evaluate itself— its mission; its performance and results; its structure and organization; the allocation of its resources; and—badly needed—its performance in attracting and using resources, both people and money. This will have to be a self-evaluation tool kit. But—and all of us agreed—it will surely lead towards some follow-up, whether a reference service to help non-profits get the kind of outside help (e.g., a consultant) they might need to work on areas that need change or strengthening, or a list of resources such as business people available to help; or perhaps, in the end, a consulting service of our own, perhaps even a profit-making subsidiary. The demand for this is so great that we—reluctantly—have come to the conclusion that this, however difficult, has to be a major priority.

> Peter F. Drucker and Joseph A. Maciariello, *Management Cases: Revised Edition*, 2009, p. 65.

2. TURNING SOCIETY'S REJECTS INTO CITIZENS

The best nonprofits devote a great deal of thought to defining their organization's mission. They avoid sweeping statements full of good intentions and focus, instead, on objectives that have clear-cut implications for the work their members perform—staff and volunteers both. The Salvation

Army's goal [mission], for example, is to turn society's rejects—alcoholics, criminals, derelicts—into *citizens* [italics mine].

> Peter F. Drucker, "What Business Can Learn from
> Nonprofits," *Harvard Business Review*, 1989, p. 89.

- A clearinghouse is needed to provide best practices for nonprofit organizations. This would allow information to be transferred to similar organizations the way Willow Creek Association transfers best practices to churches of similar size and demographics. These best practices include board development, mission development, definition of results, fund-raising, recruiting volunteers, and training volunteers.

3. A THIRD AREA IS WHAT WE HAVE COME TO CALL "PARALLEL CAREERS"

A number of organizations, e.g., the National Executive Service Corps, place retired business executives into non-profit assignments, usually full-time, for a short period of time such as a year. But there is a much larger group of people—usually younger ones—who want to find the right kind of non-profit volunteer work while staying in their work and job. Within the church segment of the Third (or Social) Sector, these people usually—or often—place themselves; they have been members of the congregation for years and now become highly active volunteers. Otherwise, however, there is no other organization that even attempts to match the strengths, values, and experiences of the person with the needs of a non-profit institution. The tools for doing this exist: the National Executive Service Corps has developed—and highly successfully—fairly simple methods for finding out both the individual's strengths and the institution's values and needs, and then matching the two—and they will make these tools available to us (they want to work

closely with the Foundation as we clearly complement
what they have been doing since 1976). And there are
good analytical tools available for the individual—Dick
Bolles's *What Color Is Your Parachute* or what Bernie Haldane
developed thirty years ago in his placement work. But, so
far they have not been adapted and applied to the parallel
career—or to the placement with a non-profit organization
altogether. Mismatches are more common than the right
fit—and there is a contribution to be made.

Peter F. Drucker and Joseph A. Maciariello, *Management
Cases: Revised Edition*, 2009, p. 66.

III. Practicum-Prompts

Using the examples of a preamble in this entry, write out what you
believe to be the true purpose of your organization.

Review the mission statement of your organization. Have there
been any changes creating the need to refocus your mission?

Convene a diverse group to discuss the currency of your mission.
Work to reconcile differences among members of the management
team over the mission.

Does your mission statement contain platitudes or is it action
oriented? If adhered to will it help to fulfill your organization's purpose?

Do all the members of your organization understand your mission? Does everyone know how his or her role fits into the purpose
and mission of your organization?

Write and revise your purpose and mission statement accordingly. Seek comments and approval. Disseminate the results widely
throughout your organization. Make sure they are widely accepted
and operational.

Accommodating Various Constituencies in a Mission

Introduction

We know that single-purpose institutions tend to be the most effective. Yet the executive has to meet the needs of a number of separate groups, and meeting these needs very often requires executives to make trade-offs. The short-term interests of stockholders, for example, weigh very heavily on the executive and often create pressures against investing in the development of people and in innovation—both required to support the long-term viability of the organization. How then can the executive reconcile the demand for short-term performance with the demand to care for tomorrow?

Clearly, the executive must meet the short-term requirements for profitability. Those who advocate taking only a long-term position fail to heed the truth John Maynard Keynes described in his criticism of classical economics with its focus on the eventual return of an economy to a position of long-run equilibrium:

> The long-run is a misleading guide to current affairs. In the long run we are all dead. Economist[s] set themselves

too easy, too useless a task if they can only tell us when the storm is long past the ocean is flat again.

John Maynard Keynes, *A Tract on Monetary Reform*, 1924, p. 65.

No, business executives, especially those of public companies, must meet certain constraints on profitability in their quarter-to-quarter performance. Yet the executive must focus on meeting the critical needs of the future. By doing so, he or she will protect the interests of employees and society, as well as other stakeholders. But in taking resources from the pursuit of short-term profitability to meet the likely future needs of its customers, an organization must be aware of the trade-offs and communicate these costs to all constituents—customers, shareholders, workers, suppliers, and the communities that rely on the organization for employment, taxes, and other forms of support.

Executives of all institutions must try very hard to reconcile the interests of each of their constituents as they manage the short-term and long-term interests of the organization. In this entry Drucker applies this advice to all nonprofit organizations, but—as indicated in the readings, reflections, and applications—the same advice holds true for profit-motivated organizations.

I. Read

THE TIME DIMENSION

Management always has to consider both the present and the future; both the short run and the long run. A management problem is not solved if immediate profits are purchased by endangering the long-range health, perhaps even the survival of the company. A management decision is irresponsible if it risks disaster this year for the sake of a grandiose future. The all too common case of the great man in management who produces startling economic results as long as he runs the company but leaves behind nothing but a sinking hulk is an example of an irresponsible managerial action and of failure to balance present and future. The immediate economic results are actually fictitious and are achieved by destroying capital. In every case where present and future are not both satisfied, where their requirements are not harmonized, or at least balanced, capital—that is, wealth producing resource—is endangered, damaged, or destroyed. . . .

Management has to live always in both present and future. It must keep the enterprise performing in the present—or else there will be no enterprise capable of performing in the future. And it has to make the enterprise capable of performance, growth, and change in the future. Otherwise it has destroyed capital—that is, the capacity of resources to produce wealth tomorrow. . . . The greater the leap into the unknown, the stronger the foundation for the takeoff has to be.

Peter F. Drucker and Joseph A. Maciariello, *Management: Revised Edition*, 2008, pp. 290–91.

II. Reflect

- Business organizations can integrate the needs of each one of their constituents around the long-term goal of maximizing the wealth-producing capacity of the enterprise while meeting the immediate needs of its most important constituents: the customer and the worker.

1. INTEGRATE INTERESTS OF VARIOUS CONSTITUENTS INTO LONG-TERM VISION

The first—but also the toughest—task of the non-profit executive is to get all of these constituencies to agree on what the *long-term* goals of the institution are. Building around the long term is the only way to integrate all these interests. If you focus on short-term results, they will all jump in different directions. You will have a flea circus—as I discovered during my own dismal failure some forty years ago as an executive in an academic institution. . . . What I learned was that unless you integrate the vision of all the constituencies into the long-range goal, you will soon lose support, lose credibility, and lose respect. . . . I began to look at non-profit executives who did successfully what I unsuccessfully tried to do. *I soon learned that they start out by defining the fundamental change that the non-profit institution wants to make in society and in human beings; then they project that goal onto the concerns of each of the institution's constituencies* [italics added].

> Peter F. Drucker, *Managing the Non-Profit Organization*, 1990, p. 110.

• It is very difficult to reconcile these conflicting interests of constituents around short-term goals, but much easier for executives to integrate them around the long-term vision of the institution.

2. DRUCKER INTERVIEW BY *LEADERSHIP JOURNAL*

Introduction

Bob Buford enlisted the support of Paul Robbins, Editor, and Harold Myra, Publisher of *Leadership Journal*, to provide impetus to Bob's work very early in Bob's founding of Leadership Network. These two men helped Buford to obtain credibility among church leaders by sponsoring the first two Leadership Network conferences. Paul Robbins, in turn, was one of the thirty-three church leaders who attended the "Peter Drucker Summit Conference" held at the YMCA Camp of the Rockies, in Estes Park, Colorado, on August 19–22, 1986.

As a result of their connections to Bob and their help to him, the editors of *Leadership Journal* came to Claremont to interview Peter Drucker early in the Drucker-Buford project. They asked Peter a number of pertinent questions, none more so than how to establish a vision and mission for churches and other nonprofit organizations with multiple constituents. Here are two of the key questions along with Peter Drucker's responses:

Interview Questions and Answers

Editors: How important is it for a local church to develop its own distinctive vision?

Peter Drucker: A unified, clear vision [purpose] is essential, and yet in nonprofits, you're almost always dealing with a number of constituencies, each of which wants something different emphasized. When you look at churches, the mission is clear. It comes straight out of the Gospels. Basically, you are to bring the gospel to all of mankind. [It is] very clear; very simple. Maybe it's the simplest mission statement [of all]. I'm not saying it's the easiest, but it's the simplest.

Editors: But the various constituencies see the specifics in sharply different ways?

Peter Drucker: This is true of all nonprofit institutions. School boards and teachers and parents and students all see different purposes for the school system. Fifty years ago, the vision was clearer: the school's purpose was to see that students learn. The school focused on skills—the ability to read, to do the multiplication table. In recent years, various constituencies began arguing about what learning means. The vision was broadened beyond skills to include traits (development of character, personality, social tasks), and as a result, the unifying focal point was lost. With so many goals to accomplish, you can't function as effectively.

Despite the conflicting visions any nonprofit faces, it has
to be held together somehow. This is the pastor's challenge
with the church—to maintain the common mission. And if
you don't, well, one of the basic weaknesses of the mainline
liberal church is that it hasn't maintained the common
mission. The leaders see the church as dedicated to social
causes outside the church. But the congregation doesn't see it
that way. The result is confusion and ineffectiveness.

> LeadershipJournal.net, "Managing to Minister: An
> Interview with Peter Drucker." [63]

• Constituents of nonprofit and for-profit institutions often have
conflicting ideas of what the mission of the institution should be.
These separate visions must be successfully reconciled in order to
effectively manage these institutions.

3. PLANNING FOR PERFORMANCE IN A NONPROFIT

Performance in the nonprofit must be *planned*. And this
starts out with the mission. For the mission defines what
results are in this particular non-profit institution. And
then one asks: Who are our constituencies? It used to be
that a business could plan in terms of one constituency,
the customers and their satisfaction—the Japanese still
do. Everybody else—employees, the community, the
environment, maybe even shareholders—were restraints.
That this has changed for American business, and quite
drastically, is the reason why many business executives
feel the world is coming to an end. But in the non-profit
institution there have been a multitude of groups, each with
a veto power. A school principal has to satisfy teachers, the
school board, the taxpayers, parents, and, in the high school,
the students themselves. Five constituencies, each of which
see the school differently. Each of them is essential, at least

to the point where they don't fire the principal, go on strike, or rebel.

> Peter F. Drucker, *Managing the Non-Profit Organization*,
> 1990, pp. 109–10.

III. Practicum-Prompts

List the constituents whose needs you must satisfy in your position and in your organization.

How are you meeting the needs of each constituent person or group?

Which demands of these various groups conflict in the short term? Can these demands be reconciled in the longer-term goals of your organization?

List the constituents again. Try to reconcile the interests of each one in your long-term goals. Which, if any, cannot be reconciled with these goals?

Can you release yourself and your organization from the responsibility of meeting the irreconcilable interests of these constituents?

The Salvation Army

Introduction

Drucker believed that certain needs of society could be met most effectively by the work of well-managed social sector organizations. If effectively managed, these organizations could become powerful vehicles for meeting human needs and for alleviating human suffering. They could also fulfill needs of their volunteers for individual achievement and citizenship within a community. No other organization earned as much praise from Drucker for its work in meeting human needs and for developing its volunteers as The Salvation Army. And I do not believe any organization he worked with brought him more joy. He told Bob Buford and Rick Warren that he looked forward to meeting with the people of The Salvation Army because "whenever I sit down with them, I just find myself transported; their spirit is so wonderful, the joy of those people." [64]

The criteria Drucker used to assess the effectiveness of The Salvation Army, unless otherwise noted in this entry, are contained in an interview with National Commander James Osborne in which Drucker leads Osborne systematically through the solutions to a number of difficult challenges faced by executives of all organizations. [65]

It is important to note that Drucker believed the critical issue facing nonprofits is to define their mission clearly and then to define results that are indicative of how the nonprofit is doing in carrying out its mission. Unlike businesses, nonprofits do not have the discipline of the bottom line. It is very important therefore that nonprofits define performance measures congruent with results and with their mission. The Salvation Army does this extremely well and is in this respect a model for other organizations.

Social programs run by The Salvation Army are meeting human needs that are very difficult for government to meet—needs of prisoners, drug addicts, the homeless, alcoholics, troubled young persons, etc. The organization has performance measures for its programs that leave little doubt about its effectiveness. These are the reasons Drucker was so committed to its work—and the reasons it has been so successful in attracting funds from the American public. The American public responds favorably to the demonstrated ability of a nonprofit to achieve measurable results.

I. Read

THE SALVATION ARMY

On Mission

"The Salvation Army is the only organization that, since its inception in 1865 in London and 1880 in this country, has succeeded in reaching the really poor, the ones whom nobody else can really reach. It has been so successful in taking the losers, the rejects of society and making self-respecting citizens out of them."

On Effectiveness

The Salvation Army is: "by far the most effective organization in the U.S. No one even comes close to it in respect to clarity of mission, ability to innovate, measurable results, dedication and putting money to maximum use. . . .

"They know how to work with the poorest of the poor and the meanest of the mean."[66]

On Providing Motivation and Achievement for Volunteers

"Whenever I sit down with them, I just find myself transported; their spirit is so wonderful, the joy of those people."[67] Peter Drucker's consulting with The Salvation Army was, for the most part, as a volunteer.

On Contributing to Drucker's Lifework by Helping to Create

"The functioning community and functioning democracy of tomorrow."

II. Reflect

- Notice how short and clear the mission statement is: "Taking the losers, the rejects of society and making self-respecting citizens out of them."
- Regarding results and performance, notice the difference between measures for individualized services and measures for categories of services.

1. DEFINING PERFORMANCE AND RESULTS

Drucker: How do you define *performance* at The Salvation Army?

Osborne: We define performance and results on the basis of work with people. For example, we have about a 45 percent success rate with the men who come to us in our adult rehabilitation centers [centers primarily for alcoholics].

Drucker: In those instances you *measure* results

quantitatively. But how do you define *what the result is?* Let's say it is probably reasonably simple for the alcoholic and maybe reasonably simple for the first-time criminal offender who would go to jail if you didn't take care of them, but how do you define *results?*

Osborne: We have specific performance measurements for each service area. For a family who has to come to us for help with food because of unemployment, we define results as their being able to hold gainful employment to support the family. For troubled youth, we define results [in terms of] getting those who have been in difficulty out of difficulty.

Drucker: Take that sixteen-year-old who has been in trouble, stealing cars or what have you. Do you set the result as staying out of trouble for the next two or three years?

Osborne: If we can keep them six months going on the straight and narrow then we have a good chance of keeping them there permanently.

Drucker: So you balance results for a group such as the alcoholics with specific results for individuals such as troubled families, and young people. The two have to work together. And who has responsibility of looking at your various clients? Who kind of thinks through their potential, and their opportunities? Is that the individual case officer?

Osborne: Each operation of The Salvation Army has a responsible individual in charge. Most are commissioned Salvation Army officers.

Drucker: So you look at every individual as an individual and you establish performance goals for categories. Do you try to find the strength of each individual in working with him or her?

Osborne: We have learned to exploit those strengths and to try to minimize those weaknesses.

Drucker: How do you judge the performance of your own people?

Osborne: We have a formal system by which they are

rated, but it is based on accomplishments and service to
people. We rate them annually on whether their service to
people has improved, whether it has declined, or whether it
has simply [been] maintained. [See also "A Second Chance
for Failures," Week 29.]

Drucker: You also have quite a few volunteers across the
country, don't you? Do you train them and monitor their
performance?

Osborne: We have about a million and a half volunteers.
We could not get along without them. We train them in the
particular areas in which they are going to function: in the
provision of services, in counseling, and in administrative
roles. And we monitor their performance but we do not have
as elaborate an evaluation system for volunteers.

Drucker: You're implying that there should be no
difference between performance by staff and performance
by volunteers. The only difference is that volunteers work
part-time and are not paid. They are just as much part of the
Army as the regulars.

• The management process has strong alignment. The mission
is converted to results for each program. Results are in turn
supported by appropriate performance measures. Programs are
evaluated periodically and resources are allocated to those most
deserving, on the basis of performance and need. Programs that
no longer serve their original intent are abandoned.

2. PERFORMANCE REVIEW, ABANDONMENT, AND ALLOCATION OF RESOURCES

Drucker: And how often do you review performance
objectives once you have set them?

Osborne: There is a review process on an annual basis.
Specific goals are adjusted annually.

Drucker: Have you ever abandoned any activity?

Osborne: Yes, we have abandoned some activities. For

example, we used to operate residences for young women who were coming into large metropolitan areas from rural America. We have discovered that in today's society that kind of service really does not meet any demonstrated needs so those programs have been closed.

Drucker: So you regularly look at your programs and progress and hold them against results?

Osborne: Yes, and if it's not working, we do not hesitate to abandon them.

Drucker: Have you ever gone into any activity where you failed?

Osborne: The Army has very carefully chosen its fields of service, recognizing that there are some things we do better than anybody else, and there are some areas in which we'd better not be involved. So if it looks like it is not for us, we don't tackle it in the first place.

Drucker: Give me one example.

Osborne: Those with serious mental difficulties.

Drucker: How do you balance your focus on immediate results with long-term objectives?

Osborne: Direct and immediate results are the aims of The Salvation Army in its programs of assistance. The family who doesn't have food needs it today. The man who doesn't have a coat on his back needs it today, and the youngster who doesn't have shoes on his feet needs [them] immediately. Meeting the immediate need is the overwhelming passion of The Salvation Army. After having done that, we address the longer-term needs as to why this family is without food, etc.

Drucker: That's how you balance—by recognizing that you must do something immediately while you address the underlying problem. How do you allocate your resources? How do you make sure that "today" doesn't swallow up all the resources you have?

Osborne: There are never enough resources to go around. So you always have to allocate the resources to the immediate need, and then exercise the faith that . . . generous people are going to provide you with additional resources to address the more long-term problems.

Drucker: So what you are saying is first things come first and then the rest you hope. So needs allocate your resources?

Osborne: I must say we are amazed by what I call the "torrid love affair" of the American people with The Salvation Army. It has resulted in a level of support that is beyond the wildest dream of any of the early founders of The Salvation Army in this country. We find that when the American people know there is a need that The Salvation Army is trying to meet, they supply the resources for us to meet it.

Drucker: I am not surprised. I have long ago learned that if you have results, you get the support. And you have the results, and the results speak for themselves. But I am impressed by that very clear concept you have of where you put the resources because in my own work with nonprofit organizations, this is a continuing problem and dilemma between taking care of the immediate need and yet being able to build on the long term, which requires not only a lot of resources but a lot of commitment. Your fund-raising activity is successful because you are enabling the average American to live up to her beliefs and values and commitments.

• The Salvation Army balances short-term and long-term demands for which it has competence by attending to all short-term demands that serve its mission. It then depends on donations to meet longer-term demands.

3. CONCLUSION: MANAGING FOR RESULTS

Osborne: How can we improve our ability to evaluate performance?

Drucker: *Put resources where the results are.* I think that is one of the most important things to learn for an institution. Your organization is way ahead of most in defining performance and results and monitoring them, and allocating its resources.

- Chester I. Barnard, in *The Functions of the Executive* (1971, p. 256), testifies, "The reward of service is more service." Do you see an illustration here of this principle of the rewards of service (e.g., fulfilling the needs for achievement, citizenship, and community) in Drucker's volunteer service to The Salvation Army?

III. Practicum-Prompts

What do you think led Drucker to describe The Salvation Army as "the most effective organization" in the United States?

Convert your organization's mission statement and the mission for your position to a definition of results for your organization and for each major programmatic activity you are undertaking. Develop appropriate performance measures for each of your direct result areas. How close are these new measures to existing result areas and performance measures? What changes, if any, should be made?

Do you have a systematic process of abandonment in place in your organization? How does it operate? What programs, products, or services have you abandoned recently? Which ones should you study for abandonment?

Describe your process of balancing the allocation of resources between immediate needs and longer-term needs. Is there a healthy balance? Do current operations result in shortchanging the future? What recommendations should you make to alter the resource allocation process that is in place in your organization?

Does your resource allocation process put resources to work in areas that you know, from past experience, have achieved results? Evaluate the people and financial resource allocation process in your organization. How can they be designed to focus more on achieving results?

Week 36

Diffusion of Innovation—Public Schools

Introduction

Tom Luce is a founding partner in the Dallas law firm Hughes and Luce, LLP. He reproduced the strategies of networking and of sharing best practices that he learned from Bob Buford at Leadership Network and applied these to primary and secondary schools in the United States. Before taking a position in the Department of Education in the Bush administration, Luce was actively engaged in promoting the transfer of best practices and launching his own social sector organization, Just for Kids. He consulted with Peter Drucker in 1994 before he began.

Drucker was very interested in education, given its central role in postcapitalist society. He describes his ideas on improving education in his book *Post-Capitalist Society* (1993). He took a continuing interest in educational innovation and public school accountability, and these subjects are discussed in his *Innovation and Entrepreneurship* (1985), *Age of Discontinuity* (1969), and *Landmarks of Tomorrow* (1959). Drucker first mentioned the "knowledge worker" on page 122 of *Landmarks of Tomorrow*. He continued to track the role of knowledge in the economy and society for approximately fifty years, and this explains his deep interest in education, and therefore in the work of Tom Luce.

Luce identified "educational successes" in approximately thirty schools in his preliminary study, in order to identify best practices; and Drucker urged him to "run with success," to try to duplicate these results in other schools using proven methods for transferring best practices.

I. Read

Tom Luce

Peter, let me tell you a little bit of the background that has led to this concept. I got involved in education reform back in 1983 when I worked on a major effort to reform Texas schools that was led by Ross Perot and that was, for Texas, a very major effort to at least move our schools into the twentieth century, if not into the twenty-first century. I have remained very interested in the issue ever since, and have worked [on] all angles of the problem whether it was from the top or from the bottom. I've worked on state policy. I've worked on local policy, local reform efforts; and the more I work in the area the more I became convinced that one of the problems was that no one was really approaching the public education issue from a systems-wide approach, and understanding that it was a very complex animal, and that you couldn't fix it with some quick fix. I began to think about how to form a more comprehensive effort to reform public schools. About that time I met Bob Buford and learned what he was doing in his Leadership Network trying to transform large churches. The first time Bob and I discussed the subject, every time he would describe a situation involving churches I would say, Well, that's the same thing with respect to schools. He would talk about [how] pastors didn't learn this and didn't learn that in theology school, and I would say, Educators don't learn that in the school of education, etc. So I began to be very

interested in what Bob was doing, and he started coaching
me as to what he had been doing, and I began to utilize
some of those principles in building my Principals Network,
but at the same time I was also cognizant of the fact that
not only did you have to affect the delivery system but you
had to affect the political environment, you had to deal with
public opinion. So I began this concept of Just for Kids,
an effort that, to me, raises the essence of the problem: too
often no one is focused on the needs of the kids. [People] are
focused more on the needs of the education establishment,
whether it is the teachers union, or administrators, or this
group or that group; or it's this group that wants school
prayer, or this group that wants something else. Very seldom
are things really looked at from the viewpoint of the child,
so I began to develop this concept, and I've reached, I
think, the point that Bob Buford describes in his new book
(*Halftime*, 1994). I'm fifty-five years old, and I would really
like to devote a significant amount of my time going forward
to try and impact public education while remaining in the
law firm.

I hope to launch Just for Kids. I'm working on a book
that will be published in January that will set forth my
agenda of how we actually need to change public schools,
and I'll use that as a way to kind of launch Just for Kids. So
I'm really at the stage where I am trying to put this together,
and it's become more than just an idea, I'm moving now to
try to think about how to implement it. I would very much
appreciate your reaction to the concept, your criticisms, your
suggestions, understanding from your perspective what holes
you see in how I'm approaching it.

Peter Drucker

I know that you say in your proposals that vouchers aren't
going to save the school system, and you're absolutely
right because as I said to you at lunch, and I found that

Check Out Receipt

Greenbelt Branch
301-345-5800
www.pgcmls.info

Saturday, March 28, 2015 2:29:17 PM
76315

Item: 31268117751228
Title: Good leaders ask great questions : your f
oundation for successful leadership
Material: Book
Due: 04/18/2015

Item: 31268118000708
Title: A year with Peter Drucker : 52 weeks of c
oaching for leadership effectiveness
Material: Book
Due: 04/18/2015

Total items: 2

Thanks for visiting the Greenbelt Library. Our
regular hours are: Mon & Tues 1-9 pm, Wed- Fri
day 10-6 and Saturday 10-5. To renew by phone pl
ease call, 301-333-3111 or go to our website. w
ww.pgcmls.info

514

you agreed, vouchers are both inevitable and necessary if only to resolve that enormous inertia of the public schools establishment. You need to build a fire under public schools; vouchers are the fire. So the vouchers will help but they will not solve the problem. I think they are an essential ingredient because for the first time a voucher movement is shaking up that enormously inert and smug and self-satisfied inward-looking public school system.

What I missed in your proposal is what you have done about your study, which shows thirty or so public schools either in Texas or [elsewhere] in the country that do perform, even though they have lots of minority students, and even though they are in the inner city, for two reasons.

First, I'm very conscious that there is no greater sin than not to be able to *run with success*, and you may find a tremendous response to your success stories, and then one has to be able to say—to that principal who comes to you and says, What do I do?—"Here are a few things you can do," and you will have results because you have a model. And second, it is probably at least as important to identify the things not to do [as] it is to identify the things to do, because one of the basic causes of the mild performance is all of the things public schools shouldn't be doing.

But the important thing in your model is that you show that schools can have results despite all the adverse pressure on them. Let me say one of the things that I would expect to come out of that study of yours is: "What characterizes the schools that had results?" You said they are reasonably small schools. I think one of the things we have learned is that the great mistake we made after World War II is that we became enamored [of] the big schools. They can do so many things a small school can't do—they can teach typing, and they can teach the trombone—and so we built [them]. I believe that in elementary schools with more than three [hundred], four hundred pupils, the principal doesn't know the kids anymore, she doesn't know the parents anymore, and she doesn't know the teachers anymore. I don't know where the limits are for junior high schools, and for high schools, maybe a thousand but certainly no bigger. Maybe one of the conclusions is not that we burn down those huge big buildings, but that we build schools within schools, which were brought into New York, in the Bronx, and it worked like a charm.

So I would sit down in small towns with the high school principal, and with the five junior high school principals and perhaps six teachers. They will all tell you of the things that they cannot do, that they are totally defeated, and I think your first job will be to show that within those horrible restraints, *things can be done without having a lawsuit.*

Drucker-Buford-Luce Dialogue, November 2, 1994.

II. Reflect

- Schools are increasingly using technology both to teach technical skills and to provide teachers and students with access to resources that enrich the educational experience for children.
- Technological advances in education should allow more time for teachers to identify the strengths and deficiencies of students and to create individual time for each student to develop his or her strengths and shore up any disabling weaknesses.

1. SCHOOLS MUST BE ACCOUNTABLE FOR PERFORMANCE

A technological revolution . . . —computers and satellite transmission directly into the classroom—is engulfing our schools. It will transform the way we learn and the way we teach within a few decades. It will change the economics of education. From being almost totally labor intensive, schools will become highly capital intensive. . . . Above all, in the knowledge society, the school becomes accountable for performance and results.

Peter F. Drucker, Post-Capitalist Society, 1993, p. 194.

- The printed book, an innovation of the sixteenth century, resulted in a technological revolution in education in the West. A new technological revolution of learning and teaching is now in progress in education.

2. TECHNOLOGICAL REVOLUTION IN EDUCATION

In the West, the school underwent an earlier technological revolution several hundred years ago, brought about by the printed book. This earlier revolution holds important lessons for today—and lessons that are not [only] technological. One lesson: that embracing the new technology of learning and teaching is a prerequisite for national and cultural success and equally for economic competitiveness.

Peter F. Drucker, Post-Capitalist Society, 1993, p. 194.

- Education in the knowledge society is much too important to be left to the school alone. All institutions of society should be involved in continuous learning and teaching. Technology should be used as a tool to increase the effectiveness of education.

3. SCHOOLING MUST PERMEATE ALL INSTITUTIONS OF SOCIETY

Technology, however important and however visible, will not be the most important feature of the transformation in education. Most important will be re-thinking the role and function of schooling—its focus and purpose, its values. The technology will be significant, but primarily because it should force us to do new things rather than because it will

enable us to do old things better. . . . The real challenge
ahead is not technology itself. It is what we use it for. So far,
no country has the educational system [that] the knowledge
society needs. . . . We can define—albeit in rough outline—
the specifications for schooling and for schools which might
answer the realities of the post-capitalist society. . . . Here are
the new specifications:

The school has to provide universal literacy of a high
order—well beyond what "literacy" means today.

It has to imbue students on all levels and of all ages with
motivation to learn and with the discipline of continuing
learning.

It has to be an open system, accessible both to highly
educated people and to people who for whatever reason did
not gain access to advanced education in their early years.

It has to impart knowledge both as substance and as
process—what the Germans differentiate as *Wissen* and
Konnen.

Peter F. Drucker, Post-Capitalist Society, 1993, pp. 196, 198.

- A principals network can be a very useful forum for discussing
common problems faced by principals in different school settings
along with potential resolutions of these problems. The Luce
studies offer much hope. There are many dedicated principals
and teachers who are eager to improve educational results among
their students, and they can learn techniques from colleagues in
different school systems.

- To improve performance and results within school systems one
not only has to deal with principals, teachers, and students; one
also has to affect the political environment by dealing with
public opinion. Luce's focus is instructive here: take on the *fewest
political issues* that allow for the improvement of educational performance and results for kids.

III. Practicum-Prompts

Innovations in the form of best practice dos and don'ts can be diffused throughout the educational system. Some of these practices are available in Tom Luce and Lee Thompson's book *Do What Works: How Proven Practices Can Improve America's Public Schools* (2005).

Consider studies that report on best practices in corporate or public service education. Investigate the process of implementation in one of these organizations.

Do you have a performance and results-based system in your local school district? If not what can you do to help implement a performance and results-based educational system in your district? Discuss this with principals and teachers in your community.

How can you put to use in your organization the strategy illustrated by Tom Luce: finding and implementing best practices? Can you find and implement best practices for the professional and skills education that currently exists in one unit of your own organization?

Application of Peter Drucker's Methodology of Social Ecology

Introduction

Peter Drucker identified himself as a social ecologist, a person who attempts to spot major future trends in society that are discernible but not widely understood. For Drucker, this included identifying new institutions, understanding their function, understanding the disruptions they create for existing institutions, and thinking through how they could be made to function effectively and have a constructive impact on society. Formally his methodology has four steps:

(1) Identify an "emerging institution of society" (if possible study the first major institution in its category, for example, General Motors in the manufacturing sector and Willow Creek in the social sector).
(2) Determine the characteristics of the institution and what makes it effective.
(3) Organize this information.
(4) Finally, help executives of similar institutions become effective.

The mega-church was the last major institution that Peter Drucker identified and helped to make successful by diffusing information on leadership and management—directly, by working with Bob Buford's Leadership Network and church leaders; and indirectly, through Willow Creek's Global Leadership Summit. Drucker never wrote directly about innovation diffusion, yet as we see in steps 1 to 4 above, diffusion of innovation is a major purpose of his methodology. He wanted to diffuse innovation in the mega-church to those affected by emerging trends *and* help them to capitalize on those trends.

In this entry we take up the diffusion of innovation from Willow Creek to the world, which holds many lessons for executives in all sectors. The primary lesson for executives is that we all can learn from executives in all sectors. Church executives have, for example, learned from Jim Collins, Jack Welch, and Colin Powell how to scale up their operations. Business executives can learn from Bill Hybels and others at Willow Creek how to very rapidly capture the benefits of innovations in other sectors of the economy and in other parts of the world. Diffusion of innovations is one of the most important topics in management, especially during times of rapid change, and the Global Leadership Summit is one of the premier initiatives involved in the diffusion of innovation. For that reason, the majority of attendees at its conferences are professionals from business.

We also will observe Drucker's significant and surprising influence on the diffusion of innovation to executives throughout the global economy.

I. Read

Drucker said on numerous occasions:

> The most significant sociological phenomenon of the second half of the twentieth century has been the development of the large pastoral church.[68]

The direction of the trend in mega-churches that he identified in his 1999 book *Management Challenges for the 21st Century* (p. 29) was confirmed in a research study six years later by Hartford Seminary—*Megachurches Today 2005*—which reported that the number of Protestant churches in the United States with weekly attendance over 2,000 people was 1,210, nearly double the number five years previously (the approximate date of Drucker's book)[69] and eight times the number reported in 1980.[70] The trend continued apace. Using a different measure of size, the same authors reported in 2007 that there were over 7,200 Protestant churches with average weekly attendance over 1,000 in 2006.[71]

I once asked Drucker how he identified this emerging trend. His answer revealed his methodology:

> Because the knowledge society is creating a new and different constituency, which the likes of Rick Warren, senior pastor of Saddleback Community Church, and Bill Hybels, senior pastor of Willow Creek Community Church, recognized and organized, all I had to do was to take a look.

He saw what Bill Hybels was doing in Illinois and concluded that Hybels was organizing Willow Creek around the spiritual needs of knowledge workers, whose numbers were increasing rapidly. Drucker began in the mid-1950s to track the emergence of knowledge workers in the United States and continued to do so for a half century, and that is how he made the connection to the growth of the mega-church. He knew that the spiritual needs of knowledge workers were different from those of manual and service workers. When he understood the forces behind the development of these early mega-churches he simply made a projection from their growing importance and went to work on their needs for professional leadership and management, which are more sophisticated in mega-churches than in smaller churches.

As noted in Week 24, Bill Hybels was very early in demonstrating what was possible with effective marketing, leadership, organization, and management alongside good preaching. Hybels was one of thirty-three attendees at the Peter Drucker Summit Conference held at the YMCA Camp of the Rockies, in Estes Park, Colorado, on August 19–22, 1986, for pastors and church leaders. He was the most experienced pastor of mega-churches in attendance and was already engaged in sharing his experience and knowledge with others. Because Hybels was inundated with requests from pastors of other churches who wanted to learn about the Willow Creek approach, he decided to set up a separate organization, the Willow Creek Association, devoted exclusively to teaching others. It is an example of what is called the "teaching church," one devoted to the diffusion of innovation.

II. Reflect

- In his 1989 article "What Business Can Learn from Nonprofits," Drucker uses Willow Creek Community Church as an example of a nonprofit organization that knows its mission: *to reach the unchurched population in its geographical region.* He attributes the success of the church to Hybels's effort to determine through systematic market research just why unchurched people don't attend church, especially in a part of the country where church attendance is relatively high. Hybels then designed a new kind of church to meet the unmet expressed needs of this segment of the population.

1. WHAT IS VALUE TO THE NONCHURCHGOER?

The starting point for management can no longer be its own product or service, and not even its own market and its known end-uses for its products and services. The starting point has to be what *customers consider value.* The starting point has to be the assumption—an assumption amply proven by all our experience—that the customer never buys what the supplier sells. . . . This applies as much to a business as to a university or to a hospital. One example is the pastoral mega-churches that have been growing so very fast in the United States since 1980, and that are certainly the most important phenomenon in American society in the last [20] years. . . . And while all denominations have steadily declined, the mega-churches have exploded. They have done so because they asked, "What is value to a *nonchurchgoer?*" And they have found it is different from what churches traditionally thought they were supplying. The greatest value to the thousands who throng the mega-churches—and do so weekdays and Sundays—is a spiritual experience rather than a ritual, and equally management responsibility for volunteer service, whether in the church itself or, through the church, in the community.

> Peter F. Drucker, *Management Challenges for the 21st Century*, 1999, p. 29.

2. JIM MELLADO LEADS WILLOW CREEK ASSOCIATION

Jim Mellado,[72] a native of El Salvador, became president of the Willow Creek Association (WCA) through an unusual series of events involving Drucker's *HBR* article. After participating in the 1988 Summer Olympics in Seoul, South Korea, he attended the Harvard Business School. While at Harvard he read Drucker's article "What Business Can Learn from Nonprofits" and got excited about the portion of the article that deals with Willow Creek Community Church. Mellado attended one of their leadership conferences. A friend was taking a course in service management from Professor Leonard A. Schlesinger, then the George Fisher Baker Jr. Professor of Business Administration and associate dean of the school. Mellado's friend shared the article with Schlesinger and shared that Mellado knew all about Willow Creek. Schlesinger asked Mellado what should be done about the church and the material in his possession. Mellado responded, "You know we study six hundred cases at the Harvard Business School. I think it'd be cool if we did a case study on a church." [Mellado continues:] "So he looked at me and said, 'This is a great idea.' So . . . Len and I studied Willow and the evangelical landscape and of course that turned into the case study and teacher's note which became a part of the first-year mandatory curriculum at Harvard. And then other business schools around the country picked it up—I've taught it at Northwestern, University of Chicago, Stanford and many others."

"And so," Mellado explains, "that is how I met Bill Hybels and others, and then later graduated [from] Harvard in 1991. And by the way—this is a key point because it reflects later on the impact of the Summit [i.e., the Global Leadership Summit discussed later in this entry] in terms of philosophy—when I asked Len why—'Why are you interested in this case study? You're not a Christian.' And he said, '*Disequilibrium.* Most case studies are forgotten one minute after the class ends. If I can create disequilibrium in a class and leverage that energy for learning, they'll never forget that case study.'"

Bill Hybels started Willow Creek Association (WCA) in 1992, so when Mellado came to Willow in February 1993 to review the initial experience using the Harvard case study, Hybels suggested that Jim join this start-up organization. He explained that the mission of WCA was *to help every local church* realize its potential. Jim accepted the offer and in 1993 became president of WCA.

Jim Mellado–Joe Maciariello interview, October 11, 2011.

• Diffusion of innovation is the purpose behind the work of both Leadership Network and the Willow Creek Association—and thus the importance of Everett Rogers's work and his expert advice.[73]

3. MELLADO'S PATH FROM HARVARD TO DRUCKER TO WCA TO BOB BUFORD

Jim acknowledged the path from Harvard to Drucker
to Willow Creek Association and to Bob Buford. Jim
reports: "And because of Bob Buford I did get a chance
to meet Peter Drucker on a couple of occasions and have
some conversations with him, and thank him for writing
that article, which changed my life. And then I would go
to various Leadership Network events over time, which
Drucker sometimes conducted. The role they have played in
WCA has been very significant and informative . . . , just
the understanding that Leadership Network really is at the
tip of the innovation curve and serving others." [This is a
reference to early adopters from Everett Rogers's seminal
book, *Diffusion of Innovations* (2003). Rogers's book is the
standard reference on how innovations spread throughout a
social system.] "And then WCA is a little further down in
the early adopter category where we really get behind certain
innovations and spread them. And for the first fourteen,
fifteen years the way we were helping churches prevail was
by spreading the message, practices, strategies, and values
of Willow Creek Community Church and so people would
come to us because they were interested in learning more
about Willow Creek and how to replicate it in their setting."

Jim Mellado–Joe Maciariello interview, October 11, 2011.

- In 1992, the WCA attracted 250 member churches but had
more than fifty denominations represented. Rogers commented,
"That is a fascinating fact because it's proof that you're attracting
the progressives in those social systems. And so keep providing a product that will attract the innovators and early adopters
and that way you don't have to spend the tens of millions of
dollars to find them because they are coming to you." By 2014,

the WCA had trained more than two million leaders from more than ninety denominations.

4. WCA'S PREMIER EVENT—THE GLOBAL LEADERSHIP SUMMIT

The Global Leadership Summit (GLS) seeks, in part, to create *disequilibrium* but not for its own sake. The intent, in Mellado's words, is to create "voracious learners." He relates a story of one pastor who said after attending a GLS conference, "I came in, foot-stomping mad that Bono was at the summit because here's a rock star and he says profanity from time to time and I don't get it." And he said, "I walked in there questioning whether Bono was a Christian. When I left the session I was questioning whether I was a Christian." Mellado went on to relate that dynamic in his consultations with Everett Rogers.[74] "And that was the key characteristic that Everett Rogers told me was typical of these early adopter types. He said, 'You have a gift, Jim.' . . . 'You have a church, Willow Creek, that's acting like a magnet attracting all the innovator and early adopters from all the different denominational settings coming to Willow Creek wanting to find out what was going on. Because innovators learn best from other innovators they will travel the world, they will go wherever they need to go to learn from those innovators. . . . Companies spend millions and millions of dollars trying to try to find the innovator and early adopters in a system because they know if they adopt their product they open up the door to the vast majority. You have been given the gift of convening this powerful group of leaders who are the key to spreading new ideas and innovations to the majority that need them the most.'"

Jim Mellado–Joe Maciariello interview, October 11, 2011.

• I asked Mellado if the strategy behind GLS was to attract the early adopters and he said, "That is exactly what we're doing. We are targeting the progressives. And we call it the 'leadership core of the churches,' but the pastors are only 10 percent of the GLS audience. The vast majority of the people that come to the GLS are the leadership core; they're businesspeople and the teachers and the people working in government and the civic organizations. . . . They're carriers of influence in the church and in society." And this is how innovations get diffused throughout the society through the GLS.

• After numerous experiments with the diffusion of innovations Rogers found (*Diffusion of Innovations*, p. 272), "The adoption of an innovation usually follows a normal, bell-shaped curve when plotted over time on a frequency basis." [75]

III. Practicum-Prompts

What are some examples where *disequilibrium*, as described by Len Schlesinger and used in the Global Leadership Summit, can be used to accelerate the process of learning in your life and organization? Note: You may have to search outside your organization and industry to find these examples. For instance, I learned from prolific inventor Alan Kay of Xerox and Apple that he came up with many of his ideas for inventions while in the shower and actually had a shower installed for himself in the Xerox PARC research facilities.

What new opportunities do demographic shifts—shifts away from mechanical industries to knowledge-based industries; changes in the composition of the workforce, and the shift from national to regional to transnational economies—create for your enterprise? What operating and strategic assumptions must you discard?

Consider abandoning unjustifiable products and activities; set goals to improve productivity, manage growth, and develop your people. This will create resources to explore and undertake new innovations.

What are the risks of being an early adopter of innovations? What are the risks of being a laggard? Where is the optimal place for you and your organization to be on the innovation diffusion curve? Make plans to get there!

Developing Oneself from Success to Significance

Pursuing Significance After Success

Introduction

In the passage below Peter Drucker asks Rick Warren his age, and suggests that his priorities may change as he ages. Rick was fifty years old at the time. Drucker offers two different scenarios for how Warren might proceed: he could continue doing what he knows how to do extremely well or attempt to make another significant and innovative contribution to society.

Peter Drucker often said that "the best way to predict the future is to create it." We know that inventor Alan Kay of Apple said something very similar in a 1971 e-mail—that "the best way to predict the future is to invent it." [76] And Abraham Lincoln, our sixteenth president, is generally believed to have said, "The best way to create your future is to invent it."

Each of these three men followed his own advice. Drucker, as we know, codified the practice of management in two early books: *Concept of the Corporation* (1946) and *The Practice of Management* (1954). In 1968 Alan Kay designed the Dynabook, which became the precursor for Apple's laptops and iPads. [77] A little-known fact is that Abraham Lincoln was an inventor long before becoming president; he was the only president to hold a patent for one of his own inventions, a device to lift boats over obstacles like sandbars. [78]

Furthermore, the last sentence of Lincoln's historic Gettysburg Address, delivered on November 19, 1863, contains these words: "that this nation, under God, shall have a new birth of freedom." [79] The new birth of freedom had been brought about by the Emancipation Proclamation, formally issued on January 1, 1863.

I. Read

In the course of life, there are the great majority of successful people who have to change their direction at about age sixty. There is a very small minority of purpose-driven people who have to concentrate and not change and I can't tell you which you are going to be. The decision is going to come up. Decision is perhaps the wrong word—as you grow older, are you focusing more on doing the things that give *you* achievement and satisfaction and growth or more on the things that have an *impact outside of yourself?* Those are the decisions one has to make. And nobody can help you make them. But the one thing to avoid is splintering yourself, trying to do everything.

Drucker-Warren Dialogue, May 27, 2004.

II. Reflect

- As knowledge workers we now have much longer life spans and potential working lives. If we have achieved success in our professional lives and accumulated sufficient resources, we may be able to engage in new careers that offer the prospect of achieving additional significance for society and for ourselves.

1. THE SOCIAL ENTREPRENEURS

These are usually people who have been very successful in their first profession, as businessmen, as physicians, as consultants, as university professors. They love their work, but it no longer challenges them. In many cases they keep on doing what they have been doing all along, though they spend less and less of their time on it. But they *start* another and usually a nonprofit activity.

Peter F. Drucker, *Management Challenges for the 21st Century*, 1999, pp. 190–91.

- Drucker suggests that social entrepreneurs may be in the minority group of those who seek significance in endeavors differing from their primary profession.

2. THESE SOCIAL ENTREPRENEURS MAY BE IN THE MINORITY

People who manage the "second half" [of their lives] may be a minority only. The majority may keep doing what they are doing now, that is, to retire on the job, being bored, keeping on with their routine and counting the years until retirement. But, it will be this minority, the people [who] see the long working-life expectancy as an opportunity both for themselves and for society, who may increasingly become the leaders and the models. They increasingly will be the "success stories."

Peter F. Drucker, *Management Challenges for the 21st Century*, 1999, p. 191.

- A number of the examples in this book are from the lives of people whom Drucker guided to accomplish significant social innovations in the second half of their lives. But, these examples should not necessarily be taken as the norm. Most social contributions may be more ordinary, yet we can learn how to achieve significance in our lives from Drucker, Kay, and Lincoln as well as from those Drucker mentored.

- Drucker himself was able to continue his lifework in management while devoting a significant amount of time to stimulating
  the development of professional management in a large number
  of social sector organizations.

3. ON MAKING THE FUTURE

Managers must accept the need to work systematically on
making the future. But this does not mean the managers
can work for the elimination of risks and uncertainties. That
power is not given to mortal man. The one thing he or she
can try to do is to find, and occasionally create, *the right risk*
and to *exploit uncertainty.* The purpose of the work on making
the future is not to decide what should be done tomorrow,
but what should be done today to have a tomorrow.

We are slowly learning how to do this work systematically
and with direction and control. The starting point is
the realization that there are two different, though
complementary, approaches: Finding and exploiting the lag
between the appearance of a discontinuity in the economy
and society and its full impact—one might call this
anticipation of a future that has already happened. Imposing
on the as yet unborn future a new idea that tries to give
direction and shape to what is to come. This one might be
called *making the future that has already happened.*

> Peter F. Drucker and Joseph A. Maciariello, *Management:*
> *Revised Edition*, 2008, p. 113.

- These dreams may be fulfilled in a parallel career, doing volunteer work for an organization whose values you deeply share,
  or following a new full-time career as a social entrepreneur or
  serving society in political office or political appointments, as
  Tom Luce did.

III. Practicum-Prompts

As you grow older, you will have a decision to make. Will you focus more on the things that give you achievement and satisfaction and growth or on things that have an impact outside yourself?

Do you aspire to create a new future by exploiting a discontinuity that has already occurred (e.g., demographic changes or growth in importance of the social sector) before its full impact is generally recognized?

Do you aspire to "impose on the as yet unborn future a new idea that tries to give direction and shape to what is to come"?

Think through the steps required and the resources needed to plan a new future. Consult with others who can help you along. If it requires a long-term effort make sure you have the motivation and the help to see the idea through to completion: otherwise it is unlikely to hold you through the inevitable ups and downs of the process.

Work in an Area of Your Unique Contribution

Introduction

In Week 38 we learned that there are two ways to make the future happen:

(1) "Anticipation of a future that has already happened."
(2) "Imposing on the as yet unborn future a new idea that tries to give direction and shape to what is to come."

In this week's passage, Drucker illustrates these two separable but overlapping approaches to making the future happen by differentiating between Bob Buford's two major social innovations: Leadership Network and Halftime. Bob Buford has been very successful in both approaches. It took a lot of Buford's time, resources, and talent along with mentoring by Peter Drucker to accomplish his two major achievements.

Buford knew in the early 1980s that big churches are like supermarkets and are quite different from small churches, which are more like a corner grocery store. To be effective, leaders of megachurches must have more professional management expertise, which Buford set out to provide by sponsoring numerous training events and publications, including sessions with Drucker. Leadership Network is involved in the diffusion of innovation and best practices. It "exploited the lag between the appearance of a discontinuity in the economy and society and its full impact."

This was very much needed in 1984. Yet now many of the mega-churches have extensive global networks of their own to disseminate innovations. There is still innovation in Leadership Network, and it is primarily at the front of Everett Rogers's diffusion of innovation curve (Week 37).

Halftime, on the other hand, is an example of "imposing on the as yet unborn future a new idea that tries to give direction and shape to what is to come." Knowledge workers have longer working lives and sometimes accumulate sufficient resources to give them freedom to do what they only could dream about earlier. They too may consider the possibility of moving from success to significance by "imposing on the as yet unborn future a new idea that tries to give direction and shape to what is to come."

I. Read

Halftime is new and provides distinct answers to very new and distinct problems. Your writing and your work through the Halftime Institute [are] likely to be as [important as] or more important than your church activities. First, one leads from strength and in your work with churches, you are unique in one respect, and in others you are just one of many. In your Halftime work, you are unique and the leader, so this is basically *your area of unique contribution.*

Secondly, you have created an enormous audience. I don't know how big it is—in the millions—and you have created, OK, an awareness of the need for the successful to make themselves capable of enduring. We have some realities that are unprecedented—early success of people and a long life. You know Barbara Tuchman, the historian, who wrote the book about the fourteenth century?[80] She pointed out

that the creative people in the fourteenth century died at
age twenty-one and, therefore, they had to be successful at
age nineteen. And you understand a good deal about the
fourteenth century if you realize that they had to be at the
top in their adolescence and they behaved as adolescents.
Now, you are at the top, amazingly early, and it's not going
to change too much, not at nineteen [as for some in the
fourteenth century], but at twenty-nine a very large number
of people are pretty successful. And at the same time, they
don't die at age twenty-nine. They live to be eighty-five.
And this is something that you pointed out. You saw it first
and it is a unique contribution. Leadership Network and
Burning Bush [i.e., Buford's church planting activities] are
very different and new answers to old and existing problems.
What you are doing in your books and in Halftime [is]
very new—distinct answers to very new and distinct
problems—so there you are in a field by yourself.

Drucker-Buford Dialogue, January 12, 2003.

II. Reflect

- Knowledge workers often have two lives. In the first they make
  a living and perhaps achieve success, and in the second they seek
  significance after they fulfill their obligations to carry out their
  responsibilities to their families. It is at this point that they may
  be in a position to "make the future happen."

1. "THE CLOCK IS RUNNING"

You may have taken some vicious hits. A good share of men
and women never make it to halftime without pain. . . .
Even if your pain was slight, you are smart enough to see
that you cannot play the second half as you did the first. For
one thing, you don't have the energy you once had. Fresh out

of college, you had no problem with working fourteen-hour days and working extra hours on your days off. It was part of your first-half game plan, something almost inevitable if you hoped to succeed. But now you yearn for something more than success. Then there is the reality of the game itself: The clock is running. What once looked like an eternity ahead of you is now within reach. And while you do not fear the end of the game, you do want to make sure that you finish well, that you leave something behind that no one can take away from you. If the first half was a quest for success, the second half is a journey to significance.

> Bob Buford, *Halftime: Changing Your Game Plan from Success to Significance*, 1994, p. 27.

2. DRUCKER ON MAKING THE FUTURE HAPPEN

Decentralization, knowledge worker, management by objectives, privatization. . . . These terms, all coined by me, may go on being used for many years to come [as cited] while I was awarded the Presidential Medal of Freedom. But fame is not the only measure of life. I would like to keep this in mind and continue what I do now [Drucker made the future happen by bringing attention to and by helping to professionalize the management of the social sector of society, after codifying the practice of management in business].

> Peter F. Drucker, *My Personal History*, Article 27, 2009.

• Our unique contributions will be found at the point where our strengths and our values meet. We will know it by the enthusiasm we feel for our work and for our life. It may take a while before we identify our area of unique contribution and it becomes a reality.

- In Reading 3 George Bernard Shaw, cofounder of the London School of Economics and Political Science, a fervent socialist, Nobel laureate in literature, and winner of an Oscar for his work on the film *Pygmalion*, shares his view of success to significance.

3. "THIS IS TRUE JOY"

This is the true joy of life, the being used up for a purpose recognized by yourself as a mighty one; being a force of nature instead of a feverish, selfish little clod of ailments and grievances, complaining that the world will not devote itself to making you happy. I am of the opinion that my life belongs to the community, and as long as I live, it is my privilege to do for it whatever I can. I want to be thoroughly used up when I die, for the harder I work, the more I live. Life is no "brief candle" to me. It is a sort of splendid torch which I have got hold of for a moment, and I want to make it burn as brightly as possible before handing it on to future generations.

> G. Bernard Shaw, *Man and Superman: A Comedy and Philosophy*, 1903, pp. xxxi–xxxii.

- I went through a change of attitude toward my work in my early thirties. I then searched for an area that I thought both used my strengths and was more compatible with my values. I next obtained the amount of retraining that I needed to make the transition. I became more fulfilled as a result.

4. "WHAT ONE DOES WELL MAY NOT BE WORTH DEVOTING ONE'S LIFE TO"

Organizations, like people, have values. To be effective in an organization, a person's values must be compatible with the organization's values. They do not need to be the same, but they must be close enough to coexist. Otherwise, the person will not only be frustrated but also will not produce results. A person's strengths and the way that person performs rarely conflict; the two are complementary. But there is sometimes a conflict between a person's values and his or her strengths. What one does well—even very well and successfully—may not be worth devoting one's life to (or even a substantial portion thereof).

> Peter F. Drucker and Joseph A. Maciariello, *The Effective Executive in Action*, 2006, p. 132.

III. Practicum-Prompts

Buford says, "Success and significance offer many of the same benefits but one brings a better night's sleep and a true level of contentment." Does this statement resonate with you and your own life's path?

Drucker had the privilege of attending the lectures of John Maynard Keynes while Keynes was working on his masterpiece, *The General Theory of Employment, Interest and Money*. By listening to Keynes's Friday afternoon seminars Drucker seems to have had a revelation about his own life's interest. He states: "Keynes and his followers focused only on the behavior of commodities. I on the other hand was more interested in the behavior of people and the function of society."[81] Perhaps Drucker's story of how he sought to make a unique contribution in the first half of his working life resonates with you. If so, look for areas to apply your talents where you not only can make a contribution but also feel more content with the way you are using your life. This may take some time to materialize.

Is what you are doing in the first half something you have been trained for and do very well? Is it something you want to devote your whole life to? If not, can you with modest effort make a change?

The clock is running! What do you want to be remembered for? Are you making progress?

Individuals May Need a Process to Help Them Move from Success to Significance

Introduction

When people who have had great satisfaction with their careers retire and try to make the shift to significance, they often flounder and become discouraged. They may flounder for many reasons but usually part of the reason is that they do not understand themselves. They know they want more in life than travel and socialization, and they know they want to continue to make a contribution. Often the coordinators of programs do not completely appreciate or fully utilize these volunteers' talents. In this entry Peter Drucker and Bob Buford discuss the need for a process to help move such people from success to significance.

These people do not understand "what is in their box"—a term coined by Mike Kami, who was a student in Peter Drucker's seminar on innovation for executives at New York University in the mid-1950s while serving as director of long-range planning for IBM.

Bob uses the expression often when discussing the misuse of volunteers by leaders in churches and other social service organizations. Individuals and leaders must understand "what is in the box" of potential volunteers in order to use them properly.

I. Read

Here are the young entrepreneur friends of yours who got a company started, maybe married the bosses' daughters as so many of your YPO [Young Presidents' Organization] people do. I knew one of them. He took over a small company that makes plastic combs. He was one of the unhappiest men I knew. When he was about forty-six he sold the combs plant to a small conglomerate for an enormous amount of money, in part because the amount of money [it] offered was irresistible and in part [because] for him to go into a new technology required a lot of money that he didn't have, and he couldn't go public.

He didn't know what to do. I think he started in combs when he was sixteen, and five, six, seven years later he ran the plant, and then married the boss's daughter. She was a very nice woman. Whatever was in his in-basket each day drove him, and suddenly he was simply totally lost. He had never planned his own vacation. His wife, Mary, always did [the planning].

I think people like this need a great deal of help in three ways. One is simply identifying the possibilities. Another is thinking through what they are trying to do. And the third is preparation, training, and learning from others and from each other.

Activities for significance are by and large an enormous opportunity, but many people don't have the imagination to identify possibilities. They don't have anyplace to go to find out what is possible, what is available, how does one go about it, whom does one talk to?

Drucker-Buford Dialogue, January 9, 1989.

II. Reflect

- Individuals ready for halftime may not have the imagination it takes to find an activity that utilizes their strengths and fits their values. They may have to seek help from others. The Halftime Institute offers a process for moving from success to significance. I have presented below, as Reading 1, relevant portions from its website for you to consider.

1. A PROCESS FOR MOVING PEOPLE FROM SUCCESS TO SIGNIFICANCE

The Halftime Institute is a powerful, twelve-month experience to help successful people discover and live out their second-half life purpose. The Institute leverages a proprietary, collaborative, results-oriented process built on five core elements:

(1) An intensive two-day workshop at our Dallas, Texas, USA office, cohosted by Bob Buford and Halftime Executives—enrollment [is] limited to a small group of high-capacity peers.

(2) Personalized one-on-one executive coaching with a certified Halftime Coach.

(3) Monthly teleconferences with your Institute peers and coach to learn, network, and encourage.

(4) Ongoing contact with influential alumni—a network of mentors, information, and resources.

(5) Introductions to organizations making groundbreaking progress on issues that match your passions.[82]

- Those who follow their interests in social sector activities early in life by volunteering their services may confirm their instinct to serve in specific capacities. This in turn may provide the imagination and inspiration needed either to begin a second career or to become a social entrepreneur.

2. VOLUNTEER IN PREPARATION FOR THE SECOND HALF

There is one requirement for managing the second half
of one's life: to begin creating it long before one enters it.
When it first became clear thirty years ago that working-
life expectancies were lengthening very fast, many observers
(including myself) believed that retired people would
increasingly become volunteers for American nonprofit
institutions. This has not happened. If one does not begin
to volunteer before one is forty or so, one will not volunteer
when past sixty. Similarly, all the social entrepreneurs I
know began to work in their chosen second enterprise long
before they reached their peak in their original business. The
lawyer [Tom Luce] mentioned above began to do volunteer
legal work for the schools in his state when he was around
thirty-five. He got himself elected to the school board at age
forty. When he had reached fifty, and amassed a substantial
fortune, he then started his own enterprise to build and run
schools. He [was] still working near full-time as the lead
counsel in the very big company that, as a young lawyer, he
had helped found.

Peter F. Drucker, *Management Challenges for the 21st Century*,
1999, pp. 191–92.

- Executives of organizations who use volunteers should avoid
their strong instinct to employ these people in areas that executives believe are important to them without first determining
an individual's strengths and values. An individual must fit the
organization and the organization must fit the individual. The
idea is to release people in the area of their specific giftedness
and values.

3. RELEASING INDIVIDUAL ENERGY RELATED TO SPECIFIC GIFTEDNESS

Bob Buford on Discouragement over
the Misuse of Volunteers

Many times I find myself angry or impatient with the church, and when I do find myself angry or impatient it's because it limits itself . . . , and people who as seekers go once every ten years to church, and they see the church doing one of these narrow things and they say, well, that's all they're doing. That doesn't either heal me or it doesn't get me into some form of useful service. As Drucker's daughter has said, "Put me to work doing what I do best." They misuse people; they do not put people *in their area of giftedness but in the area of the needs* [emphasis mine] of the church. They're filling their own boxes, so to speak. . . . They do not focus on identifying people's individual giftedness and they misuse them. So one way to qualify this release of energy, to narrow it a bit, [is to say that] it's a *release of energy in the area of specific giftedness.*

Drucker-Buford Dialogue, January 9, 1989.

• Individuals and organizations may need help in thinking through just what they are trying to accomplish with the talent available; and in obtaining the necessary contacts and making the necessary preparations to do it.

III. Practicum-Prompts

Note the man in Drucker's first example—he sold his business and was lost because he did not have an outside interest. He should have asked himself, "What am I if not my business?" If the answer is "nothing" he should have taken action to develop an outside interest. How would you answer the question "What am I if not my business?"

If you want to make a contribution in the second half of your life you must understand how to manage yourself to make the right contribution. So, "What is in your box?" What are your strengths and values? Where are you finding an outlet for them? Is your job a sufficient outlet for your talents and values?

Do you have a desire to move from success to significance? What is your plan? Have you begun to take action? What help do you need? You may want to read Bob Buford's book *Halftime* and consider the Halftime Institute if you think it can help you along the way.

If you are blocked from pursuing your genuine passions in life because of your duties to your family, then consider a parallel career volunteering your services to an organization where your services are needed and where your talent is released for the good of others.

Where Do I Really Belong?

Introduction

It is not uncommon in life to remain in a position that doesn't fulfill your greatest desires even though you are successful in that position. People, especially family members, may depend on you. A sense of duty sets in. This is one of the reasons why the advent of the knowledge society creates such opportunity. With proper planning it may be possible to retire or to leave your position and continue to fulfill your responsibilities at home, which may have receded with the passage of time. The danger is that during the first half of life you lose the vision of what would make you truly happy. It may be a time in which you have to rekindle your imagination.

The other issue is that you may have a nagging sense that you are doing damage to yourself and maybe to the organization by staying put. In addition, your unhappiness may be doing damage to others, such as members of your family, because of what is going on at your work. In this case you should try to find a way out.

We deal with both of these important topics in this week's entry. And they both start by asking the question: Where do I really belong?

I. Read

But here is a whole generation of people, young in terms of life expectancy, vigorous, well-to-do, with lots of energy, a fair amount of time, more energy than time, and a desire to grow. They do not want to retire clipping coupons! They do have cultural interests, but in the sense of doing and contributing. The old-line cultural interests of the nineteenth-century cultured gentlemen are somewhat obsolete, displaying a strong smell of mothballs. Your friends hop over the world, and are back the same day. But they are built that way; they are activists. Not all of them. Some will probably retire at age forty-five to a life of cultured leisure, but I don't think they will enjoy it. First, they are all workaholics, and will have withdrawal symptoms if they don't do things, and second they need the stimulus, but at the same time they are not terribly satisfied with putting in three or five hours a week sitting on a board discussing the budget. They want to make a contribution over and above the money, and are trained and equipped to do it. But they don't really know how to organize themselves for it. They don't know where to put their energies. They don't know things you have learned— that basically one has to concentrate; if you splinter yourself you will not accomplish much of anything. And I don't think they understand how to apply the basic lessons they have learned in their business [to the new opportunity]. In their community activities, the ones I see are very short term, largely because they are not exposed to the demands of the organization. I think they need a great deal of guidance and help and leadership to find out "Where do I really belong?" It may be at that church.

Drucker-Buford Dialogue, January 3, 1989.

II. Reflect

- A number of difficulties face knowledge workers during their long working lives. Many become bored by the daily grind of their careers. This boredom may result in seeking another job or in a complete change: a second career, perhaps in a social sector organization. Second, many find significance as long-term, sustained volunteers in church or other social sector organizations. This is what Drucker refers to as a *parallel career*. Finally, there are those who achieve success in their careers and by doing so accumulate significant financial resources. Then they try to make a difference with their lives by solving social problems. These are the *social entrepreneurs*. Bob Buford is an exemplar in this last category.

1. DRUCKER ON BUFORD'S JOURNEY FROM SUCCESS TO SIGNIFICANCE

It is the story of obscure beginnings, the story of a boy who, barely eleven, after his father's early death, had to take on the burden of being the "man of the family"; a story of great hardships, of vision and determination, of sorrow and success. While this is in itself interesting, what is unusual is that Bob Buford is one of the very few people I know who, still barely in his teens, thought through what his strengths were. . . . Even more incredible is that, when he realized that what the Lord had made him capable of doing well was very different from what he *wanted* to do, he had the intellectual honesty and courage to say to himself, "It is my duty and mission to put to work what I am good at, rather than what I would love to do." To this, of course, Bob owes his success as entrepreneur and businessman. But—and this, in my experience, is truly unprecedented—Bob never forgot his original vision and never surrendered his original values to success. He refused to write off his youthful ambition as a child's dream. He kept his nose to the grindstone and yet never lost sight of the hills. . . . [T]hese stories [in this book *Halftime*] are the stories needed by those who have reached the middle of their life span, the ones who have become successful in the sense that they have achieved—just as the very young need the stories of heroic exploits and of romantic love.

Peter F. Drucker, Foreword to the First Edition, in Bob Buford, *Halftime*, 1994, pp. 18, 22, 23.

2. WHY DON'T I BELONG HERE?

If the thoughtful answer to the question "Where do I belong?" is that you don't belong where you currently work, the next question is why? Is it because you can't accept the values of the organization? Is the organization corrupt? That will certainly damage you, because you become cynical and contemptuous of yourself if you find yourself in a situation where the values are incompatible with your own. Or you might find yourself working for a boss who corrupts because he is a politician or because she is concerned only with her career. Or—most tricky of all—a boss whom you admire fails in the crucial duty of a boss: to support, foster, and promote capable subordinates.

The right decision is to quit if you are in the wrong place, if it is basically corrupt, or if your performance is not being recognized. Promotion itself is not the important thing. What is important is to be eligible, to be equally considered. If you are not in such a situation, you will all too soon begin to accept a second-rate opinion of yourself.

Peter F. Drucker, *Managing the Non-Profit Organization: Principles and Practices*, 1990, pp. 195–96.

• Often it is our duty to do what we are good at even though we would rather do something else. There may come a time when we are mostly free of our obligations and can do what we truly love.

3. CAREER PLANNING AND PROTECTING AGAINST INEVITABLE SHOCKS

One way in which a manager can prepare to minimize the effects of this kind of experience [identity crisis, setbacks in a career, boredom, etc.] is through planning. "Take a little control over your career. . . . I am talking about career planning in the sense of: What do I have to learn, what are my strengths, how can I build on them, where do I belong, do I really belong in this company? One must take the responsibility of asking oneself these questions from time to time, and acting on the answers. . . . You build on your strengths so they stand you in good stead when you need them."

There is something else, even more important. "Develop a genuine, true, major outside interest. Not a hobby, a genuine interest, which permits you to live in a different world, with different peers whose opinions are meaningful to you." . . ."[O]ne needs a true outside interest, not just water-skiing. It not only develops your strengths, it helps to protect you against the inevitable shocks."

Peter F. Drucker, quoted in John J. Tarrant, *The Man Who Invented the Corporate Society*, 1976, pp. 101–2.

III. Practicum-Prompts

Follow Drucker's advice: "Develop a genuine, true, major outside interest. Not a hobby, a genuine interest, which permits you to live in a different world, with different peers whose opinions are meaningful to you."

Engage in career planning by clearly identifying your strengths and values. Continue to develop your strengths. Early in life, plan for a second career. Consider volunteer work that may itself provide the transition to a second career or provide enough fulfillment to achieve significance.

What will it take in your career to allow you to seriously explore opportunities to move from success to significance, assuming you cannot do so where you are right now?

If you are beginning to develop a second-rate opinion of yourself, ask yourself, Why? If it has been brought on by conditions in your current employment, seek to get out and find a place where your talents are appreciated, where you have equal opportunity to develop yourself.

Halftime Is an Entrepreneurial Enterprise

Introduction

Bob Buford met with Peter Drucker and tested his idea of making the transition from running Leadership Network to developing Halftime. He also tested with Drucker his ideas for helping gifted executives move from success to significance. Buford said, "It is an important transition that I am making, or considering, or testing. It involves working through others, or working at serving others, helping them to use their own gifts rather than being an individual performer." Drucker then proceeded to create the context and the specifics involved in this transition.

The resulting book and institute were created to help people make the transition from their primary careers to new endeavors. There are lessons for us to learn from the process Buford went through with Drucker. He first tested the *concept*. Once the concept appeared sound, he entered into *concept development* and only then into *full-scale development*.

This particular innovation ranked very high with Drucker because it addressed two major objectives of his own. First, Halftime attempted to develop the unused or underutilized talents and energy of knowledge workers. Second, many of the pursuits of

"Halftimers" do result in social innovations that improve the lives of others in society. Both the process of developing people and the end objective of social innovation are at the core of Drucker's lifework.

I. Read

But the new project [Halftime] which you are beginning to kind of grope toward involves a very different clientele [from Leadership Network], and bluntly a more interesting clientele, because what you are doing for the ministers is helping them do more effectively something they have already tried to do. What you are trying to do in the other venture is very much helping people to do what they really should be doing, and want to do. Leadership Network is very largely a *managerial task*. The new one is a very large *entrepreneurial task*.

Halftime is more like an entrepreneurial start-up company. One person sees a white space opportunity, raises angel capital, and builds a small team to complement the single entrepreneur. The sequence is something like:

(1) Aha! An idea.
(2) Launch a test market based on a hypothesis about customer value added.
(3) Prove the hypothesis—that there is a customer.
(4) Scale up—extend and expand with debt and risk capital.

Drucker-Buford Dialogue, January 9, 1989.

II. Reflect

• The very existence of civil society in the United States is a result of social innovation. Consider The Salvation Army, CARE, Alcoholics Anonymous, the Red Cross, the Girl Scouts, World Vision, and more. In 2011 there were over 1.6 million tax-exempt, 501(c)(3) organizations in the United States. These included private charities, private foundations, and religious institutions. Clearly social innovation is one of the distinguishing characteristics of American society.[83]

1. SOCIAL INNOVATION IS BADLY NEEDED IN SOCIETY

Management is the new technology (rather than any specific new science or invention) that is making the American economy into an entrepreneurial economy. It is about to make America into an entrepreneurial society. Indeed there may be greater scope in the United States—and in developed societies generally—for social innovation in education, health care, government, and politics than there is in business and the economy. And again, entrepreneurship in society—and it is badly needed—requires above all application of the basic concepts, the basic *techne,* of management to new problems and new opportunities.

> Peter F. Drucker, *Innovation and Entrepreneurship*, 1985, p. 18.

- Drucker affirms a "white space" for people who want to move from success to significance. This is the *opportunity set* that exists among relatively successful people. Drucker advises a narrow focus to help people find opportunities for utilizing their gifts in their community.

- Knowing one's strengths, weaknesses, and values helps to narrow one's set of opportunities for second-half entrepreneurial projects. If you know your strengths and core values, you will know what opportunities you should reject. Drucker's list of sources of opportunity for innovation should help you.

2. SYSTEMATIC INNOVATION

"Successful entrepreneurs do not wait until 'the Muse kisses them' and gives them a bright idea; they go to work."

Systematic innovation means monitoring seven sources for innovative opportunity. The first four sources lie within the enterprise, whether business or public-service institution, or within an industry or service sector. The *unexpected*—the unexpected success, the unexpected failure, the unexpected outside event; the *incongruity*—between reality as it actually is and reality as it is assumed to be or as it "ought to be"; innovation based on *process need*; *changes in industry structure or market structure* that catch everyone unawares. The second set of sources for innovative opportunity involves changes outside the enterprise or industry: *demographics* (population changes); *changes in perception, mood,* and *meaning*; *new knowledge*, both scientific and nonscientific.

The lines between these seven source areas of innovative opportunities are blurred, and there is considerable overlap between them. They can be likened to seven windows, each on a different side of the same building. Each window shows some features that can also be seen from the window on either side of it. But the view from the center of each is distinct and different.

> Peter F. Drucker, July 12, "Systematic Innovation," *The Daily Drucker*, 2004.

• The movement of the United States toward the European social welfare state will fail unless we become an entrepreneurial society devoted especially to solving society's most difficult problems. This will require actions from many people who care enough and who follow Drucker's basic precepts. Our fifty-year experiment with the War on Poverty has not addressed the root causes of poverty in the United States. Many of our social sector institutions, as we have discussed in this book, have been more effective in addressing the root causes and the symptoms of poverty. Yet the social sector is still much smaller than government. Much more social innovation is necessary by people in all three sectors.

3. WILL THE SUCCESSOR TO THE WELFARE STATE BE THE ENTREPRENEURIAL SOCIETY?

The emergence of the entrepreneurial society may be a major turning point in history. . . . [The modern welfare state] may survive despite the demographic challenges of an aging population and a shrinking birthrate. But it will survive only if the entrepreneurial economy succeeds in greatly raising productivities. We may even still make a few minor additions to the welfare edifice, put a room here or a new benefit there. But the welfare state is past rather than future—as even old liberals now know. Will its successor be the Entrepreneurial Society?

Peter F. Drucker, *Innovation and Entrepreneurship*, 1985, p. 265.

III. Practicum-Prompts

Pick your favorite charity or philanthropic organization. Who founded it? What were the motives of the founder? Where did these motives originate? What can you learn that can inspire and help you to go and do likewise?

Think about possibilities for social entrepreneurship that fit your strengths and values. This is a significant exercise that requires considerable thought, but out of it may come an idea for your second-half project. In his *Innovation and Entrepreneurship*, Drucker identifies seven potential sources or ideas for innovation. Four of these potential sources are the unexpected event, incongruities in processes or products, missing steps in an existing process, and changes in market structure. These four are identified within existing organizations.

Three others—changing demographics, changes in the perceptions of consumers, and innovations based on new knowledge—are found outside organizations. You may want to follow up on these sources of innovation. They have proved to be very helpful in generating opportunities for social entrepreneurship.

Many social entrepreneurs follow the pattern of Tom Luce, described in Week 36. Tom's interest in education led him to run for a school board while he was still engaged in a successful law practice. He then started his own social enterprise, the Principals Network. Tom's approach allowed him to learn before he made a more significant commitment to education reform. This process has a high probability of success.

A Catalyst to Help People Manage Themselves and Move to the Second Half of Their Lives

Introduction

Bob Buford discussed the idea of developing a systematic program that would help move people from success to significance for the benefit of society. In Drucker's body of knowledge this subject falls under the category "managing oneself."

The subject of managing oneself first appeared in published form as chapter 6 (pp. 161–96) of Drucker's *Management Challenges for the 21st Century* (1999). A portion of that chapter, with the same title, appeared in the March–April 1999 issue of *Harvard Business Review* (*HBR*) and was later reprinted as an *HBR* Classic in January 2005. It is also available on Amazon.com as a pamphlet.

I later worked with Peter Drucker to integrate additional aspects of managing oneself with themes raised by Bob Buford in his best-selling book *Halftime* (1994). These additional themes were then integrated into *The Effective Executive in Action* (Drucker and Maciariello, 2006). The basic ideas are synthesized below.

Managing oneself requires that we understand what we are good at—that is, our strengths. Next, managing oneself requires that we understand our values. Third, we should understand how we work best—alone or with others as a team. Are we good at taking on unstructured tasks, or do we do better when we understand the structure at the outset? This leads us to understand where we are likely to make the biggest and most satisfying contribution. Once we understand our strengths, our values, how we work, and areas in which we are likely to make a contribution, we are ready to manage ourselves in the second half of our lives. These of course are the same specifications for managing our first half but the answers probably will be different.

I. Read

Yes, I see a number of possibilities, which are not
necessarily mutually exclusive, but are not the same thing.
I see something . . . unique where you and the organization
become the catalyst that enables these people—young
successful people, who are not entirely satisfied with
running their business, and are not consumed with it—to
find out their sphere of community service. With some
help, people can check out possibilities, organize things,
and come together a couple of times a year to talk through
what is worthwhile doing, what are the needs, where
are the people who can be trusted? Out of this maybe
half a dozen different directions will emerge, focused
on the individuals' needs, and on the needs of their own
community.

I don't think you can do more than two or three
initiatives; one is probably the best focus, where you feel
that a small group working together can make a difference.
You have a personal interest in [it], and you feel the need is
great. You should start an initiative with a *very narrow focus*.
I think otherwise it won't work. Maybe you build a small

group in which you know the people, they trust you, and they follow you.

Drucker-Buford Dialogue, January 9, 1989.

II. Reflect

- Drucker recognized that knowledge workers often have working lives of fifty years or more. Drucker himself enjoyed a working life closer to seventy years! But a number of difficulties face knowledge workers during their long working lives. Many become bored by the daily grind of their careers and simply want to make a shift to opportunities that eliminate boredom. This requires that they "repot" themselves.

1. MANAGING ONESELF: REVOLUTION IN SOCIETY

Managing Oneself is a *revolution* in human affairs. It requires new and unprecedented things from the individual, and especially from the knowledge worker. For in effect it demands that each knowledge worker think and behave as a Chief Executive Officer. It also requires an almost 180-degree change in the knowledge workers' thoughts and actions from what most of us still take for granted as the way to think and the way to act.

The shift from manual workers who do as they are being told—either by the task or by the boss—to knowledge workers who have to manage themselves profoundly challenges social structure. For every existing society, even the most "individualist" one, takes two things for granted, if only subconsciously: Organizations outlive workers, and most people stay put. Managing Oneself is based on the very opposite realities: Workers are likely to outlive organizations, and the knowledge worker has mobility. In the United States *mobility* is accepted. But even in the United States, workers outliving organizations—and with it the need to be prepared for a Second and Different Half of One's Life—is a revolution for which practically no one is prepared. Nor is any existing institution, for example, the present retirement system.

> Peter F. Drucker, *Management Challenges for the 21st Century*, 1999, p. 194.

• Boredom leads to an underutilization of our talents. It can also lead to destructive behaviors such as drug or alcohol addiction. So, while it may be risky to attempt a move from success to significance, it may be more risky not to—especially for people who are experiencing boredom on the job.

2. MANAGING ONESELF: THE SECOND HALF

What to Do with the Second Half of One's Life

Knowledge workers are able physically to keep on working into old age, and well beyond any traditional retirement age. But they run a new risk: they may become mentally finished. What's commonly called "burnout," the most common affliction of the forty-something knowledge worker, is very rarely the result of stress. Its common, all too common, cause is boredom on the job. Managing oneself therefore requires that you prepare for the second half of your life.

> Peter F. Drucker and Joseph A. Maciariello, *The Effective Executive in Action*, 2006, p. 137.

• Parallel careers and second careers are normally easier transitions than the transition to social entrepreneurship. Discouragement often sets in when people flounder while trying to make the shift from success to significance. They flounder for many reasons— partly because they do not understand themselves and their values and partly because of the difficulties of finding opportunities that match their talents and sustain their motivation.

3. THE MOVE FROM SUCCESS TO SIGNIFICANCE CAN OCCUR IN A NUMBER OF WAYS

Significance need not be a 180-degree course change.
Instead, do some retrofitting so that you can apply your gifts
in ways that allow you to spend more time on things related
to what is in *your box* [your strengths and values]. And to do
it in such a way as to reclaim the thrill of that first deal.

Bob Buford, *Halftime*, 1994, p. 89.

III. Practicum-Prompts

Begin thinking of a parallel or second career you might find fulfilling. List areas of work that interest you, including work as a volunteer in a nonprofit organization.

Set goals now outside your current position. Begin to pursue these goals.

The book *Halftime*, and the Halftime Institute try to help individuals who are seeking to move from success to significance by matching their giftedness with the right social opportunity. With the help of expert mentoring during the process of transition, Halftime seeks to fulfill a need in the social or private sector of society by using an innovative process *that matches your giftedness and values to pressing problems.* Consider this approach or similar ones, especially if you are trying to become a social entrepreneur.

Character and Legacy

Our Society in the United States Has Lost Its Sweetness

Introduction

In this entry we get a glimpse into Peter and Doris Drucker's grand adventure when they arrived in America in 1937. It was a challenging but exciting time for the newlyweds. They found severe economic challenges but enjoyed the hospitality and warmth of the American people. The Druckers treasured this "sweetness" in Americans as they faced their new life during hard economic times.

A great sadness for Peter Drucker as he aged was observing the demise of this spirit among Americans. This observation was probably the source of his fervor for the work of the social sector in America, fueling his energy and inspiring his long-term commitment. It is the reason he considered the work of the Peter F. Drucker Foundation for Nonprofit Management, and its successors and like-minded organizations, so important to a healthy and hopeful America.

He saw great promise in the results achieved by many effective nonprofit organizations to which he gave his time and effort. There was little question in his mind that the best hope for our central cities and for the solution of our numerous social problems was in the work of effectively managed social sector institutions.

The Druckers gave tangible form to their values and concerns for America. Their lives are testimonies of service. Peter worked quietly and tirelessly to improve the management of all institutions of our society. He was acutely aware of the great promise and problems of America. He loved this country. He was devoted to developing people, a major part of his legacy. And as I write, his life partner, Doris Drucker, is 102 years old. She is constantly pushing others to think about new possibilities opened up by advances in information technology, genetics, and space exploration—to name a few areas that interest her. She has served as a volunteer for most of her adult life. Her experiences in Germany during World War I and during the period of the rise of the Nazis to power soured her on Germany. Her autobiography, *Invent Radium or I'll Pull Your Hair: A Memoir* (University of Chicago Press, 2004), is a testimony to a courageous life full of contributions.

I. Read

It is almost fifty-six years since Doris and I came to the United States from England in [the] spring of 1937. We arrived during probably the deepest point of the Great Depression. The economy collapsed again in 1936, after a very feeble recovery. The economy was in worse shape in 1937 than in most European countries, but the fight to adapt here in a very, very depressed economy provided us with tremendous excitement. I think all of you know *economically* the New Deal was a failure. We were here in the midst of a totally depressed economy. But *the society was strong*, and it was a country with almost no envy or very little, and was basically decent, with a great deal of sweetness in it. What bothers me today is not the economy. What bothers me in this country is that our society today has lost its sweetness. It's sour, terribly sour, and I think that this isn't anything government can do much about, or is likely to do very much about. In fact the way we are going, government is making the sourness worse.

It's only by this kind of activity in the nonprofits, this kind of self-respect shown to people, this kind of initiative in solving our most difficult social problems that I think we can make this a society again. That is why I think it is the work all of us associated with the Drucker Foundation for Nonprofit Management are doing, or are interested in doing, that is so tremendously important, and why our efforts and results to date are so deeply moving.

> Peter F. Drucker, address to Advisory Board of the Drucker Foundation for Nonprofit Management, November 8, 1992.

II. Reflect

- Some of our major cities have large segments that resemble war zones. There were over five hundred homicides in Chicago in 2012, in the predominantly drug-infested, gang-dominated, economically deprived areas of the South Side. A major part of the United States' third-largest city is uncivilized. The per capita murder rate is higher in Chicago than in underdeveloped Mexico City and São Paulo. Solutions seem especially elusive in Chicago. Civilizing our three largest cities—New York, Los Angeles, and Chicago—is one of the major challenges confronting our society. Per capita homicide rates in our three biggest cities are many times greater than those in Tokyo, London, and Paris.[84]

1. CIVILIZING THE CITY

"Only the social sector can create what we now need, communities for citizens."

Civilizing the city will increasingly become top priority in all countries—and particularly in the developed countries such as the United States, the United Kingdom, and

Japan. However, neither government nor business can
provide the new communities that every major city in the
world needs. That is the task of the nongovernmental,
nonbusiness, nonprofit organizations. Only the social sector
can create what we now need, communities for citizens—
and especially for the highly educated knowledge workers
who increasingly dominate developed societies. One reason
for this is that only nonprofit organizations can provide
the enormous diversity of communities we need—from
churches to professional associations, from organizations
taking care of the homeless to health clubs. . . . The
nonprofit organizations are also the only ones that can
satisfy the second need for effective community, the need for
effective citizenship. The twentieth century saw an explosive
growth of both government and business—especially in the
developed countries. What the twenty-first century needs
above all is equally explosive growth of the nonprofit social
sector in building communities in the newly dominant
social environment, the city.

> Peter F. Drucker, June 24, "Civilizing the City," *The Daily
> Drucker*, 2004.

- "Drucker calls The Salvation Army 'by far the most effective
  organization in the U.S. No one even comes close to it in respect
  to clarity of mission, ability to innovate, measurable results, dedication and putting money to maximum use.'"[85]

2. COMPASSION AND CULTURE

It would be wrong, but not far wrong, to say that all
management theory is a footnote to Peter Drucker. Asked
which management thinker had most influenced him, Bill
Gates is supposed to have replied, "Drucker, of course."
But in recent years the world has discovered that he is

more than just a "management guru," as he's often called;
he's a social theorist out to defend the human spirit. If
The Salvation Army wants to save the world—they are a
match made, perhaps literally, in heaven. No other major
organization in the U.S. has more faithfully understood
and implemented Peter Drucker's management ideas. Just
what is The Salvation Army? It enjoys near-universal name
recognition and inspires great public trust, but few people
actually know what it is, or even what it does. . . . The
Army is difficult to pin down. It is occasionally referred to
as a church, but more often as a charitable service provider.
It is probably best described as a Methodist/Holiness
ministry that came into being to deal with the worst
casualties of the early industrial era.

Gwen Purtill, *Compassion and Culture*, 2002, pp. 1, 2.

• Do you understand why Drucker believed the United States has
lost its "sweetness"? And do you now understand why Drucker
believed that our major problems in the United States are social
and not economic?

3. SPIRITUAL VALUES

"Only compassion can save—the wordless knowledge of my
own responsibility for whatever is being done to the least of
God's children."

Society needs a return to spiritual values—not to offset the
material but to make it fully productive. However remote
its realization for the great mass of mankind, there is today
the promise of material abundance or at least of material
sufficiency. Mankind needs the return to spiritual values, for
it needs compassion. It needs the deep experience that the
Thou and the I are one, which all higher religions share. In

an age of terror, of persecution, and mass murder, such as ours, the hard shell of moral callousness may be necessary to survival. Without it we might yield to paralyzing despair. But moral numbness is also a terrible disease of mind and soul, and a terrible danger. It abets, even if it does not condone, cruelty and persecution. We have learned that the ethical humanitarianism of the nineteenth century cannot prevent man from becoming beast. Only compassion can save—the wordless knowledge of my own responsibility for whatever is being done to the least of God's children. This is knowledge of the spirit.

The individual needs the return to spiritual values, for he can survive in the present human situation only by reaffirming that man is not just biological and physiological being but also spiritual being, that is creature, and existing for the purposes of his Creator and subject to Him. Only thus can the individual know that the threat of instant physical annihilation of the species does not invalidate his own existence, its meaning and its responsibility.

> Peter F. Drucker, *Landmarks of Tomorrow*, 1959, 1996, pp. 264–65.

III. Practicum-Prompts

Are you involved in a civic organization that is active in strengthening the social bonds that help create more healthy communities in the United States?

Make sure to check out the mission and performance of nonprofit organizations that you support financially. They are not all equally effective. For example, salaries paid to top executives in these organizations range from very modest to exorbitant.

Check out the salaries of the top officers of the charities and the percentage of budgets devoted to fund-raising. Finally, check out their results. You should use these data to make decisions on your giving patterns to nonprofit organizations.

Seek to promote and elect local public officials who understand the limits of government and the need for public and private co-operation to further strengthen the work of our social sector and public sector institutions.

The Power of Purpose

Rick Warren on Peter Drucker

Introduction

Rick Warren's development of purpose-driven ministries is an elaboration and application of Peter Drucker's work on the "theory of the business" (THOB). This is at the heart of Drucker's management system for all organizations. The THOB for an organization requires executives to specify the mission of the organization, how the mission fits assumptions about the specific environment facing it, and the core competencies possessed by it that are needed to accomplish its mission in the specific environment. (Drucker and Maciariello, *Management: Revised Edition*, 2008, pp. 85–96).

A valid THOB is a hypothesis about the mission required to succeed given the realities faced by an organization in a specific business or domain; its core competencies or knowledge requirements; and its own set of values. Without a valid theory, the organization simply will not produce what its customers and potential customers consider value. A THOB is a hypothesis that is tested against reality each day.

The major difference in the THOB between for-profit and nonprofit organizations is that "mission" is primary for nonprofits. These organizations are driven primarily by the values being pursued. For-profit organizations, on the other hand, must place customers in a primary position, and competencies and mission must be aligned to customer values in a specific market. The title thus changes from "THOB-driven" to "mission-driven" as we move from for-profit to public service organizations. Everything else remains the same.

If the organization has assembled the right competencies to fulfill its mission, it then needs to align members up and down the organization, using effective communications. Each person should be able to identify his or her objectives based on the THOB.

The testimony below by Rick Warren on the power of purpose is followed by readings from Drucker that specify the requirements for a valid THOB. Warren substitutes "purpose" for "mission," but the terms mean the same thing.

I. Read

Every organization and every life is driven by something. Some organizations are driven by personalities; the key leader is the driving force. What happens when that leader dies, or moves, or retires, or takes another position? We have all seen what happens. Personality-driven organizations are very unstable.

One thing Peter taught is that charisma is extremely dangerous. The most charismatic leaders of the twentieth century, Peter taught over and over, were Mao, Stalin, and Hitler. And they weren't very helpful, but they had a lot of charisma. So you don't want a personality-driven organization; you want a purpose-driven organization.

Peter says [that] the first thing you should ask is, "What is my mission? What is my business?" And you clarify that.[86] . . . Why purpose-driven?

First, purpose builds *morale*. One reason why Saddleback is the second-largest church in America—82,000 names on our church roll—is [that] we have high morale. Second, purpose *reduces conflict* in organizations. When you are all in the same boat together nobody has time to rock it; you don't get distracted; you know your purpose. Third, purpose provides *vision*. "Where there is no vision the people perish." [87] Fourth, purpose allows *concentration*. You don't have time to do everything in life, and the good news is [that] not everything in life is worth doing anyway. Quoting Peter, "Concentrate on the smallest number of activities that will focus on the greatest productivity." [88] Focus on your core competencies; focus on your strengths; don't major in the minors. If you want your life to count, if you want your organization to count, the secret is to focus. Do a few things well. Fifth, purpose provides *a system of evaluation*.

At Saddleback we align everything we do around the mission. We budget on purpose, we structure on purpose, we staff on purpose, we schedule on purpose, we program on purpose, we plan on purpose, and I preach on purpose. Everything is purpose-driven because Peter taught me that it all starts with mission. You must know your mission.

> Rick Warren, Keynote Address on Drucker Alumni Day,
> Claremont, California, November 13, 2004. The author
> transcribed and edited this from an audiotape. It is used by
> permission of Rick Warren.

II. Reflect

- Purpose-driven missions can provide vision, lead to higher morale, promote concentration, and provide the basis for a system of evaluation.

1. THEORY OF THE BUSINESS

"A clear, simple, and penetrating theory of the business rather than intuition characterizes the truly successful entrepreneur."

A theory of the business has three parts. First, there are assumptions about the *environment* of the organization: society and its structure, the market, the customer, and technology. The assumptions about the environment define what an organization is paid for. Second, there are assumptions about the *specific mission* of the organization. The assumptions about mission define what an organization considers to be meaningful results—they point to how it envisions itself making a difference in the economy and society at large. Third, there are assumptions about the *core competencies* needed to accomplish the organization's mission. Core competencies define where an organization must excel in order to maintain leadership. For example, West Point, founded in 1802, defined its core competence as the ability to turn out leaders who deserve trust.

Every one of the great business builders we know of— from the Medici and the founders of the Bank of England down to IBM's Thomas Watson . . . —had a definite idea, had, indeed, *a clear theory of the business* that informed his actions and decisions. A clear, simple, and penetrating theory of the business rather than intuition characterizes the truly successful entrepreneur, the person who builds an organization that can endure and grow long after he or she is gone.

Peter F. Drucker, July 1, "Theory of the Business," *The Daily Drucker*, 2004.

- A mission must be tested against reality. No mission lasts forever!

2. COMMUNICATE AND TEST ASSUMPTIONS

"The theory of the business is a discipline."

The theory of the business must be known and understood throughout the organization. This is easy in an organization's early days. But as it becomes successful, an organization tends increasingly to take its theory for granted, becoming less and less conscious of it. Then the organization becomes sloppy. It begins to cut corners. It begins to pursue what is expedient rather than what is right. It stops thinking. It stops questioning. It remembers the answers but has forgotten the questions. The theory of the business becomes "culture." But culture is no substitute for discipline, and the theory of the business is a discipline.

The theory of the business has to be tested constantly. It is not graven on tablets of stone. It is a hypothesis. And it is a hypothesis about things that are in constant flux— society, markets, customers, technology. And so, built into the theory of the business must be the ability to change itself. Some theories are so powerful that they last for a long time. Eventually every theory becomes obsolete and then invalid. It happened to the GMs and the AT&Ts. It has happened to IBM. It is also happening to the rapidly unraveling Japanese *keirtsu*.

> Peter F. Drucker, July 4, "Theory of the Business," *The Daily Drucker*, 2004.

- Core knowledge is essential for achieving one's mission. And knowledge is perishable. Therefore it must be updated continuously as needed.

3. CORE COMPETENCIES

"Knowledge is a perishable commodity."

A valid definition of the specific knowledge of a business
sounds simple—deceptively so. . . . It takes practice . . . to
do a knowledge analysis well. The first analysis may come
up with embarrassing generalities such as: our business
is communications, or transportation, or energy. But of
course every business is communications or transportation
or energy. These general terms may make good slogans for
a salesmen's convention; but to convert them to operational
meaning—that is to do anything with them (except repeat
them)—is impossible. But with repetition the attempt to
define the knowledge of one's own business soon becomes
easy and rewarding. . . .

   Few answers moreover are as important as the answer to
this question. Knowledge is a perishable commodity. It has
to be reaffirmed, relearned, re-practiced all the time. . . .
But how can one work at maintaining one's excellence unless
one knows what it is? Every knowledge eventually becomes
wrong knowledge. It becomes obsolete. . . . "Have our recent
experiences borne out our previous conclusions that this
particular ability gives us leadership?"

> Peter F. Drucker, *Managing for Results*, 1964, pp.
> 117–18.

• If members of an organization are secure in their own mission
  and it is aligned with the mission of the organization, which is
  also a socially constructive mission, there is no danger of following a charismatic leader such as Rick Warren.

III. Practicum-Prompts

Has your organization slipped from being a star performer to being in crisis? What does this say about your organization's mission or its theory of the business?

Establish an ongoing group for communicating your mission throughout your organization and for testing your organization's mission or theory of the business.

If your mission or theory of the business is obsolete, do not procrastinate. Rethink the assumptions and core competencies on which it is based and update the premises on which your organization is operating.

Stay focused on the things your organization must do extremely well in order to succeed in carrying out its mission. Support those areas of required excellence by offering continuing education.

The Stewardship of *Affluence* and the Stewardship of *Influence*

Introduction

The final recorded consultation between Rick Warren and Peter Drucker took place on May 27, 2004, following the unparalleled success of Rick Warren's book *The Purpose Driven Life*, and his course "40 Days of Purpose." The course, as its title indicates, guides individuals and churches through the book in forty days. Hundreds of thousands of churches worldwide have used the program, and it helped start a number of new ministries, including very effective ministries within the California prison system and within Chinese factories. The success of the book and of the course created unexpected affluence and influence for Rick and Kay Warren.

The question they were confronted with was "How should we deal with this unexpected affluence and influence?" The path they chose is an exemplary one.

Yet, as Peter Drucker saw the explosive growth in the ministry at Saddleback, he continued to be concerned about designing a structure to accommodate and not stifle this kind of growth while protecting the health and welfare of Rick and Kay Warren. The church was growing not only at its home in Lake Forest, California, but at

a number of satellite congregations in the United States and around
the world. Warren himself had trained over 100,000 ministers in the
purpose-driven paradigm. Meanwhile outreach ministries to people
with HIV-AIDS were growing in Africa, as were efforts to help developing nations. In addition, the church was being asked to produce
publications to support its global efforts. Without proper organizational structure and competent people, such overwhelming growth
could have easily toppled the organization and the Warren family.
These problems are not unique but are a regular occurrence in business organizations that experience explosive growth.

I. Read

Peter Drucker

I think the balance between maintaining *internal dynamics*
and *institutionalization* is a very delicate one. And eventually,
one always institutionalizes or one dissipates, but you haven't
reached that point where there's reason for you to rush it.

Rick Warren

You kept talking to me about our networked movement and
finally two things happened that affected the movement
when the book became so successful. First, it gave me a lot of
notoriety that I did not ask for. Pastors knew me but I wasn't
known by anybody else, because of our low-key approach to
expansion. Then all of this money started coming in. Kay
and I began to pray about the *stewardship of affluence* and the
stewardship of influence. What do I do with the fame and what
do I do with the money? I don't think God gives a pastor
fame and money to satisfy his own ego. So if it's not for me,
what am I supposed to do with it?

Kay and I made four decisions. First, we decided we
would not change our lifestyle one bit. We're not buying a
bigger house; we're not buying a second house. I still drive

a Ford. Second, I stopped taking a salary from the church. Third, I added up all that the church had paid me for twenty-four years and I gave it all back. I did that when *Time* magazine wrote an article on me a couple of months ago. They always expect pastors to be in it for money. I said, No—actually I now serve my church for free. And we are reverse-tithing. Kay and I now live on 10 percent and give away 90 percent. So, nobody can accuse me of doing this for money. Fourth, we set up three foundations to fund the PEACE Plan. That's why I sent you a little bit of material about the PEACE Plan.

Part of the plan is to expand the movement, not just by turning around old churches, but by starting new churches. As I was traveling around the world, I began to think, "What are the greatest opportunities for the church?" "Where could the church make a difference?" I now feel that God is calling me to basically lead a new Reformation. And this is a reformation not of belief but of action. The first Reformation was a reformation of "What does the church believe?" This is more about "What does the church do?"

The PEACE Plan is an acronym for: *P*lant churches. *E*quip servant leaders. *A*ssist the poor. *C*are for the sick. *E*ducate the next generation in developing nations. As I was traveling around the world, I began to think, "What are the greatest opportunities for the church?" "Where could the church make a difference?" The PEACE Plan is intended to get the church outside of itself and reach the unchurched.

We are testing the prototype for the Plan right now. There are three thousand unreached people groups around the world with no church of any denomination, no Catholic, no Protestant, nothing; three thousand unreached people groups. Most of these groups have less than half a million people in them. They consist of a language group within a culture within a culture. As we looked at these, we took the world and divided it up into ten segments. We have sixty-four groups that are going out to fifty-one different people groups this year. They're testing our new PEACE Plan.[89]

II. Reflect

• Rick and Kay Warren decided to use their affluence and influence to begin engaging in nation-building, bringing organizations from all sectors of the world together to assist needy nations to achieve higher levels of health, education, and welfare and lower levels of crime and corruption. The pilot project in Rwanda is now expanding to other nations around the world.

1. TIMELINE FOR PEACE PLAN

The decade-long Timeline for the PEACE Plan in Rwanda from the vision to the pilot to its extension to other nations of Africa is as follows:[90]

(a) 2003—The vision for the PEACE Plan was developed as Rick Warren met with a fifty-member African church whose members were caring for twenty-five orphans who were victims of AIDS.

(b) 2004—President Paul Kagame of Rwanda invited Rick and Kay Warren to help Rwanda become a purpose-driven nation, thus inaugurating the PEACE Plan in 2005.

(c) 2005—The PEACE Plan began uniting all churches in Rwanda.

(d) 2008—20,000 people gather in Amahoro Stadium (one of the few sanctuaries run by the United Nations where people could go in 1994 to escape the Rwandan genocides, which led to the murder of approximately 800,000 people).

(e) 2012—23,000 people from all Christian denominations gather to celebrate Rwanda's first National Thanksgiving Day.

(f) 2013—Rwandan PEACE board meets to establish other purpose-driven churches in seven other African nations: Burundi, Democratic Republic of Congo–East, Uganda, Tanzania, Malawi, South Sudan, and Nigeria–Niger Delta.

- Warren learned the benefits of piloting the PEACE Plan from the teachings of Peter Drucker.

2. PILOTING

Neither studies nor market research nor computer modeling are a substitute for the *test of reality*. Everything improved or new needs, therefore, first to be tested on a small scale, that is, it needs to be *piloted*. The way to do this is to find someone in the enterprise who really wants the new. As said before, everything new gets into trouble. And then it needs a champion. It needs somebody who says, "I am going to make this succeed," and who then goes to work on it. And this person needs to be somebody whom the organization respects. This need not even be somebody within the organization. A good way to pilot a new product or new service is often to find a customer who really wants the new, and who is willing to work with the producer on making the new product truly successful. If the pilot test is successful—if it finds the problems nobody anticipated, whether in terms of design, of market, of service—the risk of change is usually quite small. And it is usually also quite clear where to introduce the change and how to introduce it, that is, what entrepreneurial strategy to employ.

Peter F. Drucker and Joseph A. Maciariello, *Management: Revised Edition*, 2008, p. 403.

- Drucker was a persistent advocate of piloting innovative projects on a small scale before introducing them on a larger scale. This is especially important for complex government programs that often experience many unintended consequences of well-intended legislative programs. Public administrators should learn from experience, and piloting is a way to gain experience.

3. "MAKE SURE *YOU WILL NOT* LEARN FROM EXPERIENCE"

Surely one of the main reasons for the success of so many of the New Deal programs was that there had been "small-scale" experiments in states and cities earlier—in Wisconsin, for instance, in New York State, or in New York City, or in one of the reform administrations in Chicago. And the outstanding administrators of the New Deal program—Frances Perkins at Labor, Harold Ickes at Interior or Arthur Altmeyer at Social Security—were all graduates of such earlier small-scale experiments. . . . *"Make sure you will not learn from experience"* is the prescription for non-performance in public administration.

Peter F. Drucker, *Towards the Next Economics and Other Essays*, 2010, p. 158.

4. COMMON MISTAKES IN INTRODUCING CHANGE

There are a few common mistakes in doing anything new. One is to go from idea into full-scale operation. Don't omit testing the idea. Don't omit the pilot stage. If you do, and skip from concept to full scale, even tiny and correctable flaws will destroy the innovation. . . . Another common mistake is to patch-up the old rather than to go all out for the new. . . . It is one of the critical tasks of the executive to know when to say, "Enough is enough. Let's stop improving. There are too many patches on those pants."

Peter F. Drucker, *Managing the Non-Profit Organization*, 1990, p. 70.

III. Practicum-Prompts

Make sure the innovative projects in your organization have passionate advocates, like President Paul Kagame of Rwanda and the Warrens, to see these projects through the inevitable difficulties they will face during their design, implementation, and marketing phases.

You may have a customer who, like President Kagame, genuinely seeks a new product or service you are developing and is willing to work with you to make the product or service a success. Take advantage of the offer.

Examine one innovative change that has recently been introduced in your organization. What unintended consequences, positive or negative, occurred? What have these consequences taught you about the process of introducing change?

What innovative change would you like to introduce within your organization? Do you have enough enthusiasm for the project and its potential to give it everything you have to make it successful? Are you also able to accept failure and say "Enough is enough" if after repeated attempts you fail?

Week 47

Making Ourselves Useful to Others and to Ourselves

Introduction

Peter Drucker's article "The Unfashionable Kierkegaard" was first published in the *Sewanee Review* (1949, pp. 587–602). He considered it his finest essay.[91] It was republished in 1993 as chapter 30 in his book of essays *The Ecological Vision*.[92] In his introduction there, he explains why the article was written, and why it was so important to him (p. 426): " 'The Unfashionable Kierkegaard,' was thus written as an affirmation of the existential, the spiritual, the individual dimension of the Creature. It was written to assert that society is not enough—not even for society. It was written to affirm hope."

We share immensely in the products of prosperity, including better health care and longer life expectancies. These lead us to a whole new range of conditions and choices, especially the opportunity to move from success to significance. Peter Drucker knew that a tipping point took place in the twentieth century, and that professional management made this progress possible. And yet it created existential challenges and, for him and others, loneliness.

Peter Drucker focused on the nonprofit sector because he believed the predominant need in our culture is "existential." The "products of prosperity" do not create fulfillment, and this becomes very apparent as we achieve prosperity. There are many illustrations that fame and fortune do not in themselves create fulfilling lives. For example, Lee Iacocca, not long after leaving the automobile business, said in his book *Straight Talk* (Bantam, 1988, p. 36), "Here I am in the twilight years of my life still wondering what it's all about. . . . I can tell you this: Fame and Fortune is for the birds."

Drucker knew very well that existential purpose provides meaning and hope for life and fulfills the need Iacocca is expressing. But many find the term "existential" difficult to comprehend. For Drucker it was a universal need for inspiration, effectiveness, and hope. While these needs are important to fulfill throughout our lives, they are especially important to fulfill as we try to make the transition from success to significance. Fulfilling these needs is a way to face the reality of our own mortality.

We saw in Reading 3 of Week 39 that George Bernard Shaw, who preferred to call himself an atheist,[93] found happiness and hope in his life—or, as he expressed it, "pure joy"—by totally using himself up in the pursuit of doing whatever he could to make himself useful for the benefit of the community. He was clearly looking beyond himself for fulfillment as he faced his own mortality. He was fulfilling an existential need in his life by pursuing worthy humanitarian goals.

I. Read

My *work* has indeed been totally in society. But I knew at once, in those far-back days of 1928, that my *life* would not and could not be totally in society, that it would have to have an existential dimension which transcends society. Still my work has been totally in society—except for this essay on Kierkegaard.

Though Kierkegaard's faith cannot overcome the awful loneliness, the isolation and dissonance of human existence, it can make it bearable by making it meaningful. The

philosophy of the totalitarian creeds enables man to die.
It is dangerous to underestimate the strength of such
a philosophy; for, in a time of sorrow and suffering, of
catastrophe and horror, it is a great thing to be able to die.
Yet it is not enough. Kierkegaard's faith, too, enables man
to die; but it also enables him to live. Faith is the belief that
in God the impossible is possible, that in Him time and
eternity are one, that both life and death are meaningful.
Faith is the knowledge that man is creature—not
autonomous, not the master, not the end, not the center—
and *yet responsible and free* [italics mine]. It is the acceptance
of man's essential loneliness, to be overcome by the certainty
that God is always with man, even "unto the hour of our
death."

> Peter F. Drucker, December 25, "Human Existence in
> Tension," *The Daily Drucker*, 2004.

II. Reflect

- Drucker believed that an important existential need of person-
  hood is to integrate the two dimensions of existence—life in the
  present and life in the spirit.

1. SIMULTANEITY OF LIFE IN THE SPIRIT AND LIFE IN THE FLESH AND MEANINGFULNESS OF EACH FOR THE OTHER

Kierkegaard stands squarely in the great Western tradition
of religious experience, the tradition of St. Augustine and
St. Bonaventure, of Luther, St. John of the Cross, and Pascal.
What sets him apart, and gives him this special urgency
today, is his emphasis on the meaning of life in time and
society for the man of faith, the Christian. Kierkegaard is
"modern," not because he employs the modern vocabulary
of psychology, aesthetics, and dialectics—the ephemeral

traits which the Kierkegaard boom ballyhoos—but because he concerns himself with the specific disease of the modern West: the falling apart of human existence, the denial of the simultaneity of life in the spirit and life in the flesh, the denial of the meaningfulness of each for the other.

> Peter F. Drucker, "The Unfashionable Kierkegaard," 1949, p. 601; reprinted in *The Ecological Vision*, 1993, p. 438.

- Mega-churches can do things that smaller churches and social sector institutions cannot do. For example, they can offer opportunities for meaningful service in the community while also providing a greater sense of purpose for the volunteer. This can bring hope for the development and formation of these two kinds of community, which are badly needed in America.

2. THE MEGA-CHURCH HELPS FULFILL DRUCKER'S DESIRE FOR INSPIRATION, HOPE, AND EFFECTIVENESS

Drucker, Vince Barabba[94] points out, appreciates the use of bigness. "There are certain things an elephant can do that a mouse cannot do," he says. Through its very large scale—as many as 10,000 members per institution—the mega-church can provide social services of all kinds. Re-creating the American community eroded by the acids of modernity, the large pastoral church is realizing Peter Drucker's dream of a new postmodern social form based on commitment instead of conformity.

> Jack Beatty, *The World According to Peter Drucker*, 1998, p. 186.

- Most churches of significant size cannot fully utilize their lay talent, so placement in volunteer community service work is indispensable for the growth and development of the person as well as the church. Such work provides people with an opportunity to be useful both to themselves and to others.

III. Practicum-Prompts

Looking for *salvation by society* has failed systematically in totalitarian states and in western democracies. We know that the promises of totalitarian states, which seek to convince the individual that all that exists is the state, and that identification with the interests of the state is the primary purpose of life, are false. The cradle-to-grave social programs of some western democracies create the belief that the state will provide for all needs of its citizens. This belief too is false. We must find meaning and purpose in life for ourselves. This means we must deal with life in tension—the here and now and the hereafter. Have you made progress in rationalizing these two dimensions of life?

Are you making yourself useful to others? How?

Drucker considered "The Unfashionable Kierkegaard" to be his finest essay. Why do you think he considered it his best? (See http://www.druckersociety.at/index.php/peterdruckerhome/texts/the-unfashionable-kierkegaard.)

Think through Drucker's statement of belief in his article on Kierkegaard: "Faith is the belief that in God the impossible is possible, that in Him time and eternity are one, that both life and death are meaningful." Can this provide you with hope for the present and for the future?

What Do Leaders Stand For?

Introduction

Integrity in leadership inspires trust and commits leaders to viewing the world as it is and not as they wish it to be. Effective leaders go to work on the priorities of the *organization* rather than on those tasks they thought were going to dominate their tenure. Leaders therefore must be continuous learners and surround themselves with experts in areas necessary to solve present and emerging problems.

Leadership is responsibility. Accordingly, strong leaders select subordinates who can help them fulfill their responsibilities. Some of these subordinates may be difficult to deal with, in which case the leaders must make sure to get the contribution needed. Salmon P. Chase was appointed secretary of the treasury by President Lincoln when Lincoln took office in 1861. Chase was successful in establishing a national bank, and what later became known as the Internal Revenue Service. Each time Chase did not get his way, he resigned, and Lincoln had to humble himself and ask him to return—because Lincoln needed Chase's ability to raise money to finance the Union's effort in the Civil War. The fourth time Chase tendered his resignation, in 1864, however, Lincoln shocked him and accepted it. By then, Chase had made his contribution to the war effort and his talents, and the contention he caused, were no longer needed.

Chase had what Lincoln called "the presidential fever" and in 1864, while serving in Lincoln's cabinet, actively campaigned for the presidential nomination—a clear act of insubordination. It was a shock to many when Lincoln, after years of tolerating Chase's insubordination, appointed him as the sixth Chief Justice of the United States (to succeed Roger Taney, who had died in October 1864). Lincoln was known for his magnanimity, but some of the civil rights legislation passed during his first term were sure to be tested in the courts, and he also knew that Chase was opposed to slavery. Lincoln knew that in Chase he had a defender of emancipation. Again, Lincoln asked, "What can this man do?" and it was quite a lot!

I. Read

Let me say bluntly, I don't believe in leaders. All the talk about leaders is dangerous nonsense. It is a cop-out. Forget about it. And I am very unhappy that after the twentieth century, with Hitler, Stalin, and Mao as the great leaders— maybe the greatest leaders in hundreds of years—I'm very unhappy that anybody wants leaders with those examples of misleaders so fresh. We should be very much afraid of leaders. We should ask, "What do they stand for? What are their values? Can we trust them? Not "Do they have charisma?" We've had too much charisma the last hundred years. Truman was the best president the United States has had, and the one who accomplished the most. He was not a high-profile leader—on the contrary, everybody underrated him, including himself. So I have very little use for the superman CEO. As for the high salaries, I think they are a scandal. J. P. Morgan, who was not averse to money, said in 1906 that any organization, any company in which the top people got more than twenty times what the average people got is mismanaged. He refused to invest in it. That is still a good rule, and by that rule I wouldn't invest in a great many of our companies. . . . By the way, the CEOs I have known— and I have known quite a few—did not see themselves as supermen. They built a team. They were team leaders.

> "Management Guru Peter Drucker," WBUR for National
> Public Radio, December 8, 2004.

II. Reflect

- What a leader stands for is much more important than specific personality traits. Some very effective leaders maintain a very low profile.

1. ARE THEY THE RIGHT OR WRONG VALUES?

The question is not whether to have values—every human being has them and every human group, however organized, does too. The question is: Are they the right values or the wrong values? Are they values that give life or values that give death? And, as Lord Griffiths reminds us—and as all recent research validates—it is not the business whose values are pure opportunism, pure greed, pure selfishness and self-aggrandizement that does best, not even in the very short run. It is the business that has a set of values that enables it and the people who work for it to respect themselves, to have pride, to grow, that is the winner in the marketplace.

> Response by Peter F. Drucker to Brian Griffiths (Lord
> Griffiths of Fforestfach), "The Business of Values," 2005,
> p. 55.

- Outrageous salaries and bonuses are indicative of values that promote greed. Speaking of high salaries and bonuses Drucker argued, "Few top executives can even imagine the hatred, contempt and fury that has been created—not primarily by blue collar workers who never had an exalted opinion of the 'bosses'— but among the middle management and professional people." [95]

2. VALUES THAT HELP ORGANIZATIONS WEATHER ADVERSITY

It is also the business with these values, the business that believes it exists to contribute rather than just to take, that will weather adversity. In good times, values may look like an ornament. They may be treated—and frequently are— as something we can indulge in as a "nice little extra." It is in times of adversity, in times that try a man's soul, that values are a necessity. For if the right values are absent at such a time, there is no incentive for human beings to walk the extra mile, to make the extra commitment, to do the hard work of rethinking strategy, of trying new things, of rebuilding. People won't do that just for money. They will do it only if they believe that what their business does and can do matters. And it is this belief that is instilled by the right values.

> Response by Peter F. Drucker to Brian Griffiths (Lord Griffiths of Fforestfach), "The Business of Values," 2005, p. 55.

- Establishing and nurturing the right values is a primary result area, along with fulfilling the mission of the organization and developing its people. Values, like nutrients that sustain an organism, also sustain an organization.

- The high salaries and bonuses paid to top executives undermine values that are needed by an organization to successfully weather periods of adversity.

3. VALUES ARE COMMITMENTS TO ACTION

Preachments aren't values—they are good intentions,
at best. . . . And then one has to ask: What is the one
decisive, most unambiguous action that most expresses an
organization's values? It is the *personnel decision.* In every
organization—and not only in a business—the true and real
values of its leaders are judged by who gets promoted, who
gets fired, who gets rewarded and who gets punished. People
decisions are highly visible. . . . People in an organization,
even a very big one, are not abstractions. They are real. . . .
Even in organizations that are only medium-size a good
many people, including people pretty high up, often cannot
judge the rationale, let alone the wisdom, of this or that
business decision. But they always can—and do—judge the
values underlying a people decision.

> Response by Peter F. Drucker to Brian Griffiths (Lord
> Griffiths of Fforestfach), "The Business of Values," 2005,
> p. 56.

• Two of America's great presidents, Abraham Lincoln and Harry
Truman, surrounded themselves with strong subordinates. They
were not afraid of or intimidated by strength in subordinates.
Rather, they gloried in these subordinates, praised them, and
promoted those who could help shoulder the tremendous responsibilities of being president of the United States, especially
during extraordinary times.

III. Practicum-Prompts

What are the espoused values in your organization? How do they
match up with the values in action? Realize that perfect congruence
is elusive.

Are the values in your organization life sustaining? If not, what can you and others do to change them?

Are your values strong enough to weather adversity? Are they fair-weather values? If they are not strong enough, what can be done to fortify or correct them?

Are the people decisions in your organization life giving? Are they fair? Do they inspire confidence? If not, what can you do to alter them?

You Become a Person by Knowing Your Values

Introduction

Working where your values are not compatible with those of the organization puts you in a very uncomfortable, strained position. You must make a choice between keeping a job in which you feel increasingly disconnected from who you are, from your core values, and searching for a new position in which your core values will be in sync with the new organization.

If you surrender your values you end up losing your self-esteem. This progressive discomfort can haunt you every day as you sense your own core values eroding at the workplace. And it is difficult to separate your values at the workplace from those in the rest of your world.

There is a way to tiptoe around these value differences, but if they persist long enough they will wear down your own self-respect and make those nearest to you uneasy or distressed by the continuous changes in your personality as you lose the confidence you once had.

I. Read

I've known this wealthy man for many years. He was at my lecture in April of last year in Pennsylvania. He's a very generous man. Afterward he and I had dinner together. I looked at him as he talked about money, and money, and money. I said to him, Why do you talk of money so much? What difference does it make? What are you doing it for? He said, "What else is there to be interested in?" I said, How old are you now? Fifty-six. *Do you feel your life makes any sense?* He looked at me and said, "Funny you ask me that because I asked myself that this morning. It doesn't. It makes no sense." Of the very wealthy people I've known— and I've known quite a few—most of them are desperately unhappy people. But, fortunately they're rare. The rest of us do grow up.

You become a person by knowing what your values are, what you contribute, and it is outside yourself. It is better to give than to receive but you have to know what to give. It is very difficult to know.

> Peter Drucker–Bob Buford Dialogue, Estes Park, Colorado, August 9, 1993.

II. Reflect

- Drucker defined the existential side of life—becoming a person and what it entails. As a person he learned that "it is more blessed to give than to receive." That was a part of *his* value system. He thought it more difficult to know what to give than to know that one should give.

1. WHAT TO DO IN A VALUE CONFLICT?

"I saw no point in being the richest man in the cemetery."

There rarely is a conflict between a person's strengths and the way that person performs. The two are complementary. But there is sometimes a conflict between a person's values and the same person's strengths. What one does well—even very well—and successfully may not fit with one's value system. It may not appear to that person as making a contribution and as something to which to devote one's life (or even a substantial portion thereof).

I too, many years ago, had to decide between what I was doing well and successfully, and my values. I was doing extremely well as a young investment banker in London in the mid-1930s; it clearly fitted my strengths. Yet I did not see myself making a contribution as an asset manager of any kind. *People, I realized, were my values* [emphasis mine]. And I saw no point in being the richest man in the cemetery. I had no money, no job in a deep Depression and no prospects. But I quit—and it was the right thing. Values, in other words, are and should be the ultimate test.

> Peter F. Drucker, *Management Challenges for the 21st Century*, 1999, p. 178.

• There may be a conflict between what you do well and your own values as a human being. You need to bring this to a resolution; otherwise you will suffer in the "mirror" test.

2. WHAT ARE MY VALUES?

To be able to manage oneself, one has to know: "What are my values?" In respect to ethics, the rules are the same for everybody and the test is a simple one—I call it the "mirror test."

As the story goes, the most highly respected diplomatist of all the Great Powers in the early years of the 20th century was the German ambassador in London. He was clearly destined for higher things, at least to become his country's foreign minister, if not German federal chancellor. Yet, in 1906 he abruptly resigned. King Edward VII had then

been on the British throne for five years, and the diplomatic
corps was going to give him a big dinner. The German
ambassador being the dean of the diplomatic corps was to
be the chairman of that dinner. King Edward VII was a
notorious womanizer and made it clear what kind of dinner
he wanted—at the end . . . naked prostitutes as the lights
were dimmed. And the German ambassador resigned rather
than preside over this dinner. "I refuse to see a pimp in the
mirror in the morning, when I shave."

This is the mirror test. What ethics requires is to ask
oneself: "What kind of person do I want to see when I
shave myself in the morning, or put on my lipstick in the
morning?" Ethics, in other words, are a clear value system.
And they do not vary much—what is ethical behavior in
one kind of organization or situation is ethical behavior in
another kind of organization or situation.

Peter F. Drucker and Joseph A. Maciariello, *Management:
Revised Edition*, 2008, p. 488.

- To work in an organization that has a value system that is incompatible with your value systems forces you into compromise and
  loss of self-esteem.

3. WHAT IS THE VALUE SYSTEM OF MY ORGANIZATION?

To work in an organization the value system of which
is unacceptable to a person, or incompatible with [him
or her], condemns the person both to frustration and to
nonperformance. . . . A brilliant and highly successful
executive found herself totally frustrated after her old
company was acquired by a bigger one. She actually got a
big promotion—and a promotion into doing the kind of
work she did best. It was part of her job to select people for
important positions. She deeply believed that one only hired

people from the outside into important positions after having exhausted all inside possibilities. The company in which she now found herself as senior human resources executive believed, however, that in staffing an important position that had become vacant, one first looked at the outside, "to bring in fresh blood." There is something to be said for either way (though, in my experience, the proper one is to do some of both). But they are fundamentally incompatible, not as policies but as values. They bespeak a different view of the relationship between organization and people; a different view of the responsibility of an organization to its people and in respect to developing them; a different view [of] what is the most important contribution of a person to an enterprise, and so on. After several years of frustration, the human resources executive quit, at considerable financial loss to herself. Her values and the values of the organization simply were not compatible.

> Peter F. Drucker and Joseph A. Maciariello, *Management: Revised Edition*, 2008, pp. 488–89.

• Peter Drucker gave his wisdom, time, and resources, and this project is an example of it. He knew what he stood for. Values were not relative to him, although his values allowed for and encouraged diversity of thought. As one who served with him and had the opportunity to work with him in an organization that bore his name, I learned that he practiced what he taught. I learned that I should try to do the same. He taught that if you surrender your values you surrender self-respect.

III. Practicum-Prompts

Does what you do well fit within your value system? Is the contribution you are making something to which you want to devote your life? Is it what you want to be remembered for?

Do you pass the mirror test: "Do you like the person you see in the mirror each day?" If not, why not?

Does the system of values in your organization conflict with your personal values? If so, what are you doing about it? Consider developing a plan either to change offensive values or to join an organization whose values are more compatible with your own.

What Do You Want to Be Remembered For?

Introduction

Peter Drucker cared deeply about people. For example, my ophthalmologist has told me a number of "Drucker stories" after my appointments. His father was Drucker's ophthalmologist and friend. Drucker and his wife visited the family home for dinner when the son was a boy. At each visit, Drucker would ask about the young man, how he was doing and what he was planning for his life, not merely in a polite way, but in a way that revealed that he really cared and wanted to know.

I too was a recipient of Drucker's concern, during a long period of illness. Drucker from time to time asked me how I was doing. He called me after surgeries, once when I was not doing very well. At the depth of my illness, he just simply listened to me. To hear from Peter Drucker and to realize that he was my friend and was trying to cheer me up was encouraging. At a social gathering he asked my wife how I was getting along; she told him, with considerable irritation, that all I wanted to do was work. Surprising my wife, Drucker responded, in his deep Austrian accent, "And, Judy, don't you ever try to stop him." He knew that I loved my work as he loved his and this would help me to focus and keep my mind off the illness; it would in and of itself help the healing process. Once I started to heal, he noticed it in the way I was carrying myself and he commented on it. Drucker was an astute observer of human behavior, and he was always observing.

I learned the importance of manners from Drucker. He frequently wrote notes and made phone calls to thank people who had shown him kindness. Manners, he taught, are the lubricant of organizations. His own manners seemed to telegraph the dignity and worth he recognized in people.

Perhaps my most moving experience as a colleague of Peter Drucker came in December 2002. Our son, Patrick, had worked with me during his college years researching Drucker's work as it related to my writing projects on "work and human nature." He thought he knew Drucker's material pretty well ("Druckered-out" was the term he used), so when it came time to choose an MBA graduate school, he followed in the steps of his boss at a New York investment banking firm and attended Columbia University. When Patrick attended valuable MBA events with senior executives who were visiting Columbia, he was surprised at how many of them referred to the importance of the advice and counsel they received from Drucker. Absolutely frustrated, he came home for Christmas vacation in December 2002 hoping to discuss his life path with Drucker. I resisted his wish, not wanting to impose on Drucker. My wife insisted, so just before our son returned to New York City, I asked Peter to join us for lunch on the next Saturday afternoon. He stunned me by emphatically accepting the invitation, sending me a fax at work and leaving phone messages for me at work and at home. He then spent three hours at lunch with us giving Patrick advice on his future. My son left that meeting feeling enabled and saying to me, "I feel I gained a couple of semesters of knowledge in those three hours." Patrick was elevated and empowered. He had received three hours of counseling from a person with vast intellectual gifts, historical vision, and wisdom—all focused on Patrick's personal issues. To this day, we often talk of the specific advice Drucker offered; we sort of carry on an oral tradition about that luncheon meeting and the wise advice Patrick received. And I have always been eager to pass on to other students the advice he gave Patrick.

People were important to Peter Drucker. The artifacts from his twenty-plus years of mentoring leaders of various organizations confirm what is well developed in his writings: Drucker was fervent in his belief that organizations should develop people and that the most durable ones do![96]

I. Read

Bob Buford's last meeting with Peter Drucker took place on September 29, 2005, approximately six weeks prior to Peter Drucker's death on November 11, 2005. Bob was especially interested in what Peter wanted to be remembered for—his legacy.

Peter Drucker

I'm a writer, and so my legacy is my writings. My legacy is my books. As far as I'm concerned I consider my books my legacy, and not an institution. I am content; the books are there; they either survive or they don't, and there are reasons for their continuing to be in print. I've made the necessary provisions, which is how to keep my important books in print for a considerable amount of time. The Harvard Business School Press has agreed to take them over if and when HarperCollins lets them go out of print. The Harvard Business School Press will keep them in print for seventeen years after my death, minimum. That's all provided for. I am not worried about it.

Drucker–Buford Dialogue, September 29, 2005.

II. Reflect

- Asking yourself the question, "What do I want to be remembered for?" provides you with an opportunity to refocus your efforts and, in the process, to engage in self-renewal.

1. SELF-RENEWAL

"What do you want to be remembered for?"

When I was thirteen I had an inspiring teacher of religion [Father Pfliegler] who one day went right through the class of boys asking each one, "What do you want to be remembered for?" None of us, of course, could give an answer. So, he chuckled and said, "I didn't expect you to be able to answer it. But if you still can't answer it by the time you're fifty, you will have wasted your life."

I'm always asking that question: What do you want to be remembered for? It is a question that induces you to renew yourself, because it pushes you to see yourself as a different person—the person you can *become*. If you are fortunate, someone with the moral authority of a Father Pfliegler will ask you that question early enough in your life so that you will continue to ask it as you go through life.

Peter F. Drucker, June 8, "Self-Renewal," *The Daily Drucker*, 2004.

- Schumpeter's earliest desires were to be a great lover, a great horseman, and a great economist. Such desires, like most of our early desires, give way as we age. That is the reason to periodically ask: "What do I want to be remembered for?" Schumpeter was indeed a great economist—along with Keynes, one of the two greatest economists of the twentieth century. His emphasis on productivity, innovation, and economic development was a seminal contribution to our knowledge of economics.

2. THE ANSWER CHANGES AS WE AGE

Joseph Schumpeter, one of the greatest economists of the [twentieth] century, claimed at twenty-five that he wanted to be remembered as the best horseman in Europe, [as] the greatest lover in Europe, and as a great economist. By age sixty, just before he died, he was asked the question again [by Drucker's father, with Peter present, five days before Schumpeter died on January 8, 1950]. He no longer talked of horsemanship and he no longer talked of women. He said he wanted to be remembered as the man who had given an early warning of the dangers of inflation. That is what he is remembered for—and it's worthwhile being remembered for. Asking that question changed him, even though the answer given at twenty-five was singularly stupid, even for a young man of twenty-five.

> Peter F. Drucker, *Managing the Non-Profit Organization*, 1990, p. 202.

• Each of us can strive to make contributions to the lives of others.

3. THE DIFFERENCE ONE MAKES IN THE LIVES OF OTHERS

"One thing worth being remembered for is the difference one makes in the lives of people."

"I have never forgotten that conversation," Drucker said, because Schumpeter continued and said, "You know, Adolph, I have now reached that age where I know that being remembered for books and theories is not enough. One does not make a difference unless it is a difference in the lives of people." I learned three things from that conversation. First, one has to ask oneself what one wants to be remembered for. Second, that should change as one gets older. It should change both with one's own maturity and with the changes in the world. *Finally, one thing worth being remembered for is the difference one makes in the lives of people* [italics mine].

> Peter F. Drucker and Joseph A. Maciariello, *Management: Revised Edition*, 2008, p. 511.

• It is important, especially as one ages, to think about the purpose of one's life. To quote from Rick Warren's May 2004 keynote address to Drucker School alumni and friends, "There is no more fundamental question than, 'What on earth am I here for?'" Warren has an answer and so did Immanuel Kant, even though they are different answers. But both men asked the same question. And that is why it is important for each one of us to ask and resolve it if we can.

III. Practicum-Prompts

It is important to ask yourself the question, "What do I want to be remembered for?" from time to time in your life because it motivates you to work toward the person you can become. It is a question that if asked seriously can lead to personal revitalization in your life.

When asking the question, "What do I want to be remembered for?" focus away from yourself toward the contribution you would like to make in the lives of others.

Consider again two personal notes from Drucker on his movement toward answering the question posed in this entry: "I . . . had to decide between what I was doing well and successfully, and my values. I was doing extremely well as a young investment banker in London in the mid-1930s; it clearly fitted my strengths. Yet I did not see myself making a contribution as an asset manager of any kind. . . . And I saw no point in being the richest man in the cemetery."[97] And: "In 1934 as a young economist in a London merchant bank, I sat in the Keynes seminar in Cambridge. I suddenly realized that Keynes was interested in the behavior of commodities while I was interested in the behavior of people."[98]

What do *you* want to be remembered for?

"We Mentor... Because We Can Envision What a Person Can Become" [99]

Introduction

Peter Drucker mentored Rick Warren for twenty to twenty-five years. During that time Warren developed the purpose-driven paradigm for the management of churches, as described in his book *The Purpose Driven Church* (1995). In a 2005 survey of American pastors and ministers by George Barna, a leading market researcher on religion in America, this book was voted the second most influential, behind Warren's *The Purpose Driven Life* (2002).[100]

As Drucker neared the end of his life, he could look back at the people he mentored, such as Warren and Buford, among many others, and he knew he had made substantial contributions to their lives and, through them, to the lives of many others.

Rick Warren considered Peter Drucker one of the three most influential people in his life. I have transcribed his talk honoring Peter Drucker, delivered on November 13, 2004, at Drucker Alumni Day in Claremont. The annual event was also a celebration of Peter Drucker's ninety-fifth birthday. Interspersed with Warren's comments are his quotes from the works of Peter Drucker, which I have documented as closely as possible. Additional portions of the Warren address are contained in Weeks 8 and 45.

I. Read

Now without a doubt, I could not overestimate the influence that Peter Drucker has had on my life. If you would come to visit Saddleback Church you would see his fingerprints all over it, because of his influence, as a friend, and as a writer, and as a mentor for the past twenty to twenty-five years. I'd have to say Peter Drucker is one of the three men that have influenced my life the most. And today I have been asked to share what Peter means to me and some of the lessons and wisdom that he has taught me, the wisdom we have applied in our church that has literally helped tens of thousands of other churches. We have purpose-driven churches in 120 countries, about 37,000 of them here in the United States alone. And as I talk about Peter, as we honor him on his ninety-fifth birthday, I know he likes to have learning experiences, so I am going to show you what Peter has taught me, and then I want to give you an example of it in our situation.

I want to begin [with] two things that Peter said. The first one I have heard him say many times, at least a dozen: "The most significant sociological phenomenon of the second half of the century has been the development of the pastoral church." [101]

The second that really has influenced me is: "The function of management in the church is to make it more church-like instead of business-like." [102]

That is a brilliant statement.

We just had our twenty-fifth Easter. We had 39,000 people in church, and we have a 128-acre campus, and we started thirty-six other churches in Southern California, and we have helped tens of thousands of churches around the world. I have trained about 350,000 pastors . . . in fifty-six countries. Now, how did we go from me and my wife to where Saddleback is today, helping other churches? A large part of it is from the wisdom that I got from Peter Drucker. I learned a number of very important truths, and you may want to write some of these down. I think these are the "essential Druckers" that I am going to describe.

The first is: Leaders don't ask, "What do I want?" Leaders ask, "What needs to be done?"[103]

So I started with the question, not "What do I want?" but "What needs to be done and where does it need to be done?"

This then is the question you need to ask: "What is in my life that needs to be done, and where do I need to be doing it?"

The second Drucker principle is "The mission comes first."[104]

You all know to ask, "What is our business?" And that, I say, is being prepared to help people to *be purpose driven.*

You see successful organizations. They know what they are called to do and they know what they are not called to do, what's important and what's not important. They don't need reminding; they are clear about their identity. *They have a clear purpose.*

II. Reflect

- I have adapted the next reflection from Warren's responses to a question from the audience at the end of his talk.
- As to why *The Purpose-Driven Life* has been so popular, Warren said there is no more fundamental question than "What on earth am I here for?" It is a question that applies to everyone.
- Peter Drucker addresses this question of purpose in his article "The Unfashionable Kierkegaard,"[105] as does Immanuel Kant in his *Critique of Pure Reason.*

1. MISSION OR PURPOSE DRIVEN

Leaders communicate in the sense that people around them know what they are trying to do. They are purpose driven—

yes, mission driven. They know how to establish a mission. And another thing—they know how to say no. The pressure on leaders to do 984 different things is unbearable, so the effective ones learn how to say no and stick with it. They don't suffocate themselves as a result. Too many leaders try to do a little bit of twenty-five things and get nothing done. They are very popular because they always say yes. But they get nothing done.

> Rich Karlgaard, "Drucker on Leadership: An Interview
> with Peter F. Drucker," *Forbes*, November 19, 2004.

- If we are to become all we can be, it is simply impossible to keep adding activities to our work and to our lives without dropping other activities.

2. CREATIVE ABANDONMENT

A critical question for leaders is, "When do you stop pouring resources into things that have achieved their purpose?" The most dangerous traps for a leader are those near-successes where everybody says that if you just give it another big push it will go over the top. One tries it once. One tries it twice. One tries it a third time. But by then it should be obvious this will be very hard to do. So, I always advise my friend Rick Warren, "Don't tell me what you're doing, Rick. Tell me what you *stopped* doing."

> Rich Karlgaard, "Drucker on Leadership: An Interview
> with Peter F. Drucker," *Forbes*, November 19, 2004.

- We can learn about Drucker's work by watching his mentees practice what Drucker taught. Rick Warren has been notable for asking Drucker's question: "If we did not do this already, would we, knowing what we know, go into it?" (*Management Challenges for the 21st Century*, 1999, p. 74). Warren has abandoned numerous successful programs whose purpose was achieved in order to make room for programs and activities that were even more central to the mission.

3. WHAT NEEDS TO BE DONE

Successful leaders don't start out asking, "What do I want to do?" They ask, "What needs to be done?" Then they ask, "Of those things that would make a difference, which are right for me?" They don't tackle things they aren't good at. They make sure other necessities get done, but not by them. Successful leaders make sure that they succeed! They are not afraid of strength in others. Andrew Carnegie wanted to put on his gravestone, "Here lies a man who knew how to put into his service more able men than he was himself."

> Rich Karlgaard, "Drucker on Leadership: An Interview with Peter F. Drucker," *Forbes*, November 19, 2004. (Drucker's ninety-fifth birthday. He died November 11, 2005, just before his ninety-sixth birthday.)

III. Practicum-Prompts

Do you have a clear purpose in life? Think it through. What is your mission?

As a leader, do you ask, "What do I want?" Or do you ask, "What needs to be done?"

Once you know what needs to be done in your life, ask, "Where does it need to be done?"

Are you engaged in mentoring others? Are you having an influence for good in the lives of other people and in society?

What is it that you want to be remembered for? Does Drucker's life help you to answer this question? Does his mentoring?

Peter Drucker's Ten Principles for Finding Meaning in the Second Half of Life

As Reported by Bob Buford

Introduction

Bob Buford has done us a service in elaborating on Drucker's ten principles for finding significance. Although Bob is focused primarily on activities in the second half of life, the principles apply to every stage of our lives.

As you go through each of these principles, think about how you can put them to use today. For example, Principle 6, "Know your values," will become more important as you progress in your career. But you should try now to place yourself in a position where the values are compatible with those you hold. Staying in a position when you are out of sync with its values will either corrupt you or make you cynical. I learned this very early in my own career, and began to think about a career change, when one evening, I experienced emptiness after a hard day's work on a task that I had prepared well for and once enjoyed. The emptiness resulted from the realization that I no longer shared the values that were important to the job.

You should be alert for Principle 5, "Opportunity comes in over the transom." Once you know your strengths and values and begin thinking about the "best of all possible" positions, be alert for the unique opportunity. The difficulty is that opportunities often present themselves when the time is not right and then you have to make a tough choice. If you bypass an opportunity because the time is not right, you may live to regret it because a similar opportunity may not arise again. This too has been my experience.

Principle 8, "Know the difference between planning and harvesting," is very important background for this project. Drucker wrote so much over approximately seventy years that his wisdom has often been ahead of its time, and this has made it difficult for some of us to put it into practice. This project is one in which Drucker is harvesting and applying a lifetime of work. Although I have been a student of Drucker's work for most of my professional life, I always find that examples of applications of his principles deepen my understanding of how to apply the principles to my own work. Your study and application of these principles will also give you the opportunity to acquire wisdom that you can use right away.

Principle 9 is "Good intentions aren't enough; define the results you want." Results are needed in for-profit and nonprofit organizations, yet many nonprofits are full of well-meaning people who are very idealistic and want to save the world. They need to set realistic goals, by seeking to optimize rather than maximize the performance of their organizations. Profit-seeking organizations, on the other hand, should recognize that the definition of results and appropriate performance measures will influence behavior, so careful attention should be paid to establishing them.

Finally, with regard to Principle 10, we know that knowledge is moving very fast in most professions, so you and I must keep abreast or we will quickly become obsolete!

In summary, I have experienced the benefit of these ten principles, especially those that I have illustrated in this introduction. I encourage you to study them, apply them as appropriate, and try to finish well.

I. Read

(1) Find out who you are.

"Whenever people are on the road to success," Drucker said, "they tend to think of repositioning as something they do if they're a failure. But I would say that you ought to reposition when you're a success, because that's when you can afford it." But people cannot reposition for significance, Drucker claimed, without first knowing who they are and where they belong.

(2) Reposition yourself for full effectiveness and fulfillment.

"Early in their careers," Drucker said, "people tend to have a fairly limited time frame, of four years or so. They can't visualize what comes after that." By the time they achieve some measure of success, however, the time frame expands. "Suddenly they begin to think about options that are twenty, thirty, or more years ahead of them," Drucker said. Such a long view often brings clarity where none existed before.

(3) Find your existential core.

"There's a strong correlation between high achievement and the ability to come to terms with life's basic questions," Drucker said. "I think the most successful people are those who have a strong faith . . . ; there is a very substantial correlation between religious faith, religious commitment, and success as doers in the community."

(4) "Make your life your endgame; the only worthy goal is to make a meaningful life out of an ordinary one."

(5) Planning doesn't work.

"Opportunity comes in over the transom," Drucker insisted, and that means one has to be flexible, ready to seize the right opportunities when they come. "Too much planning can make you deaf to opportunity. . . . Opportunity knocks, but it knocks only once. You have to be ready for the accident."

(6) Know your values.

"If you don't respect a job, not only will you do a poor job of it, but it will corrupt you, and eventually it may even kill you," Drucker said. "For example, ninety-nine percent of all physicians should not become hospital administrators. Why? Because they have no respect for the job. They're physicians and they feel that hospital administration is a job for clerks."

(7) Define what finishing well means to you.

"My definition of success changed a long time ago," Drucker said. "I love doing consulting work and writing—I regularly lose track of time when I'm doing those things. But finishing well, and how I want to be remembered, those are the things that matter now. Making a difference in a few lives is a worthy goal. Having enabled a few people to do the things they want to do—that's really what I want to be remembered for."

(8) Know the difference between harvesting and planting.

"For many years, I measured my work by my output— mainly in terms of books and other writing that I was doing," Drucker said. "I was very productive for many years. I am not so productive today, because these are years of *harvesting* rather than years of *planting.*"

(9) Good intentions aren't enough; define the results you want.

Nonprofits often get poor results because "they don't ask about results, and they don't know what results they want in the first place. They mean well and they have the best of intentions, but the only thing good intentions are for (as the maxim says) is to pave the road to hell."

(10) Recognize the downside to "No longer learning, no longer growing."

"I see more and more people who make it to their mid-forties or beyond, and they've been very successful," Drucker said. "They've done very well in their work and career, but in my experience, they end up in one of three groups. One group will retire; they usually don't live very long. The second group keeps on doing what they've been doing, but they're losing their enthusiasm, feeling less alive. The third group keeps doing what they've been doing, but they're looking for ways to make a contribution. They feel they've been given a lot and they're looking for a chance to give back. They're not satisfied with just writing checks; they want to be involved, to help other people in a more positive way." And they're the ones, Drucker said, who finish well.

Bob Buford, http://www.druckersociety.at/files/ten-principles-for-life-from-peter-drucker.pdf, n.d.

II. Reflect

- Principle 3, the existential core or the coming to terms with life's basic questions, can have a powerful effect on your life and on your contributions to the lives of other people.

1. PETER DRUCKER HAS ADDED SIGNIFICANCE TO THE LIVES OF MANY PEOPLE OVER THE SPAN OF DECADES

In each of the ten principles in part 1 you can hear ideas found in most major religions. In my own life several core ideas parallel ideas found in the Bible. The overriding assumption in Peter's ten principles is that we are all created to enjoy success and ultimately significance. Peter Drucker understood life principles because he understood how individuals are fearfully and wonderfully made with eternity in mind. . . . Listen for the spiritual in Drucker's ten life principles and expect to discover your own success and more importantly your own significance.

Bob Buford, http://www.druckersociety.at/files/ten -principles-for-life-from-peter-drucker.pdf, n.d.

- Notice Drucker's "bolt from out of the blue" in Reading 2 and how closely it fits Pasteur's comment that "luck favors the prepared mind" in Reading 3.

2. PETER DRUCKER'S "LUCKY" BREAK

Late in the fall of 1943, when I was just about to mark my 34th birthday, I received an offer like a bolt from out of the blue. "My name is Paul Garrett," said a voice on the telephone. "I'm in charge of public relations at General Motors (GM) and calling on behalf of the corporation's vice president, Mr. Donaldson Brown." Mr. Brown was wondering if I might be interested in making a study of GM's management policies and structure from a third person's perspective. GM was then the largest company in the world. . . . I had yet to realize a major project to investigate a large corporation from within. I first came up with the idea for such a project in Vermont while writing my second major book, *The Future of Industrial Man* [1942]. I strongly felt I needed to find out how large companies behaved as organizations. . . . The businesses' executives to whom I could get introductions all turned me down. . . . Right at the time when I was deeply discouraged by the failure to launch the project, I received the phone call from GM. At the time GM was not only the world's largest company but also the most innovative. Under the leadership of Alfred Sloan, a key figure in helping revive the company from near bankruptcy, GM had pioneered in creating the modern-style corporate organization, becoming the first in the world to implement the concept of divisionalization or decentralization. Even today, I feel very lucky to have gotten the break.

Peter F. Drucker, *My Personal History*, Article 17, 2009.

- When innovators are asked about circumstances surrounding a specific innovation, they will sometimes attribute it to luck. Yet, if we look deeper into the circumstances surrounding most of these innovations, we find that, yes, luck creates a breakthrough idea or event—but normally the innovator has been immersed in the general area for a long time and knows and can identify a breakthrough event when he or she spots it.

3. LOUIS PASTEUR'S "LUCKY BREAKS"

Pasteur made not just one, but several discoveries in his career. This led some people to say that he was lucky. Pasteur himself said that chance favors only the prepared mind. In other words, luck only helps those who are ready to recognize it. Pasteur's greatest gift may have been his ability to notice the little things that other people missed. Some of those little things proved to be the source of his lucky breaks.

> Linda Wasmer Smith, *Louis Pasteur, Disease Fighter*, 2008, p. 10.

III. Practicum-Prompts

Make notes on Drucker's ten principles for "Finding Meaning in the Second Half of Life" as they apply to your life. Return to the principles and your notes as time passes. Revise your notes as necessary.

Try, like Pasteur and like Drucker, to "notice the little things that other people miss." Read high-quality newspapers and periodicals and ponder items that are significantly different from your expectations. Follow them to see if they are fads or genuine trends.

If you spot new, genuine trends identify the opportunities they create for you and for your organization. Think through what it would take to turn the opportunity into a reality for you and your organization.

Prepare and dream for a meaningful second half. When unexpected opportunities arise that move you closer to your dream, ask yourself, "What would it take for me to take advantage of this opportunity right now?"

Lessons Learned

This chapter summarizes the major lessons learned this past year as you have worked through the readings, reflections, and exercises. The entire book is devoted to helping you become an effective leader of your organization. This means being committed to doing the right things for your constituents, especially customers, employees, shareholders, and the society to which you are responsible.

Effective Leadership

Our premise is that while a few people are natural-born leaders most of us have to learn how to become effective leaders. And you cannot learn effectiveness as a leader simply by reading a book, no matter how inspired the book might be. It is learned by *precept,* or general principles; and *practice,* or the actual application of precepts to practical problems we encounter as leaders. The fifty-two weeks of coaching that you have completed should assist you in becoming an effective leader through the use of both precepts and opportunities to practice. The process should continue all your life. The effective leaders you have met this past year are lifelong learners.

To be a leader you must have followers, and your followers must have gained confidence in your leadership. For your followers to gain confidence, you as a leader must possess integrity of character and pursue high purpose. Integrity of character is earned when you are consistent: when your words match your actions. These qualities will result in colleagues' trusting your leadership. And this we have learned makes up "right leadership."

Right leadership in the management group of an organization has the potential to transform the lives of people for the better. For example, it can raise a person's vision of what is possible and raise an individual's performance to a much higher standard. It can even contribute to developing an individual's personality beyond what the person had thought possible.

These are the high qualities and high standards that we have sought to develop this year. What follows is a summary of the process we followed.

How to Be an Effective Leader

First, effective leaders do what their organization *needs*, and not necessarily what they *want* to do. They ask "What needs to be done?"—not "What would I like to do?" They manage in two time dimensions and make sure that their short-term goals are compatible with the longer-term mission and vision of the organization. To this end they separate the *important* tasks from those tasks that appear *urgent* at any time.

We learned that effective leaders know that the key to success is to *concentrate* efforts and apply themselves to those areas where even a small amount of success will have a great deal of impact on contribution and results. They avoid multitasking and make sure that the most important tasks are done first. They put *pressure on their time* and recognize that true opportunities often arise at the least opportune moment. They make room for these new opportunities by delegating, delaying, or abandoning activities that are currently taking up the time needed to pursue new endeavors. And they obtain the information needed to allow them to achieve a sustainable competitive advantage. They take full advantage of data analytics and make sure that people on whom they depend know what information they need from them and in what form. In turn, they know what information their colleagues need to be effective and supply it to them on a timely basis in a form that they can use.

We know how important it is that leaders develop a functioning board of trustees who are actively engaged with the management in developing, implementing, and monitoring the strategies, resources, and results of the organization. It is important for leaders to work with board members, to assign them important duties, to provide them with timely information that allows them to perform their duties, and to monitor the performance of the CEO and the organization.

Board members should participate in the major decisions facing the organization, and perform specific duties assigned to them as members of one or more subcommittees of the board. Board members are also responsible for orderly succession. They do this as a part of their regular duties by evaluating candidates who are considered qualified to assume top management responsibilities. Board members should expect to commit a substantial amount of time to their responsibilities on the board and help make the CEO and organization effective.

Management of the Pluralistic Institutions of Society

We learned that management is the "constitutive function," or the organizing force, for bringing an institution into existence and keeping it in existence. Professional management of large-scale organizations developed first in the for-profit sectors of the United States, Germany, and Japan beginning in the late nineteenth century, but the rapid growth of professional management is a product of the twentieth century.

Effective leadership and effective management are required for *each* of the multitude of institutions of society. Professional *business management* is needed by society to create the wealth to sustain itself and the other social institutions. Wealth produced by business is, through taxation, the basis for financing the activities of government, as well as the basis for supporting the work of nonprofit and charitable organizations. For society's wealth to be used most effectively the management of these nonbusiness organizations is a priority.

Nonprofit and government organizations, unlike businesses, do not have a natural bottom line, so definition of results is essential to effectively managing these institutions and their resources. A properly constructed mission statement, followed by a definition of results and appropriate performance measures, is necessary to assess progress in the management of all organizations; but these statements are especially challenging for social sector and governmental organizations, which do not have a natural bottom line. The lack of a bottom line can be quite pernicious. Consider, for example, a government agency that measures success by the size of the organization under the leader's jurisdiction. This motivates creation of bureaucracies that waste resources. The same thing can happen in a nonprofit organization that does not clearly define its mission, the expected results, and appropriate performance measures.

To rationalize the management of the society of organizations, each organization should pursue its own mission as its top priority while remembering that it owes its very existence to the society of which it is a part. It is an organ of society and no organ can function outside a healthy body. Therefore, executives of organizations have two missions: their primary mission, to generate wealth, change lives, and govern; and their secondary mission, to support programs of the communities in which they operate. For as we have seen, a number of the needs of society fall through the cracks and are not being met by the normal operations of business, nonprofit, and government organizations. These organizations, therefore, have to lead beyond their own boundaries if society's needs are to be met.

The Importance of Top Management and the Spirit of Performance

The first priority in the management of any organization, we learned, is to establish an effective top management that will provide governance and will create a spirit of performance. Without a sustaining spirit from the top, an organization is likely at best to tread water or to experience a slow decline. The human resource is the only resource that is capable of expansion—in many cases, significant expansion—in performance. For this to happen people must be properly selected, led, placed, and trained. But this all depends on establishing the right conditions or spirit, and that has to start from, and be modeled by, those at the top of the organization.

We know that effective leadership of society's organizations is especially important at this time of rapid global change and major discontinuities. At the national level, major problems such as environmental pollution and terrorism are global in scope and require cooperation among nations for their effective management. Even with global cooperation these problems will be very difficult to solve; we may just have to learn to cope with them and to minimize disruptions and damage. Domestically, the shift from manual work to knowledge work is causing dislocations that can be solved only by retraining manual workers and by increasing the productivity of service workers. Retraining service and manufacturing workers and raising their productivity are social as well as economic tasks. These tasks will require a high degree of unity in our society politic, which seems to be fractured at the present time in the United States. These tasks have been presented here not as liberal or conservative issues, but simply as pressing problems and transitions that any nation has to solve by building effective coalitions. Let us all also remember that people in our organizations need a high level of continuity of values to make it through this period of transition.

Yet periods of discontinuities, like the one we are going through now, also create opportunities for those who are actively seeking them. Resources must be freed up in order to take advantage of new opportunities. They can be freed up by abandoning the old and no longer productive programs and units. While this is never easy, it is especially difficult for governmental organizations, where established but no longer useful programs develop strong political constituencies. We reviewed a promising method for abandonment in all sectors of the economy, as proposed by Professor Robert N. Anthony. In this method, "outside experts" are used to periodically evaluate a department's or an agency's mission, results, and costs—in other words, evaluate the entity's reason for being. While this is no guarantee of eliminating waste, fraud, and abuse, it can shine a spotlight on those areas that are limiting the ability of the organization, and society, to take advantage of change by releasing resources required to introduce new and innovative programs, products, and services.

The Importance of Mission

We have seen that a good mission statement can be used by management as a powerful tool for implementing an organization's purpose and for remaining within the confines of that purpose or for adjusting its purpose as circumstances change. All those who have major responsibility to implement various aspects of the mission should be involved in negotiating it. The mission should, to the extent possible, be written to serve all constituents of the organization in priority order.

Once a mission statement is developed, it should "force people" to think through how their position contributes or can contribute to fulfilling the mission of the organization. The objective is to use the mission statement as a dynamic document to integrate the work of all members of the organization while serving customers and other constituents.

Drucker's Fundamental Questions

We know that the essence of Drucker's approach to management is to look at the organization through a marketing lens. Of Drucker's fundamental questions, variously stated depending on the sector and circumstances, two are always asked with a corollary question. The first is, "Who is the customer?" Its corollary is, "Who is the noncustomer?" The second is, "What does the customer consider value?" Its corollary is, "What does the noncustomer consider value?" This is simple, yet many executives miss it. Once we know our customers and their values, we should reflect these values throughout our management systems—for example, in advertising, product design, operations, marketing, and service.

A solid approach to marketing research, however, also asks the corollary questions. We have learned the power of this approach by going through the readings and exercises.

Phase Changes in an Organization

Entrepreneurs innovate. When an innovation is successful, it can be licensed to a larger firm that will bring it to scale quickly; but most often the entrepreneur starts a new venture. If the new venture is successful, the entrepreneur will have to secure financing, create the proper controls, and establish a top management team. Otherwise, the new venture has a high risk of failure. Assuming success, the entrepreneur will be required to make a decision as to his or her role in the new venture going forward; otherwise the venture will suffer. Will the entrepreneur make the transition and become an effective executive, learning how to become a chief executive officer? Or will the entrepreneur work with other members of the top management team to identify, on the basis of need and individuals' strengths, the key activities that each should perform? This is what we have called a *change in phase*, and every entrepreneur has to make this change if the organization is to continue to grow and develop.

Organization Structure

Organization structure is a tool of the executive, a means to an end for achieving short-term and long-term goals of an organization. A number of organizational forms can be equally effective in a specific situation, but some forms can do harm to both people and purpose. It is clear from the examples in the book that in a knowledge society of organizations, information connects the organization, and information is power. Knowledge is expanding and will continue to expand. As it expands it will continue to splinter and become more specialized. It is unlikely that any large knowledge-based organization will have all the specialized knowledge it needs to carry out its tasks. Various forms of interorganizational cooperation will continue to emerge, including joint ventures, partnerships, alliances, and networked organizations. The same organization can form numerous interorganizational teams composed of different partner organizations in order to assemble the specialized resources it requires to complete a project without trying to maintain specialized knowledge at efficient scale within the organization. Partnering can make the organization more effective. As this process continues to evolve, the knowledge society of organizations may be referred to as the *networked society.*

Developing People

Regardless of organizational structure, we know that Drucker believed the "most durable organizations develop their people both intellectually and morally." This is a tall order. Intellectual development means expanding the ability and capacity of the individual to perform on the job and in life. Developing a person morally means developing the person's character. This is even more difficult and cannot be taught but must be learned. How can it be learned? By paying close attention to examples set by those in leadership positions in the organization—especially by leaders one admires—and then by working on making these traits a part of one's character. To protect itself and society against the downside of human nature, management should establish stiff penalties for those who break the ethical norms set by the organization and reward those whose ethical behavior is exemplary.

By developing people both intellectually and morally the organization goes a long way toward enhancing the individual's status and toward helping the individual fulfill some of the noble aspirations held by a free society for its citizens. The leadership also behaves in a way that is widely perceived as legitimate by employees and by society.

Given the scandals of the recent past, and their damage to society, restoring the legitimacy of management should be accorded top priority by business and government.

The Succession Decision

The decision regarding succession to the top position of an organization is a critical topic in management. I have seen many of these succession decisions fail, and if there are two or more failures in a row, an established organization may be in deep trouble, especially in this time of rapid change. It is incumbent on a CEO and a board of directors to form a subcommittee of the board, put it in charge of succession, and look at both internal and external candidates for a sustained period of time. While it is not uncommon for a succession decision to develop unexpectedly, it is quite reasonable to expect the board to know the potential slate of likely internal candidates who can fill the top position. Board members should also make it one of their priorities to develop a large number of contacts to equip them with information about potential external candidates. Nevertheless, the decision about succession to the top position is always a gamble because no one knows the problems to be faced by a new CEO, or how the person appointed to the top position will grow to match the unknown challenges he or she will face in the future.

The Power of Purpose

We learned that one of Drucker's favorite organizations was The Salvation Army and briefly reviewed the reasons why. He liked the Army because of its simple mission, working "with the poorest of the poor and the meanest of the mean," and its effectiveness in meeting human needs—its eagerness to take on difficult social projects such as treating drug and alcohol addiction, developing troubled young people, providing prisoner probationary services, and dealing with some of the other very difficult social problems in the United States. In these social areas it often achieves results that government has difficulty achieving. It is eager to professionalize its management and to convert those people it serves into productive members of society. It meets needs as they occur and depends on the enormous generosity of the American people to continue to provide funding for unmet needs, thus practicing "just-in-time funding." As the size of its projects grows and its organization expands, it continues to scale up its capacity to lead and to manage by mapping Drucker's teachings onto its organization. It is an example for us all.

Drucker's Methodology of Social Ecology

We observed that Drucker's methodology of social ecology is useful for every executive of every organization. The idea is to spot unnoticed trends or changes in trends that are occurring in society, in demographics, in technology, in institutions, in perceptions, and in events that are unexpected, and convert certain of these changes into opportunities. We saw how Drucker identified a number of institutions that were emerging, including the mega-church. The mega-church is changing the landscape, not only within American Protestantism, but also within the culture and economy. We also observed how Tom Luce went about identifying excellent educational practices in the schools of America and diffused these practices to others.

Once these trends are identified, the next step for the social ecologist is to understand what makes for excellence in these changes within new or existing institutions. The information is then organized into best practices—in Luce's case, those that can be emulated by principals and teachers. Luce then worked with principals and teachers through his principals network to help other schools become effective.

Thus the goal of the social ecologist is to make society's citizens and institutions more effective. Social ecology, when effectively performed, results in the diffusion of innovation and best practices. It provides an outstanding method for carrying out ideas developed by Everett Rogers in his seminal book *Diffusion of Innovations*. It helps society meet the needs of citizens and organizations. We have seen just how powerful this methodology can be when used effectively, as illustrated by Willow Creek Association and its Global Leadership Summit.

Success to Significance

We saw that one of Drucker's most powerful ideas is the opportunity—which more and more people have in the knowledge society—to bring social and economic change by imposing "upon the yet unborn future a new idea" that tries to give shape to something new and useful. The success-to-significance movement is one of these new ideas. Knowledge workers have long work spans, often over fifty years, and for one reason or another no longer find satisfaction in their primary careers. Many have a pent-up desire to do what they have often dreamed of doing but have been unable to do because of their life commitment to others. And when ready for this transition, they may need assistance in clarifying their vision and testing it against reality before making a complete commitment to the dream. Many need help in matching their interests and strengths to an opportunity that is likely to bear fruit. Here is where mentoring by senior people who have made this life-altering transition earlier may help.

We have also seen examples of those who achieved their goals in second careers or in volunteer work. It is very clear, however, that it is best to start volunteering early in an area of interest and gain experience before making a transition either to a second career or to a brand-new area involving social innovation.

If one takes on a project involving social innovation, we know that it had better be in an area where the person has both enthusiasm and a unique contribution to make. Without a unique contribution and deep enthusiasm, the project is unlikely to hold a person through the ups and downs of a start-up. Learning the lessons in this book should help you to avoid the pitfalls and to choose wisely.

Moving from success to significance involves managing ourselves just as we must do as knowledge workers. The better we manage ourselves as knowledge workers, the greater the likelihood that we will effectively make the transition to significance and the greater the likelihood that we may even be able to satisfy these desires in our first career.

Character and Legacy

One of the questions frequently asked by Peter Drucker at the end of an interview is, "What do you want to be remembered for?" We have come to see that this is not a question that most of us want to deal with. We don't ask it often or early enough. It involves coming to grips with our creaturehood and the knowledge that life is finite and we will soon leave this life. Many of the people who have provided the examples for this book have died.

We have seen that if we, like Peter Drucker, take an eternal view, only people last. Therefore, it is what we do in and for the lives of people that is most likely to outlive us. We have seen that the answer to this question of legacy is likely to change as we age because as our knowledge of ourselves grows we gain a deeper appreciation of our real strengths and how our life experiences can be used to help others. Asking the question often is a real mentoring step because it keeps before us what is important and what we must abandon.

On a final note, as we age, we tend to mature in the sense that we can see our true self and the needs of others more clearly. The competitive edge is likely to drop off and our motives tend to become purer with regard to our fellow human beings. This puts us in a better position to see where we can and should make our contributions to the lives of others. Getting to know ourselves is a lifelong process that we are likely to approach more accurately as we age. And getting to know ourselves and our unique strengths puts us in the best position to help others. This can be a very satisfying process.

Conclusion

We have now reviewed some of the lessons covered by Drucker in this year of coaching. I have traveled the same road as you. You have my best wishes for the rest of your journey. I hope that as you look back at what you have accomplished this year, you do so with great satisfaction.

Appendix

Summary of Drucker's Principles

This appendix summarizes Drucker's key principles for your ongoing reference. Principles are listed in the order in which they appear in the book.

Effective Leaders

1. "Effective leaders *get the right things done* and *you can trust them.*" (p. 3)
2. "Trust is the conviction that a leader means what she says." (p. 6)
3. "Effective leadership . . . is based primarily on being consistent." (p. 6)
4. "The supreme quality for a leader is unquestionably integrity." (p. 6)
5. "It is typical of the most successful and durable organizations that they induce in their members an intellectual and moral growth beyond a [person's] original capacities." (p. 9)

Management Is a Human Activity

1. " 'Adversity is the test of leadership,' said Xenophon 2,500 years ago." (p. 40)[106]

Setting Your Sights on the Important, Not the Urgent

1. "Make the *important* rather than the *urgent* your priority in life." (p. 45)
2. "Effective leaders I have met . . . did not start off with the question,

'What do I want?' They started out with the question, *'What needs to be done?'* " (p. 48)

3. "The best proof that the danger of overpruning [eliminating urgent activities] is a bugaboo is the extraordinary effectiveness so often attained by severely ill or severely handicapped people." (p. 48)

4. "A manager must, so to speak, keep his nose to the grindstone while lifting his eyes to the hills—quite an acrobatic feat." (On the need to harmonize decisions affecting the short term and the long term.) (p. 53)

5. "So we start always with the long range, and then we feed back and say, What do we *do today?*" (p. 55)

The Road Map to Personal Effectiveness

1. "How should you define the specific pieces of work to be tackled?" (p. 59)
2. Focus on the important questions: "What is our business?" "What should it be?" "What should it not be?" "Who is our customer?" "What is value to the customer?" (p. 60)
3. "Target yourself on the areas where a little success on your part will have the greatest impact . . . because it will make a genuine difference." (p. 60)
4. "Concentration is the key to economic results." (p. 61)
5. "If leaders are not able to slough off yesterday, to abandon yesterday, they simply will not be able to create tomorrow." (p. 63)
6. "Effective executives know that time is the limiting factor" of effectiveness. (p. 65)
7. "How do you go about developing yourself?" "I put pressure on my time. . . . I force myself to get overloaded and then I look at the whole stack for something to throw out." (p. 66)
8. "Precisely because an effective leader knows that he, and no one else, is ultimately responsible, he is not afraid of strength in associates and subordinates." (p. 68)
9. "Leadership is not rank, privilege, titles, or money, it is *responsibility.*" (p. 69)
10. "Effective leaders delegate but they do not delegate the one thing that will set the standards. *They do it.*" (p. 70)

11. "What information do I owe to the people with whom I work and on whom I depend? What information do I need myself? And from whom? And in what form? And in what time frame?" (p. 74)

12. "The ultimate test of an information system is that there are no surprises." (p. 74)

13. "For *strategy*, we need organized information about the environment. For that is where results are. Inside an organization there are only cost centers." (p. 76)

14. "Leadership is lifting a person's vision to higher sights, the raising of a person's performance to a higher standard, the building of a personality beyond its normal limitations." (p. 79)

15. "Nothing better prepares the ground for such leadership than a spirit of management that confirms in the day-to-day practices of the organization strict principles of conduct and responsibility, high standards of performance, and respect for individuals and their work." (p. 79)

16. "Whenever an institution malfunctions as consistently as boards of directors have in nearly every major fiasco of the last forty or fifty years it is futile to blame men. It is the institution that malfunctions." (p. 81)

17. "[CEOs are] responsible for making their boards effective." (p. 82)

18. "What matters is not charisma. What matters is [that] the leader leads in the right direction or misleads." (p. 82)

19. "The most important function of the executive is decision making. . . . [Executives] follow a disciplined process, first defining the problem they face. . . . Once the problem is defined correctly, the next step is to establish the boundary conditions the decision has to meet." (p. 83)

Management in a Pluralistic Society of Organizations

1. "Leaders in every single institution and in every single sector . . . have two responsibilities. They are responsible and accountable for the performance of their institutions, and that requires them and their institutions to be concentrated, focused, limited. They are responsible also, however, for the community as a whole." (p. 96)

2. "We became a society of organizations in the last century. When managers were very rare you could depend on the naturals. Now you need enormous numbers of them." (p. 98)

3. *"Management* is not 'Business Management'—though it first attained attention in business—but the governing organ of *all* institutions of modern society." (p. 99)

4. "The new pluralism requires what might be called *civic responsibility: giving to the community in the pursuit of one's own interest or of one's own task.*" (p. 100)

5. " 'By their fruits ye shall know them'—this might well be the fundamental constitutional principle of the new pluralist society of institutions." (p. 101)

6. "The first job in any organization is to make top management effective." (p. 104)

7. "A business needs a central governing organ and a central organ of review and appraisal. On the quality of these two organs, which together [make up] top management, its performance, results and spirit largely depend." (p. 107)

8. "In any major institution—the Church, for instance, or the Army—the finding, developing, and proving out of leaders of tomorrow is an essential job to which the best men must give fully of their time and attention." (p. 108)

9. "National policies impose constraints on the strategy of the transnational enterprise." (p. 114)

10. "As the corporation moves towards a confederation or a syndicate, it will increasingly need a top management that is separate, powerful, and accountable." (p. 115)

11. "The purpose of an organization is to 'make common men do uncommon things.'" (p. 120)

12. "Entrepreneurial businesses treat entrepreneurship as a duty. They are disciplined about it . . . they work at it . . . they practice it." (p. 121)

13. "Spirit of performance in a human organization means that its energy output is larger than the sum of the efforts put in." (p. 121)

14. "The task of the conscience activities is not to help the organization do better what it is already doing. The task is to remind the orga-

nization all the time of what it should be doing and isn't doing." (p. 122)

Navigating a Society in Transition

1. "Social needs will grow in two areas. They will grow, first, in what has traditionally been considered *charity*: helping the poor, the disabled, the helpless, the victims. And they will grow even faster in respect to services that aim at *changing the community* and at *changing people*. In a transition period, the number of people in need always grows." (p. 129)

2. "None of the U.S. programs of the last forty years in which we tried to tackle a social problem through government action has produced significant results. But independent non-profit agencies *have* had impressive results." (p. 130)

3. "Citizenship in and through the social sector is not a panacea for the ills of post-capitalist society and post-capitalist polity, but it may be a prerequisite for tackling these ills." (p. 131)

4. "I think anybody who is not uneasy about the direction in which the world is moving is blind and deaf. The belief in progress, which we inherited from the eighteenth century, is gone. The belief in a western-dominated world is going." (p. 134)

5. "The most effective way to manage change successfully is to create it." (p. 135)

6. "When it rains manna from heaven, some people put up an umbrella. Others reach for a big spoon." (p. 136)

7. "What must I do to be prepared for danger, for opportunities, and above all for change?" (p. 136)

8. "There is a growing need for truly transnational institutions. . . . The military invasion of Iraq in the winter and spring of 1991 may have been a starting point. [F]or the first time in recorded history, practically all nation-states acted together to put down an act of terrorism—for this is what the Iraqi invasion of Kuwait represented." (pp. 137–38)

9. "We are in the midst of a very major transition in which the new, not just new structures, new organizations, but fundamentally new con-

cepts, new ways of seeing the world, new ways of relating as individuals, as organizations, and as countries, will have to be developed." (p. 140)

10. "I think we are in a period in which there is enormous uncertainty and danger. . . . It's uncertainty, it's the feeling that the ground under your feet is shaking and that you don't know whether to step down or whether to go right through or not. That is what is bothering people." (pp. 140–41)

11. "And it's a very exciting time because it is also a time in which what individuals do, what small and large organizations do, what countries and governments do, really matters." (p. 141)

12. "The upward mobility of the knowledge society comes at a high price: the psychological pressures and emotional traumas of the rat race." (p. 142)

13. "A business can be defined as a process that converts an outside resource, namely knowledge, into outside results, namely economic values." (p. 143)

14. "Management is what tradition used to call a liberal art—'liberal' because it deals with the fundamentals of knowledge; self-knowledge, wisdom, and leadership; 'art' because it deals with practice and application." (p. 144)

15. "Equally important is managing your own career. The stepladder is gone, and there's not even the implied structure of an industry's rope ladder. It's more like vines, and you bring your own machete." (p. 145)

16. "The important thing is to identify the 'future that has already happened.'" (p. 149)

17. "The important challenge in society, economy, politics is to exploit the changes that have already occurred and to use them as opportunities." (pp. 149–50)

18. "Of all external changes, demographics—defined as changes in population, its size, age, structure, composition, employment, educational status, and income—are the clearest." (p. 151)

19. "The rapidly growing aging population and the rapidly shrinking younger population means there will be social problems." (p. 152)

20. "Theory organizes the new realities; it rarely creates them." (p. 152)

21. "Perhaps the time has come for an entrepreneur to start schools based on what we know about learning, rather than on the old wives' tales about it that have been handed down through the ages." (p. 157)

22. "In the knowledge society subjects may matter less than the students' capacity to continue learning and their motivation to do so." (pp. 157–58)

23. "The achievement that motivates is doing exceptionally well what one is already good at." (p. 159)

Maintaining Your Organization Through Change

1. "An organization needs something new every so often, and yet at the same time it also needs *continuity*. The mission or purpose remains the same so you need people that are committed to the mission, but sometimes you also need to make radical *changes*." (p. 164)

2. "Precisely because change is a constant, the foundations have to be extra strong." (p. 165)

3. "A large organization is effective through its mass rather than through its agility. Mass enables the organization to put to work a great many more kinds of knowledge and skill than could possibly be combined in any one person or small group." (p. 167)

4. "Predicting the future can only get you into trouble. The task is to manage what there is and to work to create what could and should be." (p. 168)

5. "There is an old proverb in medicine that if you can't eliminate you drown in your own waste products, and very fast. That's true of every organization, and yet if you believe in a cause that's difficult to do in a nonprofit." (p. 172)

6. "If we did not do this already, would we go into it now? If the answer is no, 'What do we do now?'" (p. 173)

7. "Knowing that an existing product will be abandoned in the near future and resources freed up may help to concentrate your mind on innovation." (p. 175)

8. "The mission statement is your tool to force—and I use quite intentionally a nonpermissive word—to force your people to think

through, 'What is my objective? What is my goal? And what does it mean for me to contribute?' " (p. 178)

9. "Use dissent to achieve unity and commitment." (p. 180)

10. "You need three things [for a good mission statement]: opportunities; competence; and commitment." (p. 182)

11. "You concentrate on what you do best; you concentrate on what the market really needs and responds to; and you strive for excellence before you branch out because far too many entrepreneurial adventures immediately see all those market opportunities and start sprinkling themselves and they don't have the resources to make it first rate, and so they start cutting corners, they start getting by, and in no time at all, they've lost all [of] what the market people call 'product differentiation.' " (p. 186)

12. "The customer rarely buys what a business thinks it sells him." (p. 189)

13. "The customers have to be assumed to be rational. But their rationality is not necessarily that of the manufacturer; it is that of their own situation." (p. 189)

14. "The management of knowledge workers is a 'marketing job.' And in marketing one does not begin with the question: 'What do we want?' One begins with the question: 'What does the other party want? What are its values? What are its goals? What does it consider results?' " (pp. 190–91)

15. "I've seen any number of businesses where a star has built a business and has no successor, doesn't perpetuate himself or herself, and it becomes a bureaucracy." (p. 194)

16. "If you don't think through the roles of the key people very early you build up tribes and power struggles in the organization that in the early stages [have] to be deadly." (p. 195)

17. "The change from a business that the owner-entrepreneur can run with 'helpers' to a business that requires a management is what the physicists call a *change of phase*, such as the change from water to ice." (pp. 196–97)

Structuring Your Organization

1. "I just know that the more control there is, the less growth there is. The great lesson of the twentieth century is that central planning doesn't work." (p. 205)

2. "*Decentralization* implies a sense of rules that the units operate under. What we are actually talking about is a *confederation*. You want these churches to be independent units but carry the spirit, right? That's a confederation." (p. 207)

3. "The developed countries are moving fast toward a network society." (p. 210)

4. "But in a partnership—whether with an outsourcing contractor, a joint-venture partner, or a company in which one holds a minority stake—one cannot command. One can only gain *trust*." (p. 211)

5. "Systems organization is an extension of the team design principle. But instead of the team consisting of individuals, the systems organization builds the team out of a wide variety of different organizations." (p. 212)

Managing Your Members

1. "It is a constant fight with the stars; because every star wants to do something he or she does not perform well. If they are stars, their range is very narrow and their temperament is narrow." (p. 220)

2. "Effective executives know that their subordinates are paid to perform and not to please their superiors. They know that it does not matter how many tantrums a prima donna throws as long as she brings in the customers." (p. 221)

3. "Concentrate on turning people of high competence into star performers." (p. 222)

4. "Feature star performers to raise the performance capacity of the organization." (p. 222)

5. "Just because a person doesn't perform in the job he or she was put in doesn't mean that that person is a bad worker whom the company should let go. It only means that he or she is in the wrong job." (p. 228)

6. "People given a second chance usually come through. If people try, give them a second chance. If people try again and they still do not perform, they may be in the wrong spot. Then one asks: Where should he or she be?" (p. 230)

7. "A functioning society must always be capable of organizing the actual reality in a social order. . . . No society can function unless it gives the individual member social status and function, and unless the decisive social power is legitimate power." (p. 234)

The Succession Decision

1. "The succession problem: 'How does one manage to maintain or preserve the wisdom, the counsel, and the example of a founder and yet not have him kill off his successor?'" (p. 242)

2. "The succession decision should focus on the maintenance of the spirit that keeps an institution alive. Solutions have to fit the specific organization and maintain its spirit of performance." (p. 244)

3. "The proof of the sincerity and seriousness of a management is uncompromising emphasis on integrity of character. . . . For it is character through which leadership is exercised; it is character that sets the example and is imitated." (pp. 244–45)

4. "The spirit of an organization is created from the top. If an organization is great in spirit, it is because the spirit of its top people is great. If it decays, it does so because the top rots; as the proverb has it, 'Fish die from the head down.' No one should ever be appointed to a senior position unless top management is willing to have his or her character serve as the model for subordinates." (p. 245)

5. "Pick successors based upon their strength, not to minimize weaknesses." (p. 247)

6. "The idea that there are 'well-rounded' people, people who have only strengths and no weaknesses, . . . is a prescription for mediocrity if not for incompetence. Strong people always have strong weaknesses too. Where there are peaks there are valleys." (pp. 247–48)

7. "An organization that is not capable of perpetuating itself has failed. An organization therefore has to provide today the men and women

who run it tomorrow. It has to renew its human capital. It should steadily upgrade its human resources." (p. 251)

8. "An organization [that] just perpetuates today's level of vision, excellence, and accomplishments has lost the capacity to adapt. And since the one and only thing certain in human affairs is change, it will not be capable of survival in a changed tomorrow." (pp. 251–52)

9. "Very few of these people have thought through the succession questions: 'What kind of people do we need to succeed us? What kind of background should they have? How do we train them? How do we test them? How do we screen them?'" (p. 253)

10. "The questions I ask nonprofit organizations looking for successors are 'What are results in the job? What competencies do you need? What experiences do you need?'" (p. 253)

Lessons from the Social Sector on the Power of Purpose—Part I

1. "One priority area [for the Peter F. Drucker Foundation for Nonprofit Management]—maybe the top one judging from the responses we have been getting—is the development of ways in which a nonprofit organization (and especially one of the smaller ones) can evaluate itself—its mission; its performance and results; its structure and organization; the allocation of its resources; and its performance in attracting and using resources, both people and money. This will have to be a self-evaluation tool kit." (p. 268)

2. "The best nonprofits devote a great deal of thought to defining their organization's mission." (p. 268)

3. "Management always has to consider both the present and the future; both the short run and the long run. A management problem is not solved if immediate profits are purchased by endangering the long-range health, perhaps even the survival of the company." (p. 272)

4. "Management has to live always in both present and future. It must keep the enterprise performing in the present—or else there will be no enterprise capable of performing in the future. And it has to make the enterprise capable of performance, growth, and change in the future." (p. 273)

5. "The first—but also the toughest—task of the non-profit executive is to get all of these constituencies to agree on what the *long-term* goals of the institution are. Building around the long term is the only way to integrate all these interests." (pp. 273–74)

6. "I soon learned that they [effective executives] start out by defining the fundamental change that the non-profit institution wants to make in society and in human beings; then they project that goal onto the concerns of each of the institution's constituencies." (p. 274)

THE SALVATION ARMY

7. "The Salvation Army is: 'by far the most effective organization in the U.S. No one even comes close to it in respect to clarity of mission, ability to innovate, measurable results, dedication and putting money to maximum use.'" (p. 279)

8. [On The Salvation Army's ability to support its programs:] "I am not surprised. I have long ago learned that if you have results, you get the support. And you have the results, and the results speak for themselves. But I am impressed by that very clear concept you have of where you put the resources because in my own work with nonprofit organizations, this is a continuing problem and dilemma between taking care of the immediate need and yet being able to build on the long term, which requires not only a lot of resources but a lot of commitment." (p. 284)

9. "Your fund-raising activity is successful because you are enabling the average American to live up to her beliefs and values and commitments." (p. 284)

10. "Put resources where the results are." (p. 285)

11. "The reward of service is more service." (p. 285)

Lessons from the Social Sector on the Power of Purpose—Part II

PUBLIC SCHOOLS

12. "I know that you say in your proposals that vouchers aren't going to save the school system, and you're absolutely right because as I said

to you at lunch, and I found that you agreed, vouchers are both in-evitable and necessary if only to resolve that enormous inertia of the public schools establishment. You need to build a fire under public schools; vouchers are the fire." (p. 288)

13. "Schools can have results despite all the adverse pressure on them." (p. 289)

14. "In the knowledge society, the school becomes accountable for performance and results." (p. 291)

15. "Embracing the new technology of learning and teaching is a pre-requisite for national and cultural success and equally for economic competitiveness." (p. 291)

16. "The technology [in education] will be significant, but primarily because it should force us to do new things rather than because it will enable us to do old things better. . . . The real challenge ahead is not technology itself. It is what we use it for." (p. 291)

17. "Here are the new specifications [for education]:

    The school has to provide universal literacy of a high order—well beyond what 'literacy' means today.

    It has to imbue students on all levels and of all ages with motivation to learn and with the discipline of continuing learning.

    It has to be an open system, accessible both to highly educated people and to people who for whatever reason did not gain access to ad-vanced education in their early years.

    It has to impart knowledge both as substance and as process—what the Germans differentiate as *Wissen* and *Konnen*." (p. 292)

Lessons from the Social Sector on the Power of Purpose—Part III

THE MEGA-CHURCH

18. "The most significant sociological phenomenon of the second half of the twentieth century has been the development of the large pastoral church." (p. 295)

19. The starting point for management can no longer be its own product or service, and not even its own market and its known end-uses for

its products and services. The starting point has to be what *customers consider value.* (p. 297)

20. "Most case studies are forgotten one minute after the class ends. If I can create disequilibrium in a class and leverage that energy for learning, they'll never forget that case study." (p. 299)

Developing Oneself from Success to Significance

1. "In the course of life, there are the great majority of successful people who have to change their direction at about age sixty." (p. 308)

2. As you grow older, are you focusing more on doing the things that give *you* achievement and satisfaction and growth or more on the things that have an *impact outside of yourself?* (p. 308)

3. "It will be this minority [social entrepreneurs], the people [who] see the long working-life expectancy as an opportunity both for themselves and for society, who may increasingly become the leaders and the models. They increasingly will be the 'success stories.'" (p. 309)

4. "The purpose of the work on making the future is not to decide what should be done tomorrow, but what should be done today to have a tomorrow." (p. 310)

5. "We are slowly learning how to do this work systematically and with direction and control. There are two different, though complementary, approaches: [One approach is] finding and exploiting the lag between the appearance of a discontinuity in the economy and society and its full impact—one might call this *anticipation of a future that has already happened.*" (p. 310)

6. "[The second approach is] imposing on the as yet unborn future a new idea that tries to give direction and shape to what is to come. This one might be called *making the future that has already happened.*" (p. 310)

7. "You may have taken some vicious hits. A good share of men and women never make it to halftime without pain. . . . Even if your pain was slight, you are smart enough to see that you cannot play the second half as you did the first. For one thing, you don't have the energy you once had. . . . But now you yearn for something more

than success. Then there is the reality of the game itself: The clock is running." (pp. 314–15)

8. "Fame is not the only measure of life. I would like to keep this in mind and continue what I do now." (p. 315)

9. "This is the true joy of life, the being used up for a purpose recognized by yourself as a mighty one; being a force of nature instead of a feverish, selfish little clod of ailments and grievances, complaining that the world will not devote itself to making you happy." (p. 316)

10. "Life is no 'brief candle' to me. It is a sort of splendid torch which I have got hold of for a moment, and I want to make it burn as brightly as possible before handing it on to future generations." (p. 316)

11. "What one does well may not be worth devoting one's life to." (p. 316)

12. "To be effective in an organization, a person's values must be compatible with the organization's values. They do not need to be the same, but they must be close enough to coexist." (p. 316)

13. "Individuals may need a process to help them move from success to significance. . . . I think people like this need a great deal of help in three ways: One is simply identifying the possibilities. Another is thinking through what they are trying to do. And the third is preparation, training, and learning from others and from each other." (pp. 318–19)

14. "Activities for significance are by and large an enormous opportunity, but many people don't have the imagination to identify possibilities." (p. 319)

15. "All the social entrepreneurs I know began to work in their chosen second enterprise long before they reached their peak in their original business." (p. 321)

16. "They misuse people; they do not put people *in their area of giftedness but in the area of the needs* [emphasis mine] of the church." (p. 322)

17. "But here is a whole generation of people, young in terms of life expectancy, vigorous, well-to-do, with lots of energy, a fair amount of time, more energy than time, and a desire to grow. . . . They want to make a contribution over and above the money, and are trained and equipped to do it. But they don't really know how to organize themselves for it." (p. 325)

18. "If the thoughtful answer to the question 'Where do I belong?' is that you don't belong where you currently work, the next question is why? Is it because you can't accept the values of the organization? Is the organization corrupt? That will certainly damage you, because you become cynical and contemptuous of yourself if you find yourself in a situation where the values are incompatible with your own." (p. 327)

19. "Take a little control over your career. . . . I am talking about career planning in the sense of: What do I have to learn, what are my strengths, how can I build on them, where do I belong, do I really belong in this company? One must take the responsibility of asking oneself these questions from time to time, and acting on the answers." (p. 328)

20. "Develop a genuine, true, major outside interest. Not a hobby, a genuine interest, which permits you to live in a different world, with different peers whose opinions are meaningful to you." (p. 328)

21. "Halftime is more like an entrepreneurial start-up company. One person sees a white space opportunity, raises angel capital, and builds a small team to complement the single entrepreneur. The sequence is something like: (a) Aha! An idea. (b) Launch a test market based on a hypothesis about customer value added. (c) Prove the hypothesis—that there is a customer. (d) Scale up—extend and expand with debt and risk capital." (p. 331)

22. "Management is the new technology (rather than any specific new science or invention) that is making the American economy into an entrepreneurial economy. It is about to make America into an entrepreneurial society." (p. 332)

23. "Successful entrepreneurs do not wait until 'the Muse kisses them' and gives them a bright idea; they go to work." (p. 333)

24. "The emergence of the entrepreneurial society may be a major turning point in history. . . . [The modern welfare state] may survive despite the demographic challenges of an aging population and a shrinking birthrate. But it will survive only if the entrepreneurial economy succeeds in greatly raising productivities." (p. 334)

25. "Managing Oneself is a *revolution* in human affairs. It requires new and unprecedented things from the individual, and especially from

the knowledge worker. For in effect it demands that each knowledge worker think and behave as a Chief Executive Officer." (p. 338)

26. "What's commonly called 'burnout,' the most common affliction of the forty-something knowledge worker, is very rarely the result of stress. Its common, all too common, cause is boredom on the job. Managing oneself therefore requires that you prepare for the second half of your life." (p. 339)

27. "Significance need not be a 180-degree course change. Instead, do some retrofitting so that you can apply your gifts in ways that allow you to spend more time on things related to what is in *your box* [your strengths and values]. And to do it in such a way as to reclaim the thrill of that first deal." (p. 340)

Character and Legacy

1. "What bothers me today is not the economy. What bothers me in this country is that our society today has lost its sweetness. It's sour, terribly sour, and I think that this isn't anything government can do much about, or is likely to do very much about. In fact the way we are going, government is making the sourness worse." (p. 344)

2. "It's only by this kind of activity in the nonprofits, this kind of self-respect shown to people, this kind of initiative in solving our most difficult social problems that I think we can make this a society again." (p. 345)

3. "Only the social sector can create what we now need, communities for citizens." (p. 345)

4. "The twentieth century saw an explosive growth of both government and business. . . . What the twenty-first century needs above all is equally explosive growth of the nonprofit social sector in building communities in the newly dominant social environment, the city." (p. 346)

5. "Only compassion can save—the wordless knowledge of my own responsibility for whatever is being done to the least of God's children." (p. 347)

6. "A valid THOB is a hypothesis about the mission required to succeed

given the realities faced by an organization in a specific business or domain; its core competencies or knowledge requirements; and its own set of values. Without a valid theory, the organization simply will not produce what its customers and potential customers consider value. A THOB is a hypothesis that is tested against reality each day." (p. 350)

7. "A clear, simple, and penetrating theory of the business rather than intuition characterizes the truly successful entrepreneur." (p. 353)

8. "The theory of the business has to be tested constantly. It is not graven on tablets of stone. It is a hypothesis. And it is a hypothesis about things that are in constant flux—society, markets, customers, technology. And so, built into the theory of the business must be the ability to change itself." (p. 354)

9. "Knowledge is a perishable commodity. It has to be reaffirmed, re-learned, re-practiced all the time." (p. 355)

10. "I think the balance between maintaining *internal dynamics* and *institutionalization* is a very delicate one. And eventually, one always institutionalizes or one dissipates but you haven't reached that point where there's reason for you to rush it." (p. 358)

11. "Neither studies nor market research nor computer modeling are a substitute for the *test of reality*. Everything improved or new needs, therefore, first to be tested on a small scale, that is, it needs to be *piloted*." (p. 361)

12. Everything new gets into trouble. "And then it needs a champion. It needs somebody who says, 'I am going to make this succeed,' and who then goes to work on it. And this person needs to be somebody whom the organization respects." (p. 361)

13. " *'Make sure you will not learn from experience'* is the prescription for non-performance in public administration." (p. 362)

14. "It is one of the critical tasks of the executive to know when to say, 'Enough is enough. Let's stop improving. There are too many patches on those pants.'" (p. 362)

15. Drucker on bigness: "There are certain things an elephant can do that a mouse cannot do." (p. 367)

16. "The question is not whether to have values—every human being

has them and every human group, however organized, does too. The question is: Are they the right values or the wrong values? Are they values that give life or values that give death?" (p. 371)

17. "It is also the business with these values, the business that believes it exists to contribute rather than just to take, that will weather adversity. [Values] may be treated . . . as something we can indulge in as a 'nice little extra.' It is in times of adversity, in times that try a man's soul, that values are a necessity. For if the right values are absent at such a time, there is no incentive for human beings to walk the extra mile, to make the extra commitment, to do the hard work of rethinking strategy, of trying new things, of rebuilding." (p. 372)

18. "Preachments aren't values—they are good intentions, at best. . . . What is the one decisive, most unambiguous action that most expresses an organization's values? It is the *personnel decision.*" (p. 373)

19. "You become a person by knowing what your values are, what you contribute, and it is outside yourself. It is better to give than to receive but you have to know what to give. It is very difficult to know." (p. 376)

20. "I . . . had to decide between what I was doing well and successfully, and my values. I was doing extremely well as a young investment banker in London in the mid-1930s; it clearly fitted my strengths. Yet I did not see myself making a contribution as an asset manager of any kind. People, I realized, were my values. And I saw no point in being the richest man in the cemetery. . . . Values, in other words, are and should be the ultimate test." (p. 377)

21. "What ethics requires is to ask oneself: 'What kind of person do I want to see when I shave myself in the morning, or put on my lipstick in the morning?' Ethics, in other words, are a clear value system." (p. 378)

22. "To work in an organization the value system of which is unacceptable to a person, or incompatible with [him or her], condemns the person both to frustration and to nonperformance." (p. 378)

23. "What do you want to be remembered for?" (p. 381)

24. "I'm always asking that question: What do you want to be remembered for? It is a question that induces you to renew yourself, because

it pushes you to see yourself as a different person—the person you can *become*." (p. 384)

25. "One thing worth being remembered for is the difference one makes in the lives of people." (p. 386)

26. "We mentor . . . because we can envision what a person can become." (p. 388)

27. "You see successful organizations. They know what they are called to do and they know what they are not called to do, what's important and what's not important. They don't need reminding; they are clear about their identity. *They have a clear purpose.*" (p. 390)

28. "A critical question for leaders is, 'When do you stop pouring resources into things that have achieved their purpose?'" (p. 391)

29. "Successful leaders don't start out asking, 'What do I want to do?' They ask, 'What needs to be done?' Then they ask, 'Of those things that would make a difference, which are right for me?'" (p. 392)

30. " 'Opportunity comes in over the transom,' . . . and that means one has to be flexible, ready to seize the right opportunities when they come." (p. 395)

31. "Good intentions aren't enough; define the results you want." (p. 396)

32. "My definition of success changed a long time ago. I love doing consulting work and writing—I regularly lose track of time when I'm doing those things. But finishing well, and how I want to be remembered, those are the things that matter now. Making a difference in a few lives is a worthy goal. Having enabled a few people to do the thing they want to do—that's really what I want to be remembered for." (p. 396)

33. "Recognize the downside to 'No longer learning, no longer growing.'" (p. 396)

34. "Pasteur made not just one, but several discoveries in his career. This led some people to say that he was lucky. Pasteur himself said that chance favors only the prepared mind." (p. 399)

Notes

1. Peter F. Drucker, interview with Reverend James Flamming, 1989: "You know, Jim, when I told one of my business friends that I am doing this nonprofit tape program he said, 'Why is this important?' And I said to him, We are developing the functioning community and functioning democracy of tomorrow, not in our businesses. They may have had the chance, but I think they missed it. We are developing it in the nonprofit sector. And he looked at me as if I had just come from outer space. And I said, because you, in business, *are not developing leaders*. You are developing *functionaries*. It is in the nonprofit sector where we develop citizens who will take responsibility for community and create self-government. And I had a hard time explaining it to him. But basically what the New England town community did in a small community of four hundred farmers, you now do, in your church, which is in that sense a small community, to develop accountability, skills, and example. And I think that makes the nonprofit sector important beyond its size or contribution as the builders of a *responsible self-governing community*."

2. At http://ccdl.libraries.claremont.edu/cdm4/document.php?CISO ROOT=/dac&CISOPTR=2279&REC=2, accessed August 23, 2011.

3. Guests included Mort Myerson, CEO of Perot Business Systems and, until its sale to General Motors in 1984, president and CEO of Electronic Data Systems (EDS); C. William Pollard, CEO of the ServiceMaster Company; C. Gregg Petersmeyer, assistant to President George H. W. Bush and director of the Office of National Service (including the Points of Light Program); John Diebold, founder of the Diebold Group; John E. Jacob, chairman of the board of trust-

ees of Howard University; Andy Grove, cofounder and chief executive officer of Intel Corporation; Richard Schubert, president of the American Red Cross; William Podlich, cofounder of PIMCO, an international investment company headquartered in Newport Beach, California; James Osborne, national commander of The Salvation Army; Philip Henry, producer and editor of "The Nonprofit Drucker," an audiotape series on the management of nonprofit organizations; Father Leo Bartell, vicar for social ministries for the Diocese of Rockford, Illinois; Dolores E. Cross, first woman president of Chicago State University; Lawrence Robert Tollenaere, CEO and chairman of the board of American Pipe and Construction Company; John Bachmann, managing partner, Edward Jones; and John A. McNeice Jr., chairman and CEO of the Colonial Group.

4. LeadershipJournal.net, "Managing to Minister: An Interview with Peter Drucker," posted April 1, at http://www.christianitytoday.com/le/1989/spring/8912014.html, accessed June 24, 2011.

5. At http://www.youtube.com/watch?v=JGyQRy-Zcj4, accessed December 11, 2013.

6. At http://www.cgu.edu/pages/6627.asp, accessed December 11, 2013.

7. Father Beltran's book *Faith and Struggle on Smokey Mountain*, Orbis, 2012, is a good introduction to the problem and promise of managing at the bottom of the pyramid.

8. Drucker, "Introduction: What Makes an Effective Executive," in *The Effective Executive*, 1966, 2007, p. xi.

9. Clark Clifford, *Preserving the Free World in the Truman Presidency: Intimate Perspectives*, Vol. 2 of *Portraits of American Presidents*, ed. Kenneth W. Thompson, University Press of America, New York, 1984, p. 18.

10. The interview was published in *Academy of Management Executive*, Vol. 17, No. 3, August 2003, pp. 9–12, http://www.jstor.org/stable/4165974, accessed October 19, 2013. The question in this reading and Drucker's answer appear on pp. 11–12.

11. Revised and Enlarged Ed., IVP Books, Madison, WI, 1994.

12. Peter Drucker coined this name for the mega-church that not only worked for him but was central to his work. To Drucker, the pastoral church was one concerned with meeting the spiritual needs of its

members while also providing opportunities for their growth and development.

13. Peter F. Drucker, "The Coming of the New Organization," *Harvard Business Review,* January–February 1988, p. 3, Reprint 88105.

14. James Manyika, Michael Chui, Brad Brown, Jacques Bughin, Richard Dobbs, Charles Roxburgh, and Angela Hung Byers, "Big Data: The Next Frontier for Innovation, Competition, and Productivity," McKinsey Global Institute Report, May 2011, at http://www.mckinsey.com/insights/business_technology/big_data_the_next_frontier_for_innovation, accessed January 26, 2014.

15. Here are five recommendations for the work of the board, condensed from the extensive work of Ira M. Millstein, Holly J. Gregory, and Rebecca C. Grapass, "Six Priorities for Boards in 2006," *Law and Governance* Vol. 10, No. 3, March 2006, pp. 17–19: (1) Arrange to have *appropriate information flows* to permit the board to set its agenda and to organize its own work. (2) *Set compensation levels* that reflect performance against preset responsibilities of top management. (3) Designate a subcommittee of the board to focus on issues related to *managerial succession* for key positions. (4) Go beyond matters related to *compliance in reporting* and insist on *ethical performance throughout the corporation.* (5) Make certain that financial statements accurately reflect the true economics of the corporation and its parts.

16. Drucker, "What Business Can Learn from Nonprofits," 1989, at http://www.brynmawr.edu/businessworkshops/management/documents/Drucker-Whatbusinesscanlearnfromnonprofits.pdf, p. 4, accessed January 29, 2014.

17. Letter from Robert A. G. Monks to Jonathan G. Katz, secretary of Securities and Exchange Commission, June 2, 2003, https://www.sec.gov/rules/other/s71003/gagmonks060203.htm, accessed April 23, 2014.

18. Peter F. Drucker, "The Bored Board," in *Towards the New Economics and Other Essays,* Harper & Row, New York, 1981, p. 110. Reissued: Harvard Business School Publishing, Cambridge, MA, 2010.

19. SEC Chairman Mary L. Shapiro, "SEC Adopts New Measures to Fa-

cilitate Director Nominations by Shareholders," August 25, 2010, www.sec.gov/news/press/2010/2010-155.htm, accessed April 23, 2014.

20. "To restore management's ability to manage we will have to make boards effective again—and that should be considered a responsibility of the CEO." Drucker, "What Business Can Learn from Nonprofits," 1989, p. 5 of Reprint 89404.

21. See more at http://constitution.laws.com/10th-amendment#sthash .5PYopx34.dpuf, accessed December 26, 2013.

22. Frances Hesselbein, http://blogs.hbr.org/2010/06/how-did-peter -drucker-see-corp/, June 9, 2010, accessed December 26, 2013.

23. Rosabeth Moss Kanter; "Upsize, Downsize," *New York Times*, September 27, 1995. Archives, http://www.nytimes.com/1995/09/27/ opinion/upsize-downsize.html, accessed March 30, 2014.

24. "Is it possible to be a good governor?" At http://www.amazon.com/ Firing-William-Buckley-Possible-Governor/dp/B007QK7LTK, accessed December 26, 2013. This program is also available at hoover.org.

25. Drucker, *Innovation and Entrepreneurship*, 1985, p. 116.

26. At http://www.lincolnelectric.com/en-us/company/pages/lincoln-world wide.aspx, accessed December 19, 2013.

27. My conclusions are based on an analysis of the data at http://www. worthingtonindustries.com/, accessed December 19, 2013.

28. At http://www.nucor.com/, accessed December 19, 2013.

29. "The law of negative entropy states that systems survive and maintain their characteristic internal order only so long as they import from the environment more energy than they expend in the process of transformation and exportation." Book review, Dhiren N. Panchal, Daniel Katz, and Robert Kahn, *The Social Psychology of Organizations*, 2nd ed., Wiley, New York, 1978, http://sites.idc.ac.il/dice/files/activ-ity2.pdf, accessed December 18, 2013.

30. Winston Churchill, "Book Review, *The End of Economic Man*," *London Times Literary Supplement*, May 27, 1939, p. 306.

31. Center on Education Policy, "Are Private Schools Better Academically Than Public Schools?" 2007, p. 6.

32. Transcript of Drucker-Buford video, August 1998.

33. Robert D. Putnam and David E. Campbell, *American Grace*, Simon & Schuster, New York, 2010, p. 471.

34. Peter F. Drucker and Joseph A. Maciariello, *Management Cases: Revised Edition*, Case Number 49, "Drucker's Ideas for School Reform," HarperCollins, New York, 1999, pp. 230–38.

35. "More than 19,000 of the nearly 28,000 private schools in the United States are church-related. . . . Catholic schools remain the largest group of church-related schools in the United States, with about 8,250 primary and secondary schools, compared to about 13,000 for all religions combined." Harold G. Unger, *Encyclopedia of American Education*, 3rd ed., InfoBase, New York, 2007, p. 230.

36. Pearson Index of Cognitive Skills and Educational Attainment, http://thelearningcurve.pearson.com/index/index-ranking, accessed December 16, 2013.

37. Drucker, *Innovation and Entrepreneurship*, 1985, p. 110.

38. *Reading Recovery in North America: An Illustrative History*, Reading Recovery Council of North America, Columbus, OH, 2000, p. 8.

39. The monograph *Friedrich Julius Stahl: His Conservative Theory of the State* has been translated into English by Martin Chemers and appears in *Society*, Vol. 39, Issue 5, July/August 2002, p. 46. English translation at http://www.druckersociety.at/files/p_drucker_stahl_en.pdf, accessed December 16, 2013.

40. Schumpeter describes this process in a very accessible way in chapter 7 of his *Capitalism, Socialism and Democracy*, 1942, pp. 81–110. The quotation is on p. 83.

41. See http://health.usnews.com/best-hospitals/pediatric-rankings/neonatal-care?page=5, accessed December 18, 2013.

42. Robert N. Anthony, "Zero-Based Budgeting Is a Fraud," *Wall Street Journal*, April 27, 1977. Summarized in U.S. General Accounting Office, "Zero Based Budgeting," July 1977, pp. 5–6, http://archive.gao.gov/otherpdf1/093985.pdf, accessed December 18, 2013.

43. It is called systematic innovation in Drucker's *Innovation and Entrepreneurship*, 1985, especially chapters 1–11.

44. Robert D. Putnam and David E. Campbell (*American Grace*, Simon & Schuster, New York, 2010) have recognized the pioneering role of Bill

Hybels and Willow Creek Community Church. Formed by Hybels in 1975, Willow Creek was "the first of the major U.S. evangelical mega-churches" (p. 113). Nonchurchgoers, or noncustomers—those not attending any religious institution—are given special attention in Putnam and Campbell's study. The authors refer to this group as *nones*, people without any religious affiliation (p. 16).

45. Special Report, http://www.economist.com/node/5165460, accessed January 31, 2014.

46. Barnard, *The Functions of the Executive*, 1971, p. 256.

47. Wilson Greatbatch, *The Making of the Pacemaker: Celebrating a Lifesaving Invention*, Prometheus, Amherst, NY, p. 35.

48. The complete story behind the invention of the pacemaker and subsequent developments is found in Joseph A. Maciariello, "Innovation and Management for the Common Good: Drucker's Lost Art of Management," in *Entrepreneurial Management—Challenges and Perspectives: Festschrift for Prof. Peter Gomez*, Haupt Berne, October 2012, pp. 325–44.

49. An exhaustive and authoritative treatment of many of the issues discussed in this introduction is found in U.S. Department of State, Office of the Historian, http://history.state.gov/milestones/1776–1783, accessed January 2, 2014. An extensive discussion of federal decentralization with applications to networks, alliances, confederations, and syndicates is in Maciariello and Linkletter, *Drucker's Lost Art of Management,* 2011, chapter 4, pp. 133–80.

50. Karen L. Higgins and Joseph A. Maciariello, "Leading Complex Collaboration in Network Organizations: A Multidimensional Approach," in Michael M. Beyerlein et al., *Complex Collaboration: Building the Capabilities for Working Across Boundaries,* Elsevier, New York, 2004, pp. 203–41.

51. Drucker, *The Effective Executive*, 1967, p. 72.

52. At http://www.whitehouse.gov/about/presidents/ulyssessgrant/, accessed December 17, 2013.

53. MacArthur's assessment of Eisenhower. Confirmed retrospectively in the documentary "MacArthur," in Walter Goodman, *New York Times* archives, May 17, 1999. www.nytimes.com/1999/05/17/arts/televi

sion_review_the_general_at_center_of_the_stage.html, accessed July 18, 2014.

54. "Eisenhower Takes Command," June 25, 1942, http://www.history.com/this-day-in-history/eisenhower-takes-command, accessed January 28, 2014.

55. Peter F. Drucker, Foreword, in Don M. Frick and Larry C. Spears (eds.), *On Becoming a Servant Leader*, Jossey-Bass, San Francisco, 1966, pp xi–xii.

56. HuffPost Healthy Living, "Mindfulness in the Corporate World: How Businesses Are Incorporating the Eastern Practice," posted August 29, 2012, and updated January 7, 2013, http://www.huffingtonpost.com/2012/08/29/mindfulness-businesses-corporate-employees-meditation_n_1840690.html, accessed March 3, 2014.

57. Derek Bok served as the twenty-fifth president of Harvard from 1971 to 1991. He had served as dean of Harvard Law School from 1968 to 1971. At http://www.harvard.edu/history/presidents/bok, accessed September 9, 2013.

58. At http://www.hermanmiller.com/about-us/who-is-herman-miller/company-timeline/1990.html, accessed February 1, 2014.

59. "John M. Stropki to Retire," http://www.lincolnelectric.com/en-us/Company/NewsRoom/Pages/john-stropki-retire.aspx, accessed March 25, 2014.

60. At http://www.christianitytoday.com/ct/2013/october-web-only/chuck-smith-86-dies-after-cancer-battle.html, accessed October 3, 2014.

61. At http://calvarychapelassociation.com/national-international-regional-leadership/, accessed February 1, 2014.

62. Maciariello and Linkletter, *Drucker's Lost Art of Management,* 2011, pp. 135–40.

63. LeadershipJournal.net, "Managing to Minister: An Interview with Peter Drucker," posted April 1, 1989, http://www.christianitytoday.com/le/1989/spring/8912014.html, accessed December 30, 2013.

64. Drucker-Buford transcript, January 29, 1991, p. 19.

65. This session is based on excerpts from various Drucker interviews on The Salvation Army, but unless otherwise noted the source is a

taped interview: Vol. 3, Tape 5A of the cassette series "Leadership and Management in the Non-Profit Institution."

66. From Robert Lenzer and Ashlea Ebeling, "Peter Drucker's Picks," *Forbes*, Vol. 160, No. 3, August 11, 1997, pp. 97–99. The same enthusiastic endorsement by Peter Drucker of the work of The Salvation Army appears on the cover of Robert A. Watson, *The Most Effective Organization in the U.S.*, Crown Business, New York, 2001. Watson had just retired as national commander of The Salvation Army when this book was published.

67. Drucker-Buford transcript, January 29, 1991, p. 19.

68. I included this quote in a talk at the All-Academy symposium "Serving the Public Concern Through Virtuous management in Crises, 'Ordinary,' and Exemplary Times," at the National Academy of Management Conference, Atlanta, August 2006.

69. Thumma, Travis, and Bird, *Megachurches Today 2005: Summary of Research Findings*, p. 1, http://hirr.hartsem.edu/megachurch/megastoday2005summaryreport.pdf, accessed July 22, 2011.

70. Ibid., p. 7.

71. Scott Thumma, Dave Travis, and Warren Bird, *Innovation 2007*, Leadership Network, Dallas, TX, 2007.

72. Transcript of Jim Mellado–Joe Maciariello interview, October 11, 2011, p. 18.

73. Everett M. Rogers (1931–2004) was professor and chair of the Department of Communication and Journalism at the University of New Mexico.

74. Consultation, Jim Mellado and Bob Buford with Everett Rogers, July 30, 1996, Albuquerque, New Mexico.

75. Rogers identifies five overlapping categories of adopters of innovation: (1) innovators, (2) early adopters, (3) early majority, (4) late majority, and (5) laggards. As shown in Rogers's adoption curve, the earliest innovators, category 1, constitute approximately 2 percent of total users; followed by 14 percent early adopters; 34 percent so-called early majority; another 34 percent late majority; and 16 percent laggards.

76. "The origin of the quote came from an early meeting in 1971 of

PARC, Palo Alto Research Center, folks and the Xerox planners. In a fit of passion I uttered the quote!" E-mail, September 17, 1998, from Alan Kay to Peter W. Lount, http://www.smalltalk.org/alankay.html, accessed January 4, 2014.

77. "The design for the first tablet PC was set out in 1968, long before most of the technologies necessary to build it were even invented. That design was the Dynabook, and its author was computer scientist Alan Kay. Its intended audience was children. With its windowed software environment, graphical programming language, and no-moving-parts keyboard, it was designed to be a rugged, inexpensive machine that would unleash creativity." *Wall Street Journal*, http://online.wsj.com/ad/article/laptop-invented#top, accessed January 4, 2014.

78. For information on Lincoln's patent, see http://www.abrahamlincoln online.org/lincoln/education/patent.htm, accessed January 4, 2014.

79. Abraham Lincoln, Speeches and Writings, http://www.abrahamlin colnonline.org/lincoln/speeches/gettysburg.htm, accessed January 4, 2014.

80. Barbara Tuchman, *A Distant Mirror: The Calamitous 14th Century*, Random House, New York, 1978.

81. Peter F. Drucker, *My Personal History*, interviewer and translator Yo Makino, Nihon Keizai Shimbun, Tokyo, 2009, Article 12.

82. Halftime Institute, http://www.halftime.org/the-halftime-institute/, accessed October 23, 2013.

83. At http://www.independentsector.org/scope_of_the_sector#sthash.lBX pkCYs.dpbs, accessed October 21, 2013.

84. Source: http://www.nbcchicago.com/blogs/ward-room/The-Deadliest -Global-City-163874546.html#ixzz2lQKB3Ewa, accessed November 22, 2013.

85. Purtill, in *Compassion and Culture*, 2002, p. 2.

86. "The mission comes first and your role as a leader." Drucker, *Managing the Non-Profit Organization*, 1990, p. 1.

87. Proverbs 29:18.

88. "Concentration is the key to economic results. Economic results require that managers concentrate on the smallest number of products,

product lines, services, customers, markets, distributive channels, end-uses, and so on, that will produce the largest amount of revenue." Drucker, *Managing for Results*, 1964, 1986, p. 11.

89. Rick Warren formally introduced the new vision for Saddleback Church, the launching of the PEACE Plan in Rwanda, at the twenty-fifth anniversary celebration of Saddleback Community Church, held at Anaheim Stadium on April 17, 2005. The president of Rwanda was in attendance, as were representatives from numerous participating church, government, business, and educational organizations. At http://www.bpnews.net/bpnews.asp?ID=20603, accessed November 13, 2013.

90. Church, Community, Country, 2013, Rwanda PEACE Plan, http:// saddlebackmediawest.s3.amazonaws.com/12907-RwandaReport FINALlr.pdf?AWSAccessKeyId=02SEKEM7N07K11AZCQ02& Expires=1389299603&Signature=hAJKSa%2fZtMn8THRyudW 3fxbasDY%3d, accessed January 9, 2014.

91. According to one of his biographers. See Beatty, *The World According to Peter Drucker*, 1998, p. 98.

92. Transaction Publishers, New Brunswick, NJ, 1993, pp. 427–39.

93. See Dayananda Pathak, *George Bernard Shaw, His Religion and Values*, Mittal, Delhi, 1985, p. 19.

94. A friend of Drucker's and general manager of corporate strategy at General Motors until he retired in 2003.

95. "Seeing Things as They Really Are," *Forbes*, March 10, 1997, http:// www.forbes.com/forbes/1997/0310/5905122a.html, accessed January 5, 2014.

96. *Concept of the Corporation*, 1946, p. 28.

97. Drucker and Maciariello, *Management: Revised Edition*, 2008, p. 490.

98. January 22, "Economics as a Social Dimension," *The Daily Drucker*, 2004.

99. Walter C. Wright, *Mentoring: The Promise of Relational Leadership*, Paternoster, Eugene, OR, 2004, pp. 70–71.

100. Barna Group, "Survey Reveals the Books and Authors That Have Most Influenced Pastors," https://www.barna.org/barna-update/ article/5-barna-update/178-survey-reveals-the-books-and-authors

-that-have-most-influenced-pastors#.UlZoLWTuWFc, accessed October 10, 2013.

101. See, for example, Peter F. Drucker as quoted in *Forbes*, October 5, 1998, p. 169: "Consider the pastoral megachurches that have been growing so very fast in the U.S. since 1980 and are surely the most important social phenomenon in American society in the last 30 years."

102. "Drucker's Impact on Leadership Network," Leadership Network Advance, www.pursuantgroup.com/leadnet/advance/nov05o.htm, accessed September 28, 2013.

103. "Leadership Means to Get the Right Things Done," in Drucker, *Executive Summary: A Conversation with Peter Drucker on Leadership and Organizational Development*, 2002, pp. 5–6.

104. Drucker, *Managing the Non-Profit Organization*, 1990, p. xviii.

105. Drucker thought his essay on Kierkegaard was his best: "The Unfashionable Kierkegaard," 1949, pp. 587–602; reprinted in *The Ecological Vision*, 1993, chapter 30, pp. 427–39; accessible at http://www.druckersociety.at/files/p_drucker_kierkeg_en.pdf.

106. "The true test of a leader is whether its followers will adhere to his cause from their own volition, enduring the most arduous hardships without being forced to do so, and remaining steadfast in the moments of greatest peril." Xenophon's *Hellenika*, edited by Robert B. Strassler, www.thelandmarkancientstories.com/Xenophon.htm, accessed April 14, 2014.

Bibliography

Barnard, Chester I. *The Functions of the Executive*, 30th Anniversary ed. Cambridge, MA: Harvard University Press, 1971.

Beatty, Jack. *The World According to Peter Drucker*. New York: Free Press, 1998.

Buford, Bob. *Halftime: Changing Your Game Plan from Success to Significance*. Grand Rapids, MI: Zondervan, 1994, 2008.

Center on Education Policy. "Are Private Schools Better Academically Than Public Schools," 2007. (At http://www.edline.com/uploads/pdf/PrivateSchoolsReport.pdf, accessed September 24, 2013.)

Collins, Jim. *Good to Great: Why Some Companies Make the Leap . . . and Others Don't*. New York: HarperCollins, 2001.

Drucker, Peter F. *The End of Economic Man*. New York: John Day, 1939.

———. *The Future of Industrial Man*. New York: John Day, 1942.

———. *Concept of the Corporation*. New York: John Day, 1946.

———. "The Unfashionable Kierkegaard," *Sewanee Review* 57, no. 4 (Autumn 1949), pp. 587–602.

———. *The Practice of Management*. New York: Harper & Row, 1954.

———. *Landmarks of Tomorrow*. New York: Harper & Row, 1959.

———. *Managing for Results*. New York: Harper & Row, 1964.

———. *The Effective Executive*. New York: Harper & Row, 1967.

———. *The Effective Executive Video Series*, Washington, D.C.: Bureau of National Affairs, 1968. (Transcript of videotape series.)

————. *The Age of Discontinuity*. New York: Harper & Row, 1969. (Reissued, New Brunswick, NJ: Transaction Publishers, 1992.)

————. *Management: Tasks, Responsibilities, Practices*. New York: Harper & Row, 1973, 1974.

————. *Adventures of a Bystander.* New York: John Wiley & Sons, 1978. (Reissued, New Brunswick, NJ: Transaction Publishers, 1994.)

————. *Managing in Turbulent Times*. New York: Harper & Row, 1980.

————. *Innovation and Entrepreneurship*. New York: Harper & Row, 1985.

————. "Teaching the Work of Management," *New Management* (Fall 1988), pp. 2–5.

————. *The New Realities*. New York: Harper & Row, 1989. (Reissued, New Brunswick, NJ: Transaction Publishers, 2003.)

————. "What Business Can Learn from Nonprofits," *Harvard Business Review* (July–August, 1989), pp. 84–101.

————. *Managing the Non-Profit Organization: Principles and Practices*. New York: HarperCollins, 1990.

————. *The Ecological Vision*. New Brunswick, N.J.: Transaction Publishers, 1993.

————. *Post-Capitalist Society*. New York: HarperCollins, 1993.

————. *Managing in a Time of Great Change*. New York: Truman Talley, 1995.

————. Foreword, "Not Enough Generals Were Killed," in *The Leader of the Future*, edited by Frances Hesselbein, Marshall Goldsmith, and Richard Beckhard. San Francisco: Jossey-Bass, 1996.

————. *Management*. Oxford: Butterworth-Heineman, 1999. (Abridged version of *Management: Tasks, Responsibilities, Practices.*)

————. *Management Challenges for the 21st Century*. New York: HarperCollins, 1999.

————. "Managing Oneself," *Harvard Business Review* (March–April 1999), pp. 65–73.

————. *Executive Summary: A Conversation with Peter Drucker on*

Leadership and Organizational Development. Monrovia, CA: World Vision, February 5, 2002.

———. *Managing in the Next Society.* New York: St. Martin's, 2002.

———. *A Functioning Society.* New Brunswick, NJ: Transaction Publishers, 2003.

———. *The Daily Drucker.* New York: HarperCollins, 2004.

———. *Driving Change.* Phoenix: Corpedia Education, 2004. (Internet Module 8116.)

———. *The Next Society.* Phoenix: Corpedia Education, 2004. (Internet Module 8114.)

———. "Management Guru Peter Drucker," Radio interview Wednesday, December 8, 2004. *On Point,* Tom Ashbrook. Boston, MA: WBUR for National Public Radio. (At www.on pointradio.org/shows/2005/08/20050802_a_main.asp.)

———. *The Essential Drucker: The Best of Sixty Years of Peter Drucker's Essential Writings on Management.* New York: HarperCollins, 2008.

———. "Managing in Two Time Dimensions," *Drucker Insights,* vol. 10, uploaded February 2, 2009. (At http://www.youtube .com/watch?v=V1xppECWZPw.)

Drucker, Peter F. *My Personal History.* Interviewer and translator Yo Makino. Tokyo: Nihon Keizai Shimbun, 2009.

———. *Towards the Next Economics and Other Essays.* Boston, MA: Harvard Business School Publishing, 2010.

Drucker, Peter F., and Joseph A. Maciariello. *The Effective Executive in Action.* New York: HarperCollins, 2006.

———. *Management: Revised Edition.* New York: HarperCollins, 2008.

———. *Management Cases: Revised Edition.* New York: HarperCollins, 2009.

Eisenhower, Dwight David. Attribution by Steve Metivier, accessed January 27, 2014. (At http://www.inspirationalspark.com/ leadership-quotations.html.)

Griffiths, Brian. "The Business of Values." In Donald D. Holt (ed.), *The Heart of a Business Ethic,* Hansen–Wessner Memorial Lecture Series. New York: University Press of America, 2005. (Chapter 2.)

Harris, T. George. "The Post-Capitalist Executive: An Interview with Peter F. Drucker." *Harvard Business Review* (May–June 1993), pp. 114–22.

Hedrick, Larry (ed.). *Xenophon's Cyrus the Great: The Arts of Leadership*. New York: St. Martin's Griffin, 2007.

Hoover Institution. "The Moral Basis of a Free Society," Policy Review No. 86. Stanford, CA: Hoover Institution Press, November 1, 1997. (At http://www.hoover.org/moral-basis-free-society accessed July 19, 2014.)

Karlgaard, Rich. "Drucker on Leadership: An Interview with Peter F. Drucker." *Forbes Magazine*, November 19, 2004. (At http://www.forbes.com/2004/11/19/cz_rk_1119drucker.html, accessed October 10, 2013.)

Keynes, John M. *A Tract on Monetary Reform*. London: Macmillan, 1924.

Luce, Tom, and Lee Thompson. *Do What Works: How Proven Practices Can Improve America's Public Schools*. Dallas, TX: Ascent Education, 2005.

Maciariello, Joseph A. *Lasting Value: Lessons from a Century of Agility at Lincoln Electric*. New York: Wiley, 2000.

———. "Managing for Results, Planning for Succession: An Interview with Peter F. Drucker." *Shine a Light*, Leader to Leader Institute, *Commemorating Our Fifteenth Year*, 2005, pp. 15–19.

Maciariello, Joseph A., and Karen E. Linkletter. *Drucker's Lost Art of Management*. New York: McGraw-Hill, 2011.

McCullough, David. *Truman*. New York: Simon & Schuster, 1992.

Pollard, C. William. *The Soul of the Firm*. New York: HarperCollins, 1996.

Purtill, Gwen. "The Most Effective Organization in the U.S.: The Salvation Army and Peter Drucker." In Capital Research Center, *Compassion and Culture*, April 2002, pp. 1, 2. (At https://www.capitalresearch.org/pubs/pdf/x3760152596.pdf, accessed November 22, 2013.)

Riel, Kevin. "A Model Citizen with a Business Model to End Poverty." *Flame*. Claremont, CA: Claremont Graduate University, 2009, first page. (At http://www.cgu.edu/pages/6627.asp, accessed December 12, 2013.)

Rogers, Everett. *Diffusion of Innovations*, 5th ed. New York: Free Press, 2003.

Schumpeter, Joseph A. *Capitalism, Socialism, Democracy*. New York: Harper, 1942.

Shaw, G. Bernard. *Man and Superman: A Comedy and Philosophy*. New York: Bretano's, 1903.

Sloan, Alfred P. *My Years with General Motors*. New York: Doubleday, 1963, 1990.

Smith, Linda Wasmer. *Louis Pasteur, Disease Fighter*, rev. ed. Berkeley Heights, NJ: Enslow, 2008.

Tarrant, John J. *The Man Who Invented the Corporate Society*. Boston, MA: Cahners, 1976.

Thumma, Scott, Dave Travis, and Warren Bird. *Megachurches Today 2005: Summary of Research Findings*. Hartford, CT: Hartford Seminary, February 2006.

Warren, Rick. *The Purpose Driven Church*. Grand Rapids, MI: Zondervan, 1995.

———. *The Purpose Driven Life*. Grand Rapids, MI: Zondervan, 2002.

———. "The Influence of Peter Drucker on My Life." Keynote Address, Drucker Alumni Day, Claremont, CA, November 13, 2004.

———. "The Future of Evangelicals: A Conversation with Pastor Rick Warren." Pew Research, Religion and Public Life, November 13, 2009. (At http://www.pewforum.org/2009/11/13/the-future-of-evangelicals-a-conversation-with-pastor-rick-warren/#12, accessed October 24, 2013.)

Welch, Jack. *Winning*. New York: HarperCollins, 2005.

Zahar, Shaker. "An Interview with Peter Drucker," *Academy of Management Executive* 17, no. 3 (August 2003).

Index

About the Author

Joseph A. Maciariello is Marie Rankin Clarke Professor of Social Science and Management Emeritus and Senior Fellow at the Peter F. Drucker and Masatoshi Ito Graduate School of Management at Claremont Graduate University. He collaborated with Drucker on many publications, including *The Effective Executive in Action,* the revised edition of *Management,* and *The Daily Drucker.*